SIGNS OF THE HIDDEN

DEGRÉ SECOND 3

SIGNS OF THE HIDDEN
SEMIOTIC STUDIES

Amsterdam 1980

SIGNS OF THE HIDDEN
SEMIOTIC STUDIES

by

SUSAN W. TIEFENBRUN

ISBN: 90–6203–871–9

Printed in Great Britain by H Charlesworth & Co Ltd

To: Jonathan, Michèle and Jeremy

ACKNOWLEDGEMENTS

It would be impossible to thank all those who have in some way influenced my thinking, inspired my writing, encouraged my development, and fostered the eventual clarities of thought which hopefully appear on the surface of my text as mere signs of the intellectual dialectics and concomitant turmoil that produce such a work. But there were and always will be special people involved in what appears to be a one woman production. How can I ever sufficiently thank Michael Riffaterre for teaching me not only how to read between and below the lines, but how to gain lasting and satisfying pleasure from the discoveries of the text? How can I begin to thank David Rubin for the hours of intelligent and productive discussion which have doubtless been one of the primary sources of inspiration and motivation for this study. Jules Brody helped me considerably not only through his exceptionally incisive analyses of seventeenth-century texts but by actually reading and constructively criticizing parts of my own text. Roland Barthes' influence is obvious for he has done the impossible thing which is to render semiotics poetic. Colleagues in the field of seventeenth century—Claude Abraham, Nathan Gross, Marie Odile Sweetser, Judd Hubert, Milgorad Margitic and especially Wolfgang Leiner — to name but a few — have nurtured an atmosphere of intellectual stimulation which is immeasurable and nonetheless highly significant to the realization of this work.

CONTENTS

I

INTRODUCTION

CHAPTER I

INTRODUCTION

Ainsi rien n'est absolument droit,
simple, loyal, la surface est comme
la peau: elle cache plus qu'elle ne
révèle, elle dissimule en exhibant
et fourvoie en manifestant, mais
en fourvoyant elle manifeste,
quoique d'une manière indirecte et
oblique.
Jankélévitch, *L'Ironie*, p. 50

PRELIMINARIES

Signs of the hidden – a rather elusive title designed to capture the
scope and aim of this semiotic study of seventeenth-century French
literature. Meanings below, meanings beyond: poetic surfaces reveal
but faintly the joys of intellectual and spiritual expansion hidden
between the lines, joys which must necessarily, I regret, be
temporarily severed by the analytical knife that cuts away at this
thickened mass of complex exterior to expose truth and its ever-
increasing forms, more and more meanings, more and more sides to
a deceptively finite figure, whose changes constitute the very essence
of artistic creation.

This study involves the construction and application of an esthetic
metalanguage designed to penetrate the surface of a highly specialized
and eminently analyzable discourse known as literature. Contrary to
the current critical fad which refuses the specificity of literary
discourse and, more repugnantly, the powers of systems analysis, I
am committed to the belief in scientific method which must separate
esthetic wholes in order to identify its underlying parts and mechanisms, which must observe microscopically that which is not
immediately visible in order to explain the apparently unexplainable,
which applies direct and standardized language to describe the

symbolic and indirect, and which must piece together the parts in an even greater more satisfying creation that synthesizes the dissonance of ignorance and carries with it pleasures that come from the knowledge of order and meaning.

The esthetic metalanguage which I have constructed and applied to various genres within literary texts of seventeenth-century France is rooted in semiotics, in that elusive and fleeting relationship between form and content, signifier and signified, the rarefied place of the hidden. In literary media concealed messages are sent not directly but in coded form in which a substitute and symbolic language contains the essence of the referent or reality. This symbolic communication system is the stuff of semiotics.

This study, which is a multi-disciplinary approach to semiotic theories, involves a slightly different use of the basic notions of sign and symbol to which I attach and integrate the literary principles of metaphoric code and context. Moreover, the notions of denotation and connotation, the latter of which has more than a simple valuative dimension, I believe to be eminently functional in semiotic theory for they involve the semantic expansion potential of multiple code intersection. According to Frege signs do exist that refer to no real object and thus have no 'denotation' *per se* but 'meaning,' as in the case of esthetic signs. This rejection of denotation in artistic discourse is debatable and, as Kristeva put it, results in "une ambiguité constamment maintenue entre la possibilité d'un *sens* ... et d'une *dénotation*."[1] Moreover the notion of connotation is considered a function of contextual exposure to codes and could be called more simply 'multiple denotation.' It is in the intersection or superposition of multiple meanings that the new and poetic is created. For these meanings to be decoded legitimately, which is the task of the text analyst, a contextual marker constituting a control signal should be indicated on the surface of the text. Otherwise all readings would be legitimized giving way to hermeneutic anarchy. In view of the potential polysemy of the written word, other sciences such as anthropology, sociology, psychology, stylistics and rhetoric must necessarily enter into the inter-disciplinary study of semiotics.

When I speak of code in literary discourse I am referring to a metaphoric or metonymic semantic field founded on a relationship of contiguity or similarity.[2] Literary language is characterized by the high frequency of coded symbols which draw attention to themselves placing emphasis on form over content. Indirect or symbolic language is signalled by rhetorical figures such as the metaphor, comparison, metonymy, symbol, allusion, irony, satire, and a myriad of literary conventions which are vehicles for the conveyance of messages. The distinction between indirect, symbolic language and direct, referential language is analogous to the commonly-held distinction between literal and figurative language, and a literary message normally carries a smattering of each. During the reading process the referent of the coded message requires decoding, that is, the symbolic representation must be 'interpreted' in the strict sense of communication theory, such that the set of equivalents existing between the symbolic system and the referential system is established for meaningful communication. These equivalents or variants comprise the textual material required for the decoding. Just as the imposure of a code limits the entropy of a system, be it esthetic or other, so the imposure of context limits and controls the decoding of the message. Thus each esthetic message carries within it the seeds of its own decoding, a system which is a true destruction of symbolic creation, the key to which no one, not even the author, can fully possess without analytic investigations into the underlying sets of symbolic equivalence. The nature of this analytic quest is semiotic.

HISTORY OF SEMIOTICS

Semiotics is the science of signs. The science was born at about the turn of the twentieth century, when two scholars in different but related fields of linguistics and philosophy were investigating the elements of signifying systems. For Charles Sanders Peirce, who dealt with natural, conventionalized language or a sociolect, semiotics was another word for pure logic in the general sense. Saussure, who called this vast body of knowledge *sémiologie*, considered language the most important sign system:

La langue est un système de signes exprimant des idées, et par là, comparable à l'écriture, à l'alphabet des sourds-muets, aux rites symboliques, aux formes de politesse, aux signaux militaires etc. Elle est seulement le plus important de ces systèmes. *On peut donc concevoir une science qui étudie la vie des signes au sein de la vie sociale*; elle formerait une partie de la psychologie sociale et, par conséquent de la psychologie générale; nous la nommerons *sémiologie* (du grec *sèmeîon*, "signe"). Elle nous apprendrait en quoi consistent les signes, quelles lois les régissent. Puisqu'elle n'existe pas encore, on ne peut dire ce qu'elle sera; mais elle a droit à l'existence, sa place est déterminée d'avance.[3]

For Saussure the dichotomy between *langue* and *parole*, which is analogous to Noam Chomsky's competence and performance, situates the study of linguistics on a social level. *Langue* for Saussure is a social institution, a system of values; *parole* is an individual act of linguistic selection, a process of communication. An idiolect of language as it is spoken or written by the individual is equivalent to the style of the writer.[4] The 'esthetic' sign, which is the linguistic material for what Juri Lotman calls 'artistic' or 'poetic' discourse, is an autonomous sign system endowed with an affective as well as communicative function. In the area of artistic discourse Charles Morris distinguished two types of signs, those which possess properties in common with their referent (iconic signs) and those signs which are not like what they denote (non-iconic signs). Esthetic signs are normally iconic and analogical, that is there is a degree of motivation underlying the relationship between signifier and signified. Literary language is in the realm of the symbolic, and the symbol is a motivated sign. In other words, sign could be considered the genus and symbol the species or subset included within a broader category. Since both the linguistic system and the esthetic system are composed of symbolic forms, they are both an integral and legitimate part of semiotic investigation.

Since the Second World War an international effort to organize and coordinate a science of semiotics has been carried out in the United States, the Soviet Union, and France. In America a description of such non-verbal signifying systems as kinesics, zoo-semiotics, and proxemics has been undertaken to a great extent under the direction of Thomas Sebeok. In the Soviet Union cybernetics, information theory, and secondary modeling systems occupy the most important areas of semiotics. In France the movement is widespread, encompassing researchers in four main areas: linguistics, anthropology, philosophy, and psychoanalysis. Roland Barthes was one of the early literary scholars of linguistic orientation to introduce the study of semiotics to the art world. Greimas, Mounin, Guiraud and functional linguists like Martinet, Prieto, and Buyssens made advances in the science of signifying systems and contributed to the varied applications of this method to literary discourse analysis – Greimas in the field of structural semantics and actantial typologies, Guiraud in semantics and stylistics, and Mounin in translation. Structural linguists inspired by Roman Jakobson joined forces with anthropologists under the direction of Claude Lévi-Strauss to study the structural elements of myth, a field which has been continued on the literary level by Propp, Brémond, and Todorov analyzing the *récit*. Literary scholars with a philosophical orientation like Julia Kristeva and Jacques Derrida have contributed to the development of 'semanalysis' and what Derrida calls the science of *écriture*. Lacan and his disciples apply semiotic principles in their psychoanalytic investigations.

For Saussure the elements of semiology were relational and binary consisting of the signifier (or form of the message) and the signified (or content of the message). The famous equation is expressed in this way:

$$\text{Signe} = \frac{Sa}{Se} = \frac{\text{signifiant}}{\text{signifié}} = \frac{\text{form}}{\text{content}} \text{ (expression)}$$

Hjelmslev modified the formula slightly by placing differential emphasis on substance and form:

Saussure   Hjelmslev

Signifier	expression	substance de l'expression
		forme de l'expression
Signified	content	substance du contenu
		forme du contenu

Martinet added that natural languages are sign systems founded on the principle of double articulation. Language contains monemes (minimum units of meaning) and phonemes (minimum units of sound). Structural linguists up to the present have been engaged mainly in phonological investigation and the precise description of the form of expression (signifier) whereas the study of content or the signified has been relegated to the domain of structural semantics (Greimas, Guiraud, Ullmann, etc.) and taken up from a different point of view in the philosophy of Wittgenstein.

Opposed to the more or less classical Saussurian concepts of the sign in which balance of symmetry exists between the signifier and the signified are the more recent philosophically and psychoanalytically oriented semioticians like Derrida and Lacan who insist on the primacy of the signifier. For Derrida, semiotics is a formal game of differences — "le signifié est toujours déjà en position de signifiant" — something like a signifier, a trace, is already functioning in the signified. Lacan studies the signifying chain (*la chaine signifiante*) in the psychoanalytic experience. It should be noted, however, that Lacan's real linguistic competence at least in his earlier *Ecrits* has been put to serious question by some linguists, notably Mounin.[5] For Lacan the line establishing the relationship between signifier and signified $\left(\text{Signe} = \frac{Sa}{Se}\right)$ is a symbolic barrier resisting all signification or meaning. This line represents the repression of the signified. The signifier with all its permutations and combinations is actually the determinant of the signified, the key to hidden signification. For Lacan the definition of the signifier is dependent upon a triadic link between the subject, the object and vacillation into the signifying chain. Although the semiotic theories of Lacan, Derrida, and especially Kristeva are clearly revolutionary, many of the ideas they present are applicable to those introduced earlier by structural linguists. Lacan's notions of condensation as metaphor remind us of Roman Jakobson's axis of selection; psychological displacement as metonymy is based on the concept of an axis of combination.

While Saussure was investigating the social function of language, Charles Sanders Peirce was developing a general theory of signs in philosophy. His work was part of the domain of logic and is continued today by philosophers in semantic theory. Some of the most noted logicians and philosophers of language are Ernst Cassirer, Rudolf Carnap, Bertrand Russell, and Charles Morris. It is interesting to note that these philosophers make no mention of Saussure. Peirce considered himself a pioneer in the field of semiotics, which he defined as "the doctrine of the essential nature and fundamental varieties of possible semiosis."[6] By semiosis Peirce understood a ·elationship of three subjects such as a sign, its object, and its interpretant (the concept of the object). The notion of phenomenological perception is basic to Peirce's triadic conception of semiotics and occupies the serious and prolonged attention today of stylisticians, psychologists and philosophers.

DEFINITION OF TERMS

Semiotics, then, involves the relationship between the signifier and the signified. For Saussure the sign is arbitrary, unmotivated. Motivated relationships in sign systems are either analogical, as in the case of the metaphor and metonymy, or homological, as in the sign system of city streets where avenues are generally vertical, streets horizontal, and numbers follow in logical succession. Signification which is the study of semiotics involves the intricate relation existing between the expression (signifier) and the content (signified) of the message. Denotation should be distinguished from 'signification' or meaning for denotation is referential and involves the ·relationship between the sign and its referent or real object. Both Peirce and Saussure felt that the denotation of an object occupied a marginal role in the definition of the sign. Representation is the mental image of the object conjured up in the mind of the sign user. Representation of this object depends upon the sign user's selection of vocabulary and its evocatory potential. The Stoics distinguished three relations within the sign: the real thing (*denotatum*), the psychic image (*representatum*), and the 'dicible' or signification. Denotation and representation enter into the domain of symbolization and are thus of great concern to the semiotics of literary discourse.

'Symbol' is to be distinguished in the strict sense from 'sign.' Hjelmslev's idea of connotation and his elaboration of a 'connotative semiotics' is an enlarged view of semiotics close to the notion of symbolization. Hjelmslev distinguished between denotative semiotics and connotative semiotics. Phonetics and semantics would be the 'metasemiology' that treats denotative semiotics, whereas sociolinguistics and cultural or Saussurian 'external linguistics' would be the metasemiology designated to treat connotative semiotics. Connotative semiotics[7] involves polysemy or multiple meanings that exist within the content of a message. A message can have geographic, historic, political, social, religious, psychological, and stylistic significance, to name but a few of the potential variables. It is precisely this multifacetted aspect of literary discourse that accounts for its durability, its long-term source of intellectual and spiritual pleasure, and is one of the reasons why, despite the three hundred years of revolutionary changes, we can still read and laugh at Molière's *Tartuffe* or cry at the tragic isolation of a Bajazet.

Symbolization involves a relatively stable association between two elements on the same level, either signified or signifier.[8] Whereas the sign is arbitrary, necessary, and the relationship between signifier and signified unmotivated except for the case of the onomatopeia,[9] the symbol and relationship between symbolizer and symbolized is motivated.

Other terms besides sign and symbol enter into the domain of semiotics like symptom and signal. In medicine a symptom must be reported for it is not visible, like a high fever which is a symptom of many possible diseases. A sign is visible, like red blotches on the face which are symptomatic of any number of illnesses. The diagnostic determinant in medicine as in literary discourse is the global picture of the patient's symptoms, the interrelationships existing between the signs, and the context in which the signs and symptoms occur. A signal, in contrast to a sign, is that which produces a reaction but may have no intrinsic meaning. Bloomfield and the American linguists in his school had the tendency to reduce all signs to signals according to the behaviorist model of stimulus-response. (It is my feeling that the necessary presence of a signal is the key to the definition of ˙code,' a term which has caused innumerable problems in semiotics and which will be discussed shortly.) Animal language is composed basically of signals. Cybernetics is involved with technological or machine-produced signals. Stylistics is involved with signals, some marked, some unmarked, and generally involving rhetorical figures, conventions of narratology and poetics, contextual contrasts on . multiple levels of discourse,[10] and all forms of indirect language which draw attention to the form of its signification. The style of an author is the sign system of equivalents with which he selects to convey his perception of the referential world. Style implies, therefore, a deformation of reality, and, as Merleau-Ponty put it in *Signes*, "une déformation cohérente," due, first of all, to the distortion of perception and, secondly, to the indirect nature of poetic language. In this regard it seems to me that the role of the stylistician should be to identify and describe the structure and function of these equivalents in order to perform a 'translation,' as it were, of the meanings hidden within the perception of the author. The nature of stylistic signals, better called signs, is not altogether known, and it is the basic purpose of this study to investigate the polyvalence of stylistic stimuli and their role in signification.

Charles Peirce provided one of the most detailed classification systems for signs, symbols, icons, and indices. A sign or representamen is "anything which determines something else (its interpretant) to refer to an object to which itself refers (its object) in the same way, the interpretant becoming in turn a sign, and so on ad infinitum."[11] Thus it is possible to conceive the vastness of the field of semiotics where virtually everything is or can become a sign. Peirce distinguished a total number of sixty-six sign varieties which he divided into three main categories: appearances (qualisigns), individual objects or events (sigsigns), and general types (legisigns). Peirce defined an icon as "a sign which is determined by its dynamic object by virtue of its own internal nature."[12] An icon exhibits the same quality as the denoted object, like a painting which resembles the object painted, an onomatopeia whose sound imitates the sound of the noise heard, or representational diagrams which reproduce to scale the model in question. Peirce subdivided icons into images, diagrams, and metaphors. (Todorov and Ducrot are unwilling to see an iconic relationship between metaphor, which is based on resemblance, and the icon which they see as synechdochic.[13]) Taking icon in Peirce's sense to mean an intrinsic resemblance, it seems logical to assume that as the metaphor's iconicity is reduced, the difficulty of inter-pretation is increased and perceptual effectiveness threatened. The result is a hermetic metaphor.

An index is a sign which is contiguous to the denotated object and points to the absent presence of the object, like proper names, pronouns, smoke which is an index of fire, or a symptom which supposes a disease. A symbol according to Peirce refers to "the object that it denotes by virtue of a Law, usually an association of general ideas," like words of a language which always refer to a specific object. Thus for Peirce, in direct contrast to Saussure, a symbol is an arbitrary sign. According to Mounin the American semioticians tend to use the term 'symbol' to mean what European linguists call 'sign.' This semantic reversal has been the source of a great deal of confusion enhanced by the interference of the psycho-analytical meaning of 'symbol.' In psychoanalysis a symbol refers to a substitutive expression marking the presence of a repressed or censured thought. We will use the word 'symbol' more in the Saussurian sense which, as Kristeva carefully points out,[14] is Hegelian in origin. According to Saussure "le symbole a pour caractéristique de n' être jamais tout à fait arbitraire: il n'est pas vide, il y a un rudiment de lien naturel entre le signifiant et le signifié."[15]

Semiotics involves the basic concept of communication and the transmission of a message through a medium. The field is as extensive as a general theory of culture, and Umberto Eco calls it the substitute of cultural anthropology. A bird's eye view of the field would cover such areas of communication as zoosemiotics (animal communica-tion), cybernetics (machine communication and information theory which, incidentally, work as do all complex systems according to the principle of binary opposition or digits called 'bits'; like language, which is a system of double articulation composed of signifier and signified, computers are both analog and digital), bionics (live cellular communication), visual communication (chromatic systems, graphic systems, fashion, architectural notation, choreography, geographic and topographic mapping), mass communications (literature, journalism, radio, television, publicity), and exchange systems (currency). The function of the sign is to communicate. According to Roman Jakobson, a message is conveyed by a sender who is referred to differently either as the *destinateur*, the *émetteur*, or *énonciateur*. The message is sent through a medium (verbal or written language via televi-sion, radio, books, etc.) to a receiver called a *destinataire* or *énonciataire*. The message is not sent directly but in coded form in which a sub-stitute or symbolic language conceals the essence of the referent.

Jakobson defined six essential functions of language within the communication system. The emotive function of language refers to the sender; the conative function to the receiver; the poetic or esthetic function of language is that which occupies the core of our study; the phatic function draws attention to the communication itself; and, finally, the metalinguistic function which is language about language.

Since the advent of semiotic studies and the growing interest in communication systems, the word 'code' has become popular, a potentially devastating phenomenon which carries with it the stigma of misuse, abuse, and above all confusion. In Eliseo Veron's article on the pertinence of the term 'code'[16] Veron distinguishes no less than five uses: (1) Code is a language, an oversimplified but very common usage probably introduced by Martinet in 1955 when he entitled one of the sections of his *Eléments de linguistique générale* "Langue et Parole, Code et Message." Pierre Guiraud in 1963 also interpreted 'code' as *langue* and 'discours' as *message*.[17] (2) Code is the set of transformations which enable a message receiver to determine the equivalent meaning by moving from one system of signs to another, as in the Morse code or in information theory. (3) Code in many cases is used to mean a set of 'constraints' which define the nature of any particular sign system. (4) Code involves the signs which speakers of a signifying system use in order to communicate. (5) Code refers to the 'social' aspect of a signifying system, the institutional norms which underly the functioning of the system. With George Miller[18] and Umberto Eco, who has given one of the most complete accounts of the complexities of the term 'code,'[19] I would agree that the second of the above definitions is the most precise, for it is specific enough to avoid confusion and general enough to allow for applicable and intelligent extension. Eco defines a code as follows: "tout système de symboles qui par convention préalable, est destiné à représenter et à transmettre une information d'une source à un point de destination."[20] This definition is particularly important with regard to literary discourse, the medium through which a writer (sender) transmits a coded (indirect and therefore symbolic) message to his reading audience (receiver).

At the base of all code systems is the notion of convention, an established and accepted set of equivalents. Upon the receipt of a given sign, be it technological like dot/dash or esthetic like the metaphor of a flower whose base is beauty, an instantaneous response is emitted from the receiver who presumably possesses the key to the code and access to the referent of the symbolic representation. The problem with esthetic signs is their essentially iconic nature which makes them much less conventionalized. But the relativity of esthetic codes is also true of other code systems which merit the distinctive title of behavioral science, such as sociology where society's norms are rarely if every universalizable. And yet there are obvious conventions in literature like myths, archetypes, legends, and text typologies which have occupied the profound and fruitful interest of English and American scholars in New Criticism, the Germans in *Literaturwissenschaft*, and the French in *La Nouvelle Critique* since the 1960's. Their studies are in two major areas of form or morphology (Propp, Emile Souriau, Brémond, Todorov, Greimas, etc.) and symbolic or thematic archetypes (C. G. Jung, Northrup Frye, Gaston Bachelard, etc.). Readers with a wide range of literary experience can usually identify rhetorical and poetic conventions, but these are never absolute. Esthetic codes are less standardized than social or scientific codes. Moreover the diversity, polysemy, and creative nature of signs in literary discourse necessitate the reliance upon context for a reliable decoding of the message.

Code typology is conveniently divided into three main categories: logical codes, social codes, and esthetic codes with overlapping in each.[21] Logical codes contain alphabetical systems like Morse, braille, digital, and the alphabet of the deaf and dumb (called 'sign language'). In each of these alphabet systems sets of signals are substituted for another language; communication is established when the equivalents are determined and correlated. The kinesic code (gestures, body language) is another type of multi-conventional system dependent largely upon cultural difference and context. (In Italy, for example, the hand gesture used to signify 'good-bye' is equivalent to the American 'come here' signal.) Proxemics or the distance between speakers which can convey a subtle if not unconscious message is an area of sociological investigation receiving a great deal of interest today. This distance is particularly important in Spanish-speaking countries. Paralinguistic noises and non-verbal language involve suprasegmental traits of communication which appear more and more to be institutionalizable and systematic (cf. Fónagy, Stankiewicz, Mahl and Schulze, Trager, etc.). Scientific codes exist like the chemical symbolic notation system which is partially motivated, mostly arbitrary, but designed to facilitate memory; the conventionalized but unsystematized algebraic symbol notation; astrological codes which, like superstition, involve archetypal conventions — Virgo and the black cat, for example, carry special significance.

Social codes are vast, endlessly all-consuming, and virtually everything is a sign of something. Names, labels (a coat from Neiman Marcus has intrinsic significance, added quality, and probable price value than one marked, for example, Korvettes), signs of politeness, kinesics, rites, ceremonies, fashion, proxemics — all these are signs, the starting point of communication.

Aesthetic codes involve four main areas of investigation: poetics and/or stylistics; symbolic and thematic archetypes; rhetoric or the communication system of persuasion; and morphology or typology of the *récit*. In our semiotic study of seventeenth-century French literature, we make use of the findings in each of these areas of aesthetic codes in an attempt to achieve a truly interdisciplinary approach to semiotic analysis of literary discourse.

APPLICATION OF SEMIOTIC THEORIES

This collection of essays hopes to identify more specific signs of generic distinction, hidden signs that rhetoric has up to now failed to uncover. In the course of the studies on the novel, satire, fable, comedy and tragedy, the presence of similar structural models places serious question on the criteria currently existing for generic specificity. Perhaps new methods of analysis are necessary for the more accurate detection of specific signs. This re-evaluation is merely a suggestion to point scholars in the methodological direction of further investigative research.

The first section of the book examines aspects of the early and late seventeenth-century novel, *Astrée* and *La Princesse de Clèves*. Honoré D'Urfé's novel, *Astrée*, is studied as a symbolic representation of the erotic. Never before classified as erotic literature, *Astrée* has always been considered the early seventeenth-century pastoral, sentimental, and philosophical novel *par excellence*. An interdisciplinary approach applying principles of semiotics, psychoanalytics, and rhetoric is used first to distinguish the underlying elements of eroticism and then to determine the relationship of the literary representation of these elements within the narrative discourse. Since virtually all perceptual stimuli are potential signs of eroticism according to the psychological phenomenon of erotogenicity, it must necessarily be in the formal representation of the object that the erotic message is conveyed. The structural model underlying the formal representation of the erotic is a threatened stasis of dynamic equilibrium observed diversely as a profoundly embedded tension between oppositions, reality and fiction, evil and goodness, Eros and Thanatos.

In the chapter entitled "Hidden Patterns in the French Classical Novel," which is a computer-assisted study of Madame de Lafayette's novel *La Princesse de Clèves*, a decoding of the text for marked or active linguistic and rhetorical categories was performed in accordance with the theory of necessary perception. Results obtained have significant implications for a redefinition of the term 'classical' novel. While restraint and moderation, which are generally accepted non-specific signs of classical discourse, are thought to be articulated formally through generalizing signifieds, proverbial constructions, and the almost deified 'litotes,' a more precise description of the genre should include the counteractive but cohesive function of such intensifying agents on the levels of signifier and signified as hyperbole, surprise, mimetic effects, and disjunctive interruptions. Thus hidden deeply within complex linguistic and literary matrices of *La Princesse de Clèves* is a smoothly operating system of interrelated and fundamentally binary, if not oppositional, components which, when perceived by an attentive reader, will produce the esthetically satisfying effect of classical symmetry commonly associated with great works of art.

The French formal verse satire is a genre not usually given much attention by rhetoricians. To uncover the morphological patterns inherent to the genre and the signs of its most widespread technique for ridicule and persuasion, which is that elusive phenomenon known as irony, two celebrated seventeenth-century texts of rather different scope were selected for investigation: one satire by Mathurin Regnier entitled *Macette* and the entire collection of Boileau's *Satires*.

Mathurin Regnier's *Macette* is a poem which appears on the surface to advocate an abominably Machievellian system. The satirist equates love and money, denounces sanctioned values, and destroys archetypal heroes. But a close textual analysis of this satire reveals the critical role of connotative and denotative manipulation at the base of codal intersection in the establishment of a general atmosphere of ironic contradiction and unreliable commentary. Irony is defined as a fundamentally relational phenomenon in which juxtaposition and equation of disparate elements produce contradiction. When an identity is created between at least two opposed, if not incompatible, structures, the resultant disparity produces an ironic effect. The reader senses a gap between what is said and what is meant, a multiplicity of meaning which places added attention on the signifier whose signified is threatened. The most critical sign of irony which can occur on any level, be it thematic, stylistic, semantic, narrative, actantial, and functional, is the simultaneity of mutually exclusive oppositions. This is observed most clearly in the oxymoron. The incompatibility of the related elements jolts the reader and encourages the perception of the linguistic game of connotative juggling. In this manner the Satirist can simultaneously praise and blame the evil which he intends to ridicule and hopefully weed out with minimum risk.

Within Boileau's *Satires*, and because of the contradictions inherent to the genre, a conflict between the satirist and his critical targets is comically sustained by highly ambivalent verbal combat. Throughout the collection of satires and in contrast to an overriding comic tone, the poet's pathetic sense of defiant purposelessness looms forth as a heightened awareness of the inanity of his profession despite its history of beneficial reform. Satiric criticism is characterized formally by an ·interplay of contrasts referred to as the poetics of opposition, a characteristic which is not specific to satire alone but rather reflective of language in general. The targets move in two directions: inwardly towards the poet himself, his very own enemy, and outwardly towards the Other, that complex of mutable forms which are sometimes more friendly than foul. The Enemy is manifested by numerous variants on the levels of both form and content, each of which receives the persuasive wrath, invective, comic indifference, and mockery characteristic of the satirist. His Enemy is the King, ambiguity, satire, poets, poetry itself, the public, society in general, women in particular, human folly, false nobility and honor, and evil incarnate which Boileau calls *l'Equivoque*. Truth is the essence of Boileau's esthetics, his criterion of excellence, the unattainable otherside of his ever-encroaching Enemy, hypocrisy. The p⌐ ᵊt's ambivalent perception of himself naturally affects the poetic expression of his subject and his critical perception of others. This study investigates the transformations of the Enemy and the network of oppositional relationships existing between this archetype and the poet's own dual self-image.

The symbolic discourse of La Fontaine's *Fables* is constructed on an illogical assumption of animal communication in imitation of humans, an incongruity which renders the readings highly ironic.

There is a disparity between statement and intention, theory and practice, authorial promise and literary delivery. The fables constitute a complex orchestration in counterpoint, a deceptively smooth mixture of the epic and the familiar, the lyric and the eloquent. Irony as observed in literature is a surface phenomenon, a fused entity of harmonious uniformity which hides a deeper schism of incompatible contrasts. The aim of the chapter entitled "Signs of Irony in La Fontaine's *Fables*" is to penetrate the hidden, the elusive, the oblique by identifying signs of irony in the fable which work imperceptibly to create and expand meaning in poetic discourse.

The fable, which originated in the primitive allegory and has a strong link to the ancient parable, is a legitimate genre composed of political and social satire, allegory, maxim, and moral. Like allegory, fables involve the dissimulation of one series of incidents under another, and the narrative fiction is usually subordinate to the abstract moral. It is an old form of didactic poetry, and the famous formula "plaire et instruire" are its primary goals. Most critics speak of the fable with disdain, declaring that it is a form for children, for the *animae vulgares* or the *ingenia rudia*, a depreciation which runs parallel to that of the formal verse satire. Both the fable and the satire are structured oppositionally with contrast and contradiction as a basic constituent of their ironic fabric. What is common to the fable, the allegory, and the satire is the necessary presence of hidden elements, messages concealed within a symbolic system that requires decoding and translation. Irony like language itself is an allegory, for it says one thing and means another, is not meant to be believed but understood, and its symbols require interpretation for successful communication.

It is the fable's affinity with the primitive allegory that accounts for its fundamentally binary system of alterity and equivalence. Allegory means *allos* or 'other'. Alterity is the essence of irony's deceptive powers by which surface language expresses the exact opposite of its intended meaning. In the allegory characters, events or ideas are hidden below the surface of other characters, events or ideas. The historical, political, moral, philosophical, or religious referent is situated beyond allegorical structures which are purportedly described in the narrative fiction. Thus a system of equivalence develops in which A represents B, C represents D, the cicada represents parasitism and the ant industriousness, and so forth with underlying archetypal motivation, thus creating a basically symbolic mode of discourse. What matters in the fable is the sign value of the animal, its archetypal profile, which enables a system of metaphoric equivalence to be established between the referent and the symbol, between the representation and its reality. This codal system presupposes a procedure of translation to be performed by the reader wishing to commute intellectually from one code to the other in order to achieve meaningful communication.

Multi-level readings of the fable are encouraged because of the system of codal intersection and metaphoric equivalence whose polysemy · constitutes the very stuff of irony. In La Fontaine's fables there are at least four levels of meaning: the immediate or literal which is the animal or plant communication, a ridiculous and comic absurdity meant obviously for children; the implied and indirect meaning which is general, involving man in society, politics, and the satiric attack on institutions such as justice, court slavery, plagiary, war, etc. In contrast to the universal level is the topical, the social and political attack on institutions of the time; and, fourthly, the least obvious target of satiric attack, which is the direct opponent of the 'other,' that is, the absent 'I,' the poet, the fabulist, and, by extension, the reader.

Contrast is in the very nature of irony whose rhetorical signs fall into oppositional patterns: understated silence carries the same evocative power as exaggeration; sarcasm and euphemism avoid direct truth by oblique and attenuated surface language; periphrasis achieves by abundance what ellipsis effects by absence. Structural signs like rhythmic contrasts and doubling are higher-level manifestations of an antithetical state of mind at the very heart of irony. For every sign there is a basic clash between the expected and the represented, a destruction of established patterns, be they archetypal, rhetorical, structural, codal, or other. This destruction, observed primarily on the level of expression, is represented in the content of the fables by the thematics of alterity, the enemy of familiarity and expectation. Signs specific to the fable involve the unusual range of tones from the most serious and didactic carried through the medium of maxim, proverb, and generalizing direct language which runs counter to the childlike gaiety achieved through the symbolic language of the animals. The synthesis of these dissonances is irony, unwritten but implicit signification, writing between the lines, whose flashing but nonetheless subtle and almost imperceptible signals like insights light across the mind and force a searching reader to see more than before, to find satisfying and serious intellection amidst the joys of light-hearted comedy.

In the section devoted to the theatrical genre, a Molière comedy is examined for its generic relationship to satire. Fundamental generic similarity is a rather conventional given noted since Aristotle, especially with regard to comedy and tragedy. For example, Corneille's tragedy *Cinna* is as dependent on the reversal principle of irony as satire is, but for decidedly different purposes. In Racine's play, *Bajazet*, which is considered by some to be the most tragic of tragedies and the poetic illustration of a Cartesian quest for certainty, underlying causes for its unreliable communication systems are investigated, causes which result in the need by message receivers to rely on an intuitive reading of verbal and non-verbal signs to arrive at the essence of truth.

Tartuffe like *Macette* is a depiction of a hypocrite. In *Tartuffe* a double-level language involving the collocation of sensual and spiritual metaphoric codes constitute the stylistic marker of *Tartuffe*'s idiolect and one of the major signs of the play's verbal irony. The comic effects of non-verbal language and gestures like coughing are shown to cause a functional disparity between the literal and figurative significance of the act. This disparity is the irony of multiple meaning. The outlandish incongruities and oppositions within *Tartuffe*'s cast of characters and their roles, the scenic arrangements and production management are merely a few preliminaries for the sophisticated linguisitc trickery that emerges in Scene V, a play within the play. A sequential and selective rather than exhaustive analysis of this small segment of the play is conducted in the hopes of abstracting the models upon which the comic and satiric effects are articulated.

In the chapter entitled "The Big Switch: A Study of *Cinna*'s Reversals," a necessary relationship of the structure of reversal to dramatic and verbal ironies within tragedy is proposed and examined. By a varied and extensive use of poetic tools, Corneille manages to raise the expectation level of the reader to the heights of assurance only to have his self-confidence dashed by the re-arrangement of a carefully established pattern, a process of contradiction and surprise referred to as the big switch. The perceptual process involved in irony which stuns the reader into the realization of an illogical or impossible identity of oppositions is homologous to the process of reversal which is dependent upon the principles of similarity and difference. Irony is thus structurally inherent to tragedy. In *Cinna* through a masterful display of linguistic duplicity, the suggestion of actantial identities and exchanges, and the creative application of a reversal model hidden within the structural designs of the play, Corneille formally dramatizes the irony of his message: the power of pardon and the hatred of love.

In the chapter entitled "Signs of the Hidden: Semiotic Study of

Racine's *Bajazet*," the role of semiotics is examined in the establishment of a new order, a theatre of deception, which overthrows
the previous order of constraint, seclusion, and prohibition of
vision normally associated with the seraglio. In this atmosphere of
unaccustomed freedom and unreliable commentary, indirect and
symbolic language is the medium of communication. The *récit*,
indirect discourse, and intermediaries are transformations of the
indirect or symbolic language motivating the characters' tragic quest
for truth. Caught up in a network of conspiracies, undercover surveillance, and unreliable communication systems, the characters in
Bajazet crave the truth, a precious essence hidden deeply 'within'
but discernible from 'without' by seers endowed with phenomenological power. And yet, in a play written as a poetic quest for knowledge, the greatest of all ironies is Roxane's willful ignorance, her
desire for a return to the hidden. Unlike Descartes, who put faith in
the power of reason, the players in *Bajazet* demand evidence of
fact before the senses. The obscure path of their quest for reliable
knowledge is marked by silent, secret communications between the
outside and inside sources of threatened power – Babylon and
Byzantium, Amurat and Acomat – whose alliterations, assonances,
and symmetry are symptomatic of the hidden structural and stylistic order of the play. Coded communications are transmitted in
the prisonlike palace through the channels of false tales, gossip,
rumor, and espionage by disguised conspirators acting in a desperate
fear of distant oppression. The messages of this communication
system have various sign systems – some gestural, some scriptural,
some verbal, some physical – and two major operative principles:
truth and illusion. These sign systems are not universally coded and
are subject to diverse interpretations controlled primarily by the
presence of an immediate context. The receiver of the coded message
must first distinguish truth from illusion by sheer perception, and
then decode the message according to the accepted cultural significance of that particular sign. The polyvalence of blushing, for
example, causes Bajazet's lover great anguish. A peculiar ethos
develops in Racinian tragedy in which virtue lies not in the good
but in the power of vision, in the ability to read signs of the hidden,
an epistemological phenomenon encoded in the ever-present shadow
metaphor. Communication in *Bajazet* is depicted as the reading
of signs where the eyes of the reader assume the vital function of
the lens, and the face of the observed is the book on which signs
are written. Crying, fainting, blushing, sighs and moans are some
of the many *discours du visage* or body languages which *Bajazet*'s

characters must learn to decode in order to penetrate the hidden messages of the heart. Unmitigating scrutiny, the impossibility to hide from the inescapable and hostile *regard d'autrui*, this is the claustrophic atmosphere of Racine's tragedy where words, gestures, facial expressions, and even silence reveal the sacred hidden.

NOTES

[1] Julia Kristeva, *La Révolution du language poétique* (Paris: Seuil, 1974), p. 52.

[2] Cf. Roman Jakobson, *Essais de linguistique générale* (Paris: Minuit, 1963), pp. 61-67.

[3] *Cours de linguistique générale* (Paris: Payot, 1916), p. 33.

[4] Jan Mukařovský, one of the celebrated linguists of the Prague circle, considered the study of the arts, literature, painting, sculpture, and architecture a legitimate part of semiotics. See his article in *Poétique* 3 (1970) entitled "*Littérature et sémiologie*", 386-398.

[5] *Introduction à la sémiologie*, "Quelques traits du style de Jacques Lacan" (Paris: Minuit, 1970), pp. 181-188.

[6] Charles Sanders Peirce, *Collected Papers* (Cambridge: Harvard University Press, 1931-1935), V, 588.

[7] Cf. Umberto Eco, *La Structure absente* (Paris: Mercure de France, 1972), pp. 33-35; Roland Barthes, *Eléments de sémiologie* (Paris: Editions Gonthier, 1964), pp. 163-168; and Louis Hjelmslev, *Prolégomènes à une théorie du langage* (Paris: Editions de Minuit, 1966), pp. 144-157. The Danish edition appeared in 1943.

[8] Cf. Oswald Ducrot and Tzvetan Todorov, *Dictionnaire encyclopédique des sciences du langage* (Paris: Seuil, 1972), pp. 134-135.

[9] Cf. Emile Benveniste, "Nature du signe linguistique," *Problèmes de linguistique générale* (Paris: Gallimard, 1966), pp. 49-55, where he discusses the necessary relationship between the signifier and the signified. See also E. F. K. Koerner, *Contributions au débat post-Saussurien sur le signe linguistique* (The Hague: Mouton, 1972).

[10] Michael Riffaterre, "Le Contexte stylistique," *Essais de stylistique structurale* (Paris: Flammarion, 1971), pp. 64-94.

[11] Peirce, II, 300.

[12] Peirce, VIII, 288.

[13] *Dictionnaire encyclopédique des sciences du langage*, p. 115.

[14] *Le Texte du roman* (The Hague: Mouton, 1970), p. 26.

[15] *Cours de linguistique générale* (Paris: Payot, 1916), p. 101.

[16] "Pertinence idéologique du code," *Degrés* (7/8 juillet-octobre, 1974), 3-13.

[17] *Etudes de linguistique appliquée* (Paris, 1963), II, 37.

[18] *Language and Communication* (New York: McGraw Hill, 1951).

[19] *La Structure absente*, pp. 171-257, et passim. See also Pierre Guiraud, *La*

Sémiologie (Paris: PUF, 1971), pp. 37-38, and George Mounin, *Introduction à la sémiologie*, pp. 77-86.

[20] Eco, p. 13.

[21] Pierre Guiraud, *La Sémiologie*, pp. 55-115.

[22] See Roland Barthes' excellent semiotic and synchronic study entitled *Système de la mode* (Paris: Seuil, 1967).

II

NOVEL

CHAPTER 2

EROS AND THANATOS IN *ASTRÉE*

Eros is reborn in *Astrée* on the fertile plain of Forez in the valley of Lignon. Nurtured by oozing rivers and massive mountains, this fictional paradise is the birthplace of erotic experience.[1] Freud's famed struggle between "unregenerate instincts and overbearing culture" resembles the dialectics of eroticism: pleasure and pain, life and death, Eros and Thanatos.[2] Eroticism is a familiar but none-theless unfathomable concept to define. Its literary representation, which is the subject of this study, is in the realm of the symbolic. Honore D'Urfé's novel, *Astrée*, has never before been classified as erotic literature; it has always been the seventeenth-century pastoral, sentimental, and philosophical novel *par excellence*. We shall see that these classifications are not incompatible with the erotic. In order first to distinguish the underlying elements of eroticism and then determine their relationships within the literary or poetic discourse, and I use the word poetic in the larger sense, I will engage in an interdisciplinary approach. Applying principles of semiotics, psychoanalytics, and rhetoric to the definitional problem on hand. I hope to defamiliarize the familiar, and expose the deeply complex nature of eroticism whose very depth makes it a subject dear to creative artists.

Eroticism is not merely that which treats of sexual love, as the dictionaries say. Its concept is bound up in a highly complex connotational matrix involving the mythology of Eros, the philosophy and religion of love, the psychology of sexuality, to name but a few. Eroticism in literature is further complicated for it is representational, a signifying system. The literary representation of the erotic functions like a sign language with a code or set of equivalent transformations that allows the reader to move from one signifying system to another. In this manner the concepts of the erotic are observed indirectly in lit-erature as transforms, representations, signs. But many of these signs are not wholly arbitrary and by virtue of the frequency and stability of their association have a strong tendency toward symbolization.

Symbolic representation exists on at least two levels in *Astrée*. Overt symbols involve associations in which a speaker identifies an object or occurrence explicitly as a symbol, as for example in Book I when Celadon delivers an apostrophe to Astrée's ribbon – symbol of the unbinding ties of his affection,[3] or in Book IV when Celadon interprets Astrée's mysterious dream, the symbolic significance of which I will discuss in detail later in the study. Covert symbols, the more common form of implicit representation, involve motivated, relatively stable associations of elements on the same level, either between signifiers or between signified, between the symbol and the concept symbolized.[4] The association between these elements is either one of resemblance or contiguity. Thus the term *flamme*, which signifies "flame," in certain literary texts may symbolize *amour*.

What is erotic symbolism in psychology? According to Havelock Ellis, "erotic symbolism is that tendency whereby the lovers' attention is divorced from the central focus of sexual attraction to some object or process which is on the periphery of that focus, or is even outside of it altogether, though recalling it by association of contiguity or similarity."[5] Thus the semiotic and psychological approaches to symbolism are compatible and complementary. In contrast, the psychoanalytical approach to symbolism is at once all-inclusive and more specific, more descriptive but too reductive. Psychoanalytics "transforms all men into poets – incurable symbolists betraying unknown secrets with every word."[6] Freudian symbolism as expressed in his *Interpretation of Dreams* constitutes a model of containers and the contained. Objects are also governed by the principles of power and passivity. Every visible object depending upon its shape either as a container or the contained has potential as a genital symbol. In fact all objects, acts, and parts of the body have latent erotic significance; the determinant is not the object but the substance of its association. Psychoanalysis has a term for it, 'erotogenicity', which is the capacity of all body regions to be the source of sexual excitation, that is, to behave like an erotogenic zone. As Stanley Hall put it: "There is almost no feature, article of dress, attitude, act or even animal or perhaps object in nature, that may not have to some morbid soul specialized erogenic and erethic power."[7] Stated in semiotic terms, eroticism involves fundamentally arbitrary signs which by association become symbols linked with the very nature of perception.[8]

The relationship between the psychology of perception, the semiotics of symbolization, and rhetoric is based on an associative process common to all. For example, the perception of such rhetorical figures as comparison and metaphor depends upon the association of vehicle, base, and tenor.[9] Metonymy and synecdoche involve binary associations of part to whole, cause to effect, container to the contained, etc. There is little doubt that the rhetorical concepts of metaphor and metonymy influenced the formation of the Freudian concepts of displacement and condensation. Since virtually all perceptual stimuli are *potential* signs of eroticism, it must necessarily be in the literary and formal representation of the object that the message is conveyed.

This analysis which concentrates on the symbolic representation of erotic forms will follow the natural order of the psychological situation, that is the climate encouraging the birth of sexual desire, the sociological taboos, interdiction, and repression which motivate erotic sublimations, and finally the transgression, or erotic act itself.

I. CLIMATE OF EROS

Civilization, says Freud, thwarts Eros, and represses man's libidinal instincts.[10] D'Urfé depicts a primordial state of nature in the golden age of man. Lignon is a representation of unfettered civilization in which carefree, unrepressed shepherds and shepherdesses work the rich earth and roam the fertile fields. D'Urfé describes this idyllic enclosure of perfect symmetry with an abundant use of hyper-bolizing qualifiers that lend a fairy tale atmosphere to the larger context of the novel: As the novel opens, we read:

Auprès de l'ancienne ville de Lyon, du côté du soleil couchant, il y a un pays nommé Forez, qui en sa petitesse contient ce qui est *de plus rare au reste des Gaules*, car étant divisé en plaines et en montagnes, les unes et les autres sont *si* fertiles, et situées en un air *si* tempéré, que la terre y est capable de *tout ce que peut désirer* le laboureur. *Au coeur du* pays est *le plus beau* de la plaine, ceinte, comme d'une forte muraille, des monts assez voisins et arrosés du fleuve de Loire, qui prenant sa source assez près de là, passe presque par le milieu, non point encore trop enflé ni orgueilleux, mais doux et paisible. (p. 25)

The idealism of this romance motif is interrupted sporadically by the encroachment of reality — the threat of an insurrection by cruel invaders — part of a parallel epic motif that continues throughout *Astrée*. Thus, working in opposition to the creation of a magical climate outside of reality is the insistence on realism achieved by detailed documentation, mimetic description, and the frequent use of positioning signifiers (*au près de, du côté de, étant divisé en, au coeur de, près de, par le milieu, en divers lieux depuis ...).* In fact, it is my hypothesis that eroticism is perceived in *Astrée* as a threatened stasis of dynamic equilibrium, as the tensions of opposition, of reality and fiction, of Evil and Goodness, of Eros and Thanatos. As Merleau-Ponty put it in *Signes*: "Il n'y a fleurs du mal que s'il y a un Mal et un Bien, et de postulation vers Satan que s'il y a une postulation vers Dieu. Un certain érotisme suppose tous les liens traditionnels."[11]

The personification of the Loire and later the river Lignon is a conventional sign of the "paysage comme état d'âme" motif. The framing of this Cytherean paradise will naturally issue forth a depiction of its inhabitants who are reflections of an unrepressed civilization. In a short passage, it is possible to determine how the semiotic transference operates.

Or sur les bords de ces *délectables* rivières on a vu de tout temps quantité de bergers, qui pour la *bonté* de l'air, *la fertilité* du rivage et leur *douceur naturelle*, vivent avec autant de bonne fortune, qu'ils reconnaissent peu la fortune. (p. 25)

In this passage the reader is actually distracted from the transference of latent sensuality and attracted to the more manifest paranomasia, i.e., the signifiers 'fortune,' 'fortune,' an obvious play on words whose perception potential is heightened by its repetition and terminal position in the sentence. The more latent but nevertheless functional sense of eroticism can not remain unnoticed. They constitute the trace of a semantic paragram, to use a Saussurian term dear to Julia Kristeva but redefined and systematized by Michael Riffaterre.[12] The *para* – or, more accurately, the *hypo*gram, or that concept which is hidden under the surface signifiers, is in this instance Eros. The sensuality of the topographic context is transferred indirectly to the shepherds by association. Their simple life is a sociological index of Lignon's geographic perfection. (The word 'index', as Peirce defined it, is a sign whose referent is invisible, hidden, but whose relation to that object is real and accepted, like smoke which is an index of fire.) The transference is accomplished semiotically by the signifieds *délectables, fertilité*, and *douceur*. These terms are semic equivalents, tautological transformations of one and the same system of eroticism. They are displaced signs of the repressed, literary cover-ups for the desired but forbidden. The plural qualifier *délectables* transmits the pleasures of abundance – excess is a conventional sign of eroticism. *Douceur naturelle* is a sensory, and in that sense 'sensual', metaphor derived from agriculture. *Bonté de l'air* is a generalizing cliché whose specific attribute can be determined only by the senses. The semiotic system of the passage which is overdetermined[13] by sensuality and latent eroticism, is actually laid bare in the connotational matrix of the sign *fertilité*. The erotic suggestion in the word *fertilité* is due to an intersection of two codes, the sexual and agricultural. Since all the key words in the passage bear a tautological relation to the kernel but absent word, 'Eros,' it is no wonder that the sudden switch to the oxymoric, to a relationship of dissimilarity in "fortune-peu la Fortune," should capture the reader's attention. The message of Eros is hidden, suggested, muted under the masks of language and its multiple codes. Wittgenstein understood the mechanism when he said: "The aspects of things that are most important for us are hidden because of their simplicity and familiarity (one is unable to notice something — because it is always before one's eyes)."[14]

Lignon is a valley of unspeakable beauty,[15] a sacred place of temples, goddesses, nymphs, and lovers who gaily dance around bountiful fountains. The spiritual atmosphere of solitude and secrecy is favorable to the birth and continued development of erotic experiences:

De tout temps ce bocage avait été sacré au grand Hésus, Teutates et Tharamis. Aussi n'y avait-il berger qui eût la hardiesse de conduire son troupeau, ni dans le bocage, ni dans le préau; et cela était cause que personne n'y fréquentait guère, de peur d'interrompre *la solitude* et *le sacré silence* des nymphes, Pans et Egipans. (p. 115)

George Bataille discusses the relationship of religious and erotic experience in his excellent book entitled *Erotisme*. Bataille says:

Tout érotisme est sacré ... la recherche d'une continuité de l'être poursuivie systématiquement par delà le monde immédiat, désigne une démarche essentiellement religieuse.[16]

The spirituality of eroticism is suggested throughout *Astrée* by references to druids, temples, rites, and vows. The relationship is verbalized explicitly in the theoretical discussions of Adamas, the great priest, and Sylvandre who believes that man's instinct for love is given naturally by the gods for the preservation of the race (p. 131). In fact Bataille's discussion of the three forms of eroticism ("erotisme des corps, érotisme des coeurs, et érotisme sacré") corresponds to Adamas' metaphysical definition of beauty as love:

... l'amour n'est qu'un désir de beauté, y ayant trois sortes de beautés, celle qui tombe sous la vue, de laquelle il faut laisser le jugement à l'oeil, celle qui est en l'harmonie, dont l'oreille est seulement capable, et celle enfin qui est en la raison, que l'esprit seul peut discerner, il s'ensuit que les yeux, les oreilles et les esprits seules en doivent avoir la jouissance. (p. 104)

Love for Adamas is pure, saintly, a god in fact whose attributes are inscribed by the shepherd Sylvandre in a code of courtly love on the Twelve Tables of the Laws of Love. Perfection, idolatry, servitude, suffering, and death are some of the surfacing semes:

Qui veut être *parfait amant*
Il faut qu'il aime infiniment:

Qu'il n'aime jamais qu'en un lieu,
Et que cet amour soit *un dieu*
Qu'il adore pour *toute chose*

Qu'il arrête tous ses désirs
Au *service* de cette belle

Qu'épris d'un amour *violent*
Il aille sans cesse *brûlant*,
Et qu'il *languisse* et qu'il *soupire*
Entre *la vie* et *le trépas*. (pp. 120-122)

The courtly code, an appropriate vehicle for the romance motif, is especially apparent in the incongruous description of the shepherd Celadon who is portrayed as an admirable knight ready to fight to the death for his beloved. Dressed as a shepherdess, his accoutrements are those of a *chevalier*:

... l'habit de Bergère qu'il portait rendait toutes ses actions plus admirables. Son rondache était tellement hérissé de flèches qui s'y étaient plantées, que les dernières ne trouvaient plus de place vide, et fallait que par nécessité elles frappassent sur d'autres flèches. Son épée était toute teinte de sang, et la poignée même en dégouttait. Il était blessé en deux ou trois lieux ... une grande plaie ... la perte du sang ... (p. 281)

In fact Celadon's system of values — his courage, his undying service to his lady, his passion for glory and honor — bespeak the courtly tradition in a seventeenth-century world where men are *généreux* and women struggle to keep their reputation:[17]

Cruel devais-tu si longuement abuser de mon innocence pour me perdre enfin de réputation — on remarque sur mon front les apparences d'un crime que je ne commis jamais. (p. 308)

Only those imbued with saintly love can enter the temple dedicated to the adoration of Astreae, Goddess of Peace, Abundance, and Justice, an ironic name for the mythological symbol of Celadon's intractable mistress. In this temple all of nature contains symbols of love. Just as 'semen' came from the word 'seed,' there is no wonder that male and female organs and the whole process of human sexuality are represented metaphorically by signs of plant life. In the temple, for example, above a tree whose leaves are in the shape of an alter, there is an unusual painting containing symbols from agriculture. As an example of what was referred to earlier as overt symbolism, Pâris will subsequently explain the significance of the icon. As Peirce put it, the icon is the most direct means of representing an object which bears a natural, internal relationship of similarity to the sign:

... deux Amours étaient peints, qui essayaient de s'ôter l'un à l'autre une branche de myrte, et une de palme, entortillées ensemble. (p. 117)

Ces deux Amours, dit-il, gentille troupe, signifient l'Amant et l'Aimé. Cette palme et ce myrte entortillés signifient la victoire d'amour, d'autant que la palme est la marque de la victoire et le myrte de l'amour. Donc l'Amant et l'Aimé s'efforcent à qui sera victorieux, c'est-à-dire à qui sera plus amant. (p. 118)

Moreover, this sacred temple is built in a mysterious grove in which the most abundant growth of mistletoe in all Forez is to be found. The mistletoe, which is cut so that it may grow again in greater abundance, is traditionally symbolic of rebirth as the harbinger of new life. In its death (cutting) and rebirth, the mistletoe parallels the death of Celadon's identity and rebirth in the shape of Alexis who finally returns to life as Celadon in the Fountain of the Truth of Love.

Love, embodied in the portrait of the Roman goddess, is portrayed in dual terms. Both cruel and kind, a serpent symbolic of evil temptation whistles above her black and white head. She is painted as the archetypal *femme fatale*, the icon of Celadon's own Astrée who by rejection caused his near death in the river Lignon. Like a set of diminishing Russian dolls that fit neatly within each other's replica, Astreae symbolizes Astrée, and Astrée represents Eros in all his flamboyant ambivalence. Eros, Astreae, and Astrée are symbols of the same reality – love – each differing in degree of concretization.

Mont-verdun is another of Lignon's temples whose topographical description is rich in Freudian symbols, the imitation of coitus, and the portrayal of the phallus:

Mont-verdun est un grand rocher qui s'élève en pointe de diamant au milieu de la plaine du côté de Montbrison, entre la rivière de Lignon, et la montagne d'Isoure. Que s'il était un peu plus à main droite du côté de Laigneu, les trois pointes de Marcilly, d'Isoure et de Mont-verdun feraient un triangle parfait. On dirait que la nature a pris plaisir d'embellir ce lieu sur tous les autres de cette contrée. Car l'ayant élevé dans le sein de cette plaine, si également de tous côtés, il se va étrécissant peu à peu, et laisse au sommet le juste espace d'un temple, qui a été dédié à Teutates, Hésus, Tharamis, Bélénus ... Il y a trois ouvertures si spacieuses qu'un chariot y pourrait entrer: elles demeurent ordinairement closes ... (p. 157-158)

More meaningful, perhaps, than the disputable symbols of coitus is the emergence in this passage of an esthetics in which beauty is the expression of perfect harmony. Signs of symmetry in the topography mark the classical concept of beauty. The number three, the circle and the triangle, the diamond or purest of all precious stones, the middle or heart of the plain, and signifiers like "également," and "le juste espace" help in the decoding of the esthetic message.

Within the walls of enclosed temples, like the womb of Lignon's surrounding mountains, there are many enchanting fountains with truly magical powers. The Fountain of the Truth of Love is in the Palais d'Isoure where three ravishing nymphs keep Celadon captive, after Galathée rescues him from the waters of Lignon, like Ulysses on the isle of Calypso. The fountain is depicted in a plethora of hyperboles and signs of secrecy which invite eroticism:

Il y avait près de sa chambre *un escalier dérobé*, qui descendait en une galerie basse, par où avec un pont-levis on entrait dans le jardin agencé de *toutes les raretés* que le lieu pouvait permettre, fût en fontaines et en parterres, fût en *allées* et *en ombrages*, n'y ayant *rien* été oublié de tout ce que l'artifice y pouvait ajouter. (p. 47)

The fountain itself is a metonym for a larger motif of waters. In *Astrée* water functions not only as the traditional literary symbol of life and rebirth, but also as the agent of death. In its duality water is a perfect symbol of Eros. The river Lignon, for example, is the source of life for the valley and near death for Celadon. The description of the Fountain of the Truth of Love (even the name associates water and love) continues the codes of magic and mystery implicit in the signifiers "merveilleuse," "caverne," "l'antre de la vieille Mandrague," "raretés," and "sortilèges:"

Assez près de là dans un autre carré, était la fontaine de la Vérité d'amour, source à la vèrité merveilleuse ... à l'autre des carrés était la caverne de Damon, et de Fortune, et au dernier, l'antre de la vieille Mandrague, plein de tant de raretés et de tant de sortilèges, que d'heure à autre, il y arrivait toujours quelque chose de nouveau; (p. 48)

Like the nymphs who customarily presided over the streams, and for whom the term *labia minora* or *nympha* is derived, wetness is intimately associated with the erotic process. The labia minora direct the urinary stream. And I refer to Ellis' discussion of the magic powers of urine and the role of wetness in eroticism.[18] He says rather emphatically that there is indeed no excretion or product of the body which has not been a source of ecstacy: "the sweat from every part of the body, the saliva and menstrual fluid, even wax from the ears" (p. 57). Moreover, the erogenic zones are primarily located in mucous areas. Water is the sign of fertility, life, and thus Eros, whereas dryness implies aridity, impotence, and death. Wetness *is* erotic, which explains the current cosmetic fashion for lip gloss and the previous fad in clothing for the 'wet look,' the 1960's greasy-shiny look, the black leather jacket fad, the rage for patent leather, etc., In *Astrée* the kingdom of Forez was once covered entirely by water, until a mysterious stranger opened passageways in the surrounding mountains to let the water out. Like Venus surging from out of the sea, Forez was born.

The river Lignon, "fâcheuse rivière," "le malheureux et diffamé Lignon," is a metonym of Death, "un demon" it is called, and therefore the perfect symbol of love's duality. In a poem written to and about the river Celadon verbalizes its symbolism through the vehicle of comparison:

Rivière que j'accrois couché parmi ces fleurs, *Je considère en toi ma triste ressemblance*: De deux sources tu prends en même temps naissance. Et mes yeux ne sont rien que deux sources de pleurs. (p. 160)

The narrator expresses the parallel between Lignon and Celadon less explicitly by antithesis:

Mais la vue de cette rivière qui avait été presque présente à tous *ses bonheurs* passés et qui aussi avait vu naître le commencement de son extrême *malheur*. (p. 225)

The symbolism of the river reaches its most manifest state in Book V where Lignon is personified as a fatal aggressor striving for glory:

Lignon, qui n'est jamais plus orgueilleux que lorsqu'il a reçu, comme en dépôt, des montagnes voisines, toutes les marques qu'elles ont eues de la colère de l'air, s'enfla si fort en moins de deux heures, par le moyen des nuées qui se fondirent en eau, que tenant en cela de la nature des torrents, il sembla qu'il fût plutôt destiné pour *noyer* les campagnes, que pour les *arroser*. Dans cette *gloire* ... (p. 339)

Latent erotic symbolism is rendered more overt in the rest of the personified description of Lignon by the surfacing of semes of water. (*mouillés, mer, humide*), fetal serenity (*sein, mère, ouvrant les bras*), and more explicitly by reference to the customary metonym of the sex act (*lit*). With the symbolism uncovered and the message laid bare, the passage can be read as a veritable simulacra of erotic experience:

Dans cette gloire, par laquelle il prétendait se faire craindre à Loire même, qui le reçoit tous les jours dans son sein pour le rendre à la mer, qui est sa mère, il ouvrit ses bras, et portant ses bords en des lieux qu'il n'avait jamais mouillés, il enferma dans son humide lit toutes les fleurs qui auparavant étaient nées sur ses rivages. (p. 339)

The physical setting of Lignon – its temples, fountains, rivers, grottos, caverns, and palaces – assumes a semiotic function as a sign of the lovers' threatened peace. The strife of other lovers like Diane and Sylvandre also reflects the main characters' situation. Nature imitates the lovers' emotions according to the principle of pathetic fallacy. In one of the more erotic and suggestive passages in the novel in which Celadon enters the Fountain of the Truth of Love and is greeted by lions and unicorns who fight to the kill, all of nature reacts in sympathy to the bestial combat:

... tout à coup ils virent que le Ciel, qui un peu auparavant était aussi beau et aussi serein qu'il eût jamais été, se couvrit de brouillards, et retira tellement à soi toute la lumière du soleil, qu'il sembla que la Terre eût périr dans l'effroi des ténèbres qui l'environnèrent. (p. 353)

Flowers are transformed into "puanteur du soufre"; the light of day disappears and is seen only in streaks of lightning; thunder rages to compete with the anger of the gods, and the whole setting becomes a miraculous sound and light performance. Darkness, in the form of shadows, acts as a symbol of violence, death, and Thanatos while light from the sun represents clarity, love, life, and Eros:

Mais lorsqu'ils étaient le plus avant dans la créance de *périr*, tout à coup les *éclairs* et les *tonnerres* cessèrent, mais non pas l'*obscurité*, car elle demeura aussi grande qu'elle était auparavant ... enfin les *ténèbres* commencèrent à se dissiper, et *le soleil*, redonnant le jour au monde, rendit l'émail aux fleurs, et aux arbres *l'ombre* et la couleur qu'il leur avait ôtées ...
Après avoir été quelque temps à considérer ces prodiges ... ils aperçurent au milieu de cette *obscurité* un *Amour* tout brillant de *clarté* s'élévant peu à peu, parut enfin tout droit sur l'amortissement d'une pyramide de porphyre ... ce dieu se perdit sous la fontaine ... n'y resta plus *d'obscurité*. (p. 354-355)

But the symbolism of lightness and darkness does not have an altogether stable association for earlier in the book, in a continuous alternation between pleasure and pain, "clarté" is related to death, suffering, and the tormenting sight of the temptress Astrée:[19]

Et maintenant, qu'est-ce que tu ne lui fais pas souffrir, *l'éblouissant*, pour ainsi dire, de trop de *clarté*, et le faisant soupirer pour *voir trop* ce qu'autrefois il regrettait de voir trop peu? (p. 221)

D'Urfé manipulates the signifier as well as the signified, especially with regard to names. Astrée, whose name is a derivative of *astre* or any celestial body, comet, planet, or star, represents by metonymy the appreciative concept of light in all its mystical, spiritual senses. 'Astre' is the vehicle of the precious metaphors *Astre du ciel* and *Astre du jour* and, by virtue of its frequency as a literary cliché, the initial meaning of *astre* is extended to include the sun. Astrée, herself, as the quintessential beauty and source of Celadon's life, is naturally identified with the sun and other variants on the paradigm of light: *clarté, jour, lumière, vue*:

... le soleil était déjà fort haut, et n'eût été que la bergère Astrée se tourna sans y penser d'un autre côté, et par ce moyen lui ôta *cette agréable vue*, elle y eût bien été retenue encore plus longtemps, mais *privée de la clarté de ce beau soleil*, elle demeura comme *l'oeil dans les ténèbres*, lui semblant que *l'obscurité* était partout, puisque l'on lui avait caché ce que seulement elle jugeait digne d'employer et de retenir *sa vue*. (p. 221)

D'Urfé plays linguistic tricks with the referents implied in the name Astrée and creates a symbolic system in which alternating light and dark imitate human emotions vacillating in response to the pleasure-pain principle. Darkness, represented by *ténèbres, obscurité, brouil-lards, la nuit*, is symbolically polyvalent signifying the pains of ignorance, guilt, and the absence of love:

L'aurore le surprit dans cet assoupissement et, comme si elle eût voulu donner des larmes à la disgrâce de ce berger, elle lui mouilla le visage de l'humidité de sa rosée ... C'est aux coupables, continua-t-il, à fuir *la clarté*, mais à ceux qui ne font point d'action qui ne soit louable, *le jour* ne saurait jamais *luire* trop *claire-ment*. (p. 338)

II. INTERDICTION

The causes of love's pain are many – jealousy, rejection, silence, absence of the loved one, and total interdiction. In the resultant process of repression the lover, entrapped by love's powers and unable to resist, is forced against all nature to avoid the object of his affection. The force of love is represented literarily by the metaphor of the magnet (*aimant*) whose orthographic affinity with the verb *aimer* facilitates the perception of the symbolic association. The lover's state of mind is frequently described through the meta-phor of a prison, not unlike the platonic image of love's heart encased within the body.[20] Impossible to remain in this unnatural state of emotional and physical deprivation, the lover resorts to erotic sub-limations for gratification which accords untold pleasures. Psychic compensation for repressed desires takes many forms all of which tend to imitate that which is painfully denied. When the imitation approaches reality, rejection is reenacted and the lover, forced once again to avoid his temptress, will experience the tumultuous alterna-tions of pain and pleasure for the rest of the cycle. Celadon and Astrée reciprocally experience sadness and happiness in their mutual states of unrequited love. This duality is expressed by proximal anti-thesis:

Fut-il jamais amant plus *heureux* et plus *malheureux* que moi? (p. 235)

Mais voyez quels sont les enchantements d'amour: elle recevait *un déplaisir extrême* de la mort de Celadon, et toutefois elle n'était point sans quelque *contentement* au milieu de *tant d'ennuis* connaissant que véritablement il ne lui avait point été infidèle. (p. 42)

As the icon of love's duality, Astrée is represented oppositionally as goodness and evil, sun and darkness, source of life and death. Not the Freudian mother figure of warmth, protection and unqualified love (although Astrée calls Celadon significantly "mon fils"), Astrée is rather the cold and untouchable *femme-fatale* who inflicts ceaseless tortures upon her lover:

O que de *mortelles* mémoires lui remit-il en l'esprit! Il se représenta *tous les courroux* qu'en cet instant-là elle avait peints au visage, *toutes les cruautés* que son âme faisait paraître et par ses paroles et par ses actions, et *tous les dédains* avec lesquels elle avait proféré les ordonnances de son bannissement. (p. 49-50)

Not appreciably different from the courtly *Dame* in medieval romances, Astrée sees herself, and not without recrimination, as the *bourroux*, the irresistible man-killer whose cruel, punishing nature[21] literally transfigures Celadon:

Je suis tant *insupportable* que ce n'est guère moins entreprendre que l'impossible. Il faudra servir, souffrir, et n'avoir des yeux, ni de l'amour que pour moi: car ne croyez point que je veuille avoir à partir avec quelque autre, ni que je reçoive une volonté à moitié mienne. Je suis *soupçonneuse,* je suis *jalouse*, je suis *difficile à gagner*, et *facile à perdre*, et puis *aisée à offenser* et très *malaisée à rapaiser* ... (p. 52)

She is unquestionably the aggressor. Even in love-making she reduces her man to a blithering, frightened servant, "pâle et transi plus que n'est pas une personne morte" (p. 29).[22] Adamas, the great priest and moral conscience of the community, reminds Astrée that it was she, in fact, and not Celadon who initiated and controlled all acts of love:

... vous avez presque toujours commencé de le caresser et de le baiser. (p. 332)

Her unusual boldness shocks even her lover who, revelling in the ecstasies of sensual pleasure, inappropriately opens his eyes:

... elle (Astrée) le baisa encore une fois, mais elle demeura si longtemps attachée sur ses lèvres que le berger se laissant transporter à l'excès de ce plaisir, ne put s'empêcher de soupirer et d'ouvrir les yeux. (p. 302)

Astrée's supernatural power to transform Celadon is a necessary condition of platonic love as D'Urfé conceived it. His theories are discussed philosophically by Hylas and Sylvandre, each of whom represents respectively the pains and pleasures of love. Espousing constancy and extremity toward the attainment of idealized love, Sylvandre understands that transformation, unification, and ineluctable death come of a unique match made in heaven:

Savez-vous bien que c'est qu'aimer? C'est *mourir en soi* pour revivre en autrui, c'est ne se point aimer que d'autant que l'on est agréable à la chose aimée, et bref, c'est une volonté de *se transformer*, s'il se peut entièrement en elle. (p. 78)

Celadon will interpret this definition literally first by an attempted suicide and later by disguise which is a form of self-destruction. In accordance with the cyclical structures of the novel, death and destruction appropriately begin the story and life will end it with Astrée's ultimate commandment to love and "vivre" (p. 365). On Celadon's "vain tombeau" an epitaph is inscribed beneath a picture of sorrowful Cupid whose torch is out and whose bow and arrow are now broken. Love is named as the cause of Celadon's death:

... amour qui par imprudence fut cause de la mort de Celadon (p. 187).

Rites are performed at this sacred tomb where traditional symbols of fertility (fish, lamb, and a young bull) are offered in sacrifice to Ceres, goddess of all living things. Simulated deaths also occur when Celadon loses consciousness during the ecstacies of an embrace: Fainting is here as in Racine's famous "évanouissement" in *Bajazet* a tell-tale symptom of some illness, here the index of love:

... il fut *mort* sans doute dans les douceurs de ce ravissement ... n'ayant pu *mourir* de tristesse dans l'excès de vos vigueurs, il *meure* de contentement au milieu des faveurs (p. 367).

Celadon's transformation takes place more inventively by the voluntary adoption of a feminine disguise, a symbolic renunciation of his rights to manhood:

Si cela est, ajouta le druide, *vous cessez d'être homme.* – Il y a longtemps, répliqua le berger, que ce souci ne me touche nullement. (p. 164)

The total dissolution of the being will occur when Astrée eventually adopts Celadon's disguise and Celadon reciprocally becomes Astrée. Celadon's symbolic death is accompanied by a blight on nature, and his final resurrection in Book V sees a resurgence of vegetation.[23] Fearful of the self-destruction implicit in spiritual love, Hylas refuses to submit to its powers and is satisfied, instead, with lower level sensual pleasures:

Mais pour lui plaire, il faut au rebours fuir comme poison l'extrémité de l'amour, puisqu'il n'y a rien entre deux amants de plus ennuyeux que cette si grande et extrême affection. (p. 75)

The pleasures of pain, the flowers of evil, love as death — these themes developed most notably by Sade, Baudelaire, and more recently Bataille and Klossowsky — are not unfamiliar in the history of French literature. Like Deleuze who patterns the sex drive after the life instinct but links sexuality with destruction,[24] Bataille sees death as a necessary part of eroticism, the natural extension of violence, violation and transgression. Bataille defines eroticism as follows:

L'érotisme est, je crois l'approbation de la vie jusque dans la mort. La sexualité implique la mort;[25]

Although Bataille does not seem to differentiate sexuality from eroticism in this instance — eroticism being the surface manifestation of an internal experience and sexuality the libidinal drive — he distinguishes the two rather clearly in the book on the basis of a spiritual element:

L'activité sexuelle des hommes n'est pas nécessairement érotique. Elle l'est chaque fois qu'elle n'est pas rudimentaire, qu'elle n'est pas simplement animale.[26]

Spirituality is reciprocity in *Astrée* where love is a system of exchange. The motivations of the exchange are referred to by Freud as the duplicity of erotic sentiment. Freud contended that satisfaction gained from an object or person is nothing more than a narcissistic, underhanded means of self-love. Reciprocal self-interest is transmitted linguistically in *Astrée* through the subtle establishment of a materialist code whose signifieds belong to the field of economics — losses, gains, receipts, payment, services:

Il est vrai que si en *la perte* de soi-même on peut faire quelque *acquisition,* dont on se doive contenter, il se peut dire heureux de s'être *perdu* si à propos, pour *gagner* la bonne volonté de la belle Astrée, qui assurée de son amitié, ne voulut que l'ingratitude en fût le *paiement,* mais plutôt une *réciproque* affection avec laquelle elle *recevait* son amitié et ses *services.* (p. 26)

In sympathetic response to Celadon's suicide, Astrée partially fulfills her own death-wish by falling into the river Lignon:

Plût aux dieux qu'au même temps qu'il se précipita, je me fusse noyée avec lui, je ne languirais pas à cette heure dans la peine où je suis (p. 309).

Astrée becomes Alexis, and Alexis Astrée. Both are temporarily united in a spiritual bond through the duplicity of mask:

Il jure sur le sein d'Astrée *une union éternelle* avec elle (p. 266).

J'ordonne donc qu'*Astrée sera Alexis*, et qu'*Alexis sera Astrée*, et que nous bannirons de nous, non seulement toutes les paroles, mais toutes les moindres actions que peuvent mettre quelque différence entre nous (p. 255).

The transference is completed semiotically when Astrée, immediately after the exchange of identity, asks Celadon to issue a commandment — formerly she had been the dispenser of all orders. Her symbolic function as authority figure is created by the sheer repetition throughout the novel of the obsessional command: "Va t'en déloyal et garde — toi de te faire jamais voir à moi, que je ne te le commande" (p. 29).

Vous me permettrez donc, madame, répliqua Astrée, de vous en demander un commandement ... (p. 255).

The unification of lovers is so complete that their identities are dangerously confused by the insurgent Polémas (whose name is symbolic of war, a necessary facet of the violence in Eros). In a furious search for the death of Alexis, Polémas takes Astrée as a hostage. Astrée as Alexis is resolved to die in the place of her lover, but all is saved by the miraculous intercession of fate acting in compliance with a grandiose exchange system. Semire, the original cause for Astrée's jealousy, subsequent banishment and death of Celadon, will now die in the place of Astrée/Alexis.

III. SUBLIMATION

Disguise is only one of the many forms of sublimated behavior developed as a topos in *Astrée* and intricately allied with erotic elements such as nudity, voyeurism, lesbianism, and transvestitism. The first incidence of disguise occurs during the judgement of Pâris, immediately following Astrée's rejection and Celadon's subsequent attempted suicide. Like a fateful wish fulfillment, three beautiful half-naked nymphs dressed as huntresses appear before Celadon. Erotic effects in the description of these nymphs are achieved explicitly by reference to erogenic zones (*le sein*) and implicitly by reference to parts of the body traditionally representative of erotic processes. Hair, which in this case is long and scattered according to the cliché "cheveux épars," has enjoyed a long history of symbolism as sexual power since the Samson-Delila legend. Less explicitly but, in my opinion, most successfully is the effect of eroticism achieved by suggestion. Nudity is never complete, only implied, and always partial; hair is never straight always scattered and sometimes undulating, suggesting the intrinsically erotic semes of liquid and flow:

Et lorsqu'il était entre la mort et la vie, il arriva sur le même lieu trois belles Nymphes, dont les *cheveux épars* allaient *ondoyant* sur les épaules, couverts d'une guirlande de diverses perles: elles avaient le sein découvert, et les manches de la robe retroussées jusques sur le coude (p. 32)

Celadon's first disguise as a shepherdess enables him as voyeur to see three partially naked beauties without himself being seen. His disguise in the judgement scene is a preparation for the major transvestitism in the novel, that is when Celadon becomes Alexis. Transvestitism, a perversion resulting from repressed erotic desires, develops in this case to suggested lesbianism as Astrée and Alexis fall furiously in love. Astrée appears troubled by her own feelings:

... je suis tellement éloignée de toutes ces affections que plusieurs autres filles de mon âge pourraient ressentir que jamais je n'ai aimé *homme* quelconque pour ce sujet ... je prenais autant de plaisir à être caressée d'elle, que si j'eusse été *un homme* et non pas *une fille*. (p. 253)

... la bergère lui donnant le bonjour la convia de la recevoir en ses bras pour la baiser, et se la pressant contre le sein, et la sentant presque toute nue ... ces caresses étaient un peu plus serrées que celle que les filles ont accoutumé de se faire; (p. 234)

However, lesbianism does not seem to carry the same stigma in D'Urfé's *Astrée* that it has up until very recently in western civilization:

Et en disant ces paroles, elle lui baisait tantôt les yeux, tantôt la bouche, et quelquefois le sein, sans que la bergère en fît point de difficulté, *la croyant être fille*. (p. 234)

The misunderstandings of gender due to Celadon's adoption of a feminine disguise and the general atmosphere of promiscuity throughout the novel are not without some ironic effects:

... et parce que c'était la coutume que celle qui recevait la pomme, baisait le juge pour remerciement, je fus contrainte de la baiser; mais je vous assure, que quand jusques alors je ne l'eusse point reconnu, j'eusse bien découvert que c'était un berger, car *ce n'était point un baiser de fille.* (p. 70)

During the judgment of Pâris three beauties undress with pain-staking slowness, exposing their unspeakable charms for Celadon to admire in the Temple of Beauty dedicated appropriately to Venus. Time is extended in the description of this voyeur scene whose intrinsic taboo enhances the erotic effect:

Nous commençâmes, selon l'ordonnance, à nous déshabiller ... Celadon, à qui le temps semblait trop long, après avoir peu entretenu Malthée, voyant que je n'y allais point, m'appela paresseuse. (p. 68)

The antepositioned sentence with three interruptive clauses post-poning the climax formally imitates Celadon's impatience. The passage, like a slow strip-tease, continues with appropriately exclama-tive signs seen in the finalizing and emotive "Enfin," the expletive "Mon Dieu" followed by an exclamation mark itself. Astrée, like Godiva in all her enticing nudity, is covered almost entirely by her long and scattered hair adorned with nothing but a token of Celadon's love; a garland of flowers. The ironic juxtaposition of nakedness and flowers (traditional symbol of beauty, freshness, purity, and by extension of virginity and, thus, "cultural repression"), is a perfect example of the literary representation of the erotic as the threatened stasis of dynamic equilibrium. D'Urfé varies a garland of flowers with a garland of "diverses perles," but the effect is the same. Pearl, in its whiteness and roundness is the homologous symbol of purity, the hymen, that which is contained within a tight clam, the hidden, the forbidden. Against a backdrop of nakedness or shameful taboo, the pearl and the flower represent the oppositional goodness. Together the image represents a threat, instinct and culture at odds, Eros.

Enfin ... j'y fus contrainte, mais mon Dieu! j'avais les cheveux épars, qui me couvraient presque toute, sur lesquels pour tout ornement je n'avais que la guirlande que le jour auparavant il m'avait donnée. (p. 68)

Nudity is an unleashing of Eros from the bonds of civilization. As an index of relaxed taboo, loss of modesty, and an attempt at symbolic unification with the observer, nudity is a literary symbol of beauty and its reference in suggested form enhances its erotic effect:

Quand les autres furent retirées, et qu'il me vit en cet état auprès de lui, je pris bien garde qu'il changea deux ou trois fois de couleur, mais je n'en eusse jamais soupçonné la cause; de mon côté la honte m'avait teint la joue d'une si vive couleur, qu'il m'a juré depuis de ne *m'avoir jamais vue si belle,* et eût bien voulu qu'il lui eut été permis de demeurer tout le jour en cette contemplation. (p. 68)

The sight of Astrée during the judgment of Pâris is an actualization through voyeurism of Celadon's fantasies:

Tout *son plaisir* était en ses imaginations, avec lesquelles il passait les jours et les nuits. (p. 137)

The portrait of Astrée which Celadon carries about his neck allows him hours of pleasurable contemplation which he describes poetically in a chiasmus representing love's antithetical nature:

Privé de mon vrai bien, ce bien faux me soulage. (p. 140)

The fabulous atmosphere of Lignon – its enchanted fountains, talking genie,[27] and sacred mistletoe, the miraculous apparition of the God of Love, the magical transformation of stone statues into big as life ferocious lions and unicorns – these are metaphors of Celadon's fantasizing, a psychological process motivated largely by wishfulfillment and most clearly illustrated in Astrée's dream. But the dream in D'Urfé's *Astrée* does not correspond to Freud's concept of a dream as an unconscious fantasy containing the day residue, having a manifest and latent dream-content which is subject to the distortion processes of repetition, displacement and condensation. The dream in *Astrée* is a conscious fantasy of a dream, a literary motif of the prophetic whose interpretation or more strictly whose decoding is determined more by the elements of a *platonic* code than by a psychoanalytical model. D'Urfé's dream motif is a vehicle for the prophesy of impending doom, a sign of the dreamer's fear, a literary device like that used frequently by Petrarch. Despite the obvious influence that the rhetorical concepts of metaphor and metonymy must have played on the Freudian concepts of displacement and condensation, the literary dream is created with linguistic, stylistic, and symbolic mechanisms, the real dream with only symbolic mechanisms. Thus the application of the Freudian model must necessarily be done with great caution. As Henri Meschonnic put it: "des signifiants textuels – ne sont pas des signifiants du rêve."[28]

D'Urfé provides proof for the literary motif of the dream as prophesy in Book II.[29] Like a preparation for the big dream scene in Book IV, Astrée dreams that she has seen Celadon's soul. Phillis denies the prophetic value of dreams in perfect accordance with the Freudian operation of negation, *Verneinung*, or, more accurately termed in French, *la dénégation*:

Ma soeur – c'est une folie de croire aux songes, car l'imagination nous représente en dormant ce que nos yeux ont vu en veillant, ce que nous avons fait ou pensé, si bien qu'ils ne sont pas présages du futur, mais seulement images du passé. (p. 182)

The elements of the dream in Book IV are nevertheless over-determined by erotic symbolism.[30] In the dream Astrée enters a thick brushwood forest full of trees and brambles, a context indicative of the dreamer's complicated internal conflicts and fears of impending danger. Thorns rip most of her clothes, and her sight is hindered by darkness. Physical danger is symbolized here by thorns; darkness represents the fear of the unknown. Her modesty and psychological protection are threatened as expressed by the suggestion of nudity and violence in the torn clothes. This atmosphere of sensual stimulation (thorns, brambles, loss of sight) and psychological inhibition which she calls "une peine" reaches its climax when she verbalizes hyperbolically and in poetic language the threat to her body:

Je sentais à tous coups *la pointe* de ces *épines* jusques dans *la chair.* (p. 263)

And if one subscribes to the Lacanian dominance or insistence of the signifier, it is not too difficult to see the repressed distortion and phonemic displacement of the male genital organ in the surface signifiers *peine, pointe,* and *épines.* Still amidst the darkness, whose obsessive repetition indicates the extent of the dreamer's fears, an unknown person approaches her and says, curiously hiding his face and extending his hand, that if she followed him, he would take her out of her misery. Unidentifiable strangers with empty faces occur frequently in dreams, and by virtue of their imprecise physiognomy and resultant abstraction assume a greater symbolic function. This anonymity is carried over into the environment (a non-descript woods), and is translated by the dreamer's constant use of an expres-

sion os imprecision, "ill m'a a semblé que" and the equally vague
"l'autre." Even the stranger's gender is initially unknown for Astrée
refers to him as "une personne" whose object pronoun is logically
"elle" despite the neuter value of the noun. Later she speaks of
"*ma* guide," clearly identifying the gender as feminine. A confusion
results, not unlike the bizarre but coherent use of "elle" to refer to
Celadon disguised as Alexis. The stranger, who represents help and
security[31] in this forest of darkness that is life, is, by situational and
linguistic similarity, Celadon's symbol. However, his strangeness, his
secrecy, and the extension of his hand which, according to Freud, is
a threatening phallic symbol, reveal the dreamer's fears of this agent
of good will. After having thanked him, a sign of politeness in
civilization and an index of the dreamer's inhibition, she followed
him, still unable to see although seeing somewhat better than before.
Increased vision is an indication that the dreamer's fears of the unknown are abating. But rather than the progression to a happy
ending at this turning point, the dominant stranger, in perfect reciprocity like the attributes of spiritual love, now assumes the identically
passive role of the dreamer lost in the woods:

... mais nous ne pouvons sortir *ni l'un ni l'autre* du bois où nous étions.
(p. 263)

By the association of similar attributes wherein love is a system of
exchange, transformation, and unification, the dream of the two lost
and groping people symbolizes love itself. Finally someone intercedes
between her and the guide for the explicit purpose of separating
them – a physical manifestation of the dreamer's fear of disturbance
in the love affair. The guide and she squeeze each other's hands so
hard, and the interceptor pulls with such force, first on one side then
on the other, that the hand which Astrée was holding becomes
detached from the guide's body. At precisely this moment, like
a spontaneous miracle, she sees a little bit of light. This sequence is a
metaphoric representation of the transformation and self-destruction
characteristic of love's powers. It is a repetition and more concretized
symbolic representation of the first scene in which the stranger
extends his hand and the dreamer's vision then increases. The gradual
acquisition of reciprocal identities is indicated linguistically in the
elongated sentence below by the interplay of representative signifiers like the pronouns "elle et moi," "nous," the metonym "d'un
côté et d'autre," and the periphrasis "celle qui me conduisait," all of
which refer to the stranger without actually naming him.

Enfin il m' a semblé que quelqu'un s'étant mis entre *ma guide et moi* pour nous séparer, elle m'a tellement serré la main, *et moi à elle* pour ne la lâcher point, que l'autre y mettant toute sa force, enfin a tant tiré, et *d'un côté et d'autre*, que la main que je tenais s'est détachée du bras de celle qui me conduisait, et en même temps il m'a semblé de voir quelque peu de lumière. (p. 263)

The hand is a concretized symbol (by synechdoche) of the stranger's body and more specifically of the spiritual and physical help which his presence as guide accords to the lost dreamer. The detachment of the hand is a sign of self-destruction and unification with the other. When this unification begins, which is spiritual and sacred, enlightenment ("quelque peu de lumière") simultaneously occurs, enabling the dreamer to better observe the hand. The simultaneity of the situations is signalled not only by the time indication "en même temps" but more subtly by a repetition at the beginning and end of the syntagm of "il m'a semblé que." That this hand represents the essence of the other is corroborated by its subsequent transformation into a throbbing heart, the traditional literary and metonymic symbol of spiritual love in the platonic code. In a different but related code "heart" is a metonym of life (the heartbeat is a medical sign of life); thus the relationship of Eros and the life instinct is established semiotically by an intersection of codes. The attribute "throbbing" indicates love's intensity and introduces sensuality into the spiritual context. At this moment the interceptor comes back with a big knife in his hand, symbol of violence and death, both of which are elements of eroticism.[32] He strikes the heart such a great blow, that the dreamer is covered completely with blood. This scene represents the ominous nature of the outside world and the dreamer's increased fears of love's destruction, formerly represented more abstractly by the interceptor's presence. Since she and her guide are now one, this destruction would mean self-annihilation, a fear which is signified in the dreamer being covered with blood, the life force of the other. The knife, perhaps another phallus indicative of the nature of the threat, but more certainly a metonym for destruction, is the symbol of death, and the heart a symbol of life. The scene then becomes a representation of the external struggle between the life and death instincts, Eros and Thanatos. The dreamer, horrified at what has happened, throws the broken heart down on the ground and sees it change into Celadon. This frightens her; she screams and wakes up. The end of the dream renders explicit the symbolic system in which the stranger, the guide, the hand, and the heart represent Celadon, the lover. The aggregate which is gouverned by a process of symbolic repetition and increased concretization is a representation of love itself.

When Celadon (as Alexis) briefly interprets this dream for Astrée, he is indirectly revealing his mask. His interpretation is thus another attempt at wise fulfillment and a need to declare his true identity. The confession, however, is without any real significance for Astrée does not know that behind Alexis's symbolic language lay the bittersweet reality that Alexis is Celadon:

Ce bois où vous étiez si plein de ronces et d'obscurité, dit Alexis, c'est quelque peine où vous êtes, et de laquelle vous avez peu d'espérance de sortir. Cell qui se présente, et qui vous rend le chemin dans le bois plus aisé, c'est moi. Celui qui veut séparer, c'est que je serai contrainte de m'en retourner aux Carnutes par Adamas. Enfin l'on nous séparera, mais je vous laisserai mon coeur, qui vous tiendra lieu de celui de Celadon, et avec la connaissance que vous en aurez, vous vivrez à plus contente que vous n'avez pas été par le passé, ce qui vous est montré par la clarté qui depuis vous est apparue. (p. 264)

Voyeurism, like dream and fantasy, is a form of sublimation intricately related to the initial interdiction by the loved one and usually involving nudity. The eyes have always occupied a privileged position in eroticism from the time of medieval romances when Cupid's arrow shot through the eye of the victim. In his famous anthropological study entitled *The Sexual Life of Savages in North-western Melanesia* (1962) Malinowski, reporting on the role of eyes in the lovemaking process, found that lovers in one ancient tribe actually ate each other's eye lashes. Moreover, any woman found with eye lashes was considered either an unsuccessful lover or a maiden. All through seventeenth-century French novels, and especially in *La Princesse de Clèves*,[33] the ominous "vue de Madame" will captivate the lover and trap him into love's fatal snare. In *Astrée* the importance of the eyes is expressed poetically in a comparison to Argus:

... il n'y eut ni beauté du sein, ni presque de tout le reste du corps, qui ne fût permise à ses *yeux* qui, ravis de tant de perfections, désiraient que tout Celadon fût comme un autre *Argus, couvert de divers yeux*, pour mieux contempler tant de parfaites raretés. (p. 247)

Voyeurism in *Astrée* loses much of its stigma as a perversion because of the consistently appreciative description of its context. The settings resemble a portrait whose onlooking donor contemplates the classical beauty of a reclining nude on a sofa. In some cases the sight of the seductive female is not altogether deliberate (*de fortune, par hasard*):

> ... elle (Alexis) jeta de fortune *les yeux* sur le lit où était Astrée ... ces belles filles avaient laissé leurs rideaux ouverts ... *l'oeil curieux* de cette feinte druide put aisément *voir* Astrée, qui par hasard était couchée au devant du lit. (p. 220)

In an unusually detailed portrayal of the female body, an index of the voyeur's visual and emotional intensity, nudity is explicitly evoked in the expression "laissait à nu le côté droit de son sein." Nudity is suggested more subtly by a sign of relaxation in the decorum: "la chemise retroussée," "le bras paresseusement étendu hors du lit":

> Jugez donc quelle vue fut celle qu'Alexis eut alors d'Astrée. Elle avait un bras paresseusement étendu hors du lit, duquel la chemise retroussée débattait la blancheur contre le linge même sur lequel il restait. L'autre était relevé sur la tête qui, à moitié penchée le long du chevet, laissait à nu le côté droit de son sein, sur lequel quelques rayons du soleil semblaient, comme amoureux, se jouer en le baisant. O Amour! que tu te plais quelquefois à tourmenter ceux qui te suivent, de différente façon. (p. 221);

Alexis' heightened stimulation at the sight of Astrée is signalled diversely by the exclamative expressions "quelle vue fut ..." and "que tu te plais ..." and the poetic apostrophe to love. The comparison of the fall of the sun's rays to a kiss is another form of fantasy which simultaneously tortures ("tourmenter") and titillates the unfulfilled lover.

Celadon's ability to invade Astrée's privacy constitutes a form of voyeurism which at times has comic implications. In the example below the comic effect is derived from the unexpected mention of an erogenic zone in an atmosphere of Astrée's excessive inhibition which, given the context of permissive voyeurism, appears inappropriate:

> Cependant Astrée si empêchée autour de la chère Alexis, qu'elle ne lui pouvait laisser ôter une épingle sans y porter soigneusement la main, et la druide, tant qu'il lui fut possible lui laissa faire cet amoureux office; mais quand il fallait ôter sa robe, craignant qu'elle ne reconnût le défaut de ses tétins ... (p. 218)

Because of the recurrence of these erotic portraits and the constancy of certain descriptors, a virtual esthetics of erotic beauty can be derived. Let us examine one of the most detailed portraits included within a voyeur setting to determine the elements of eroticism:

Elle avait *un mouchoir* dessus les yeux qui lui *cachait* une partie du visage, *un bras sous la tête,* et l'autre étendu le long de *la cuisse,* et le cotillon, *un peu retroussé* par mégarde, ne *cachait* pas entièrement *la beauté de sa jambe.* Et d'autant que son corps de jupe la *serrait* un peu, elle *s'était délacée,* et *n'avait rien* sur *le sein*[34] qu'un *mouchoir de reseuil* au travers duquel *la blancheur de sa gorge* paraissait merveilleusement. Du bras qu'elle avait sous la tête on voyait *la manche avalée jusques sous le coude,* permettant ains la vue d'un bras *blanc et potelé,* dont *les veines,* pour *la délicatesse de la peau,* par leur couleur bleue, découvraient leurs divers passages. Et quoique de cette *main* elle tînt sa coiffure qui la nuit *s'était détachée,* si est-ce que pour la serrer trop négligemment, une partie de ses *cheveux s'était éparse* sur sa joue, et l'autre prise à quelques ronces qui étaient voisines. O quelle vue fut celle-ci pour Céladon! (p. 178)

The first sign, and one we have seen before, is the suggestion of partial nudity manifested in the expressions "cacher une partie," "ne cachait pas entièrement," "n'avait rien sur le sein que," and "la manche avalée, jusques sous le coude." The suggestion of voyeurism, implicit in the veil motif, is actualized twice by "un mouchoir" whose transparency is evoked in the qualifier "mouchoir *de reseuil*" which is lace and, by definition, dainty, highly civilized, and see through, thus the perfect literary superimposition of instinct and culture. This tempting sight is rendered all the more erotic in the voyeur context ("on voyait," "permettant ainsi la vue de," "découvraient," "O quelle vue") which constitutes a transgression and violation of taboo. The erotic female is invariably in a relaxed pose, resembling the dreamer, "un bras sous la tête et l'autre étendu le long de la cuisse." The slight disorder of her clothes and hair reflect this relaxation which can potentially be extended to a socio-logical and psychological shirking off of inhibition. Her hair is most natural — one half tied, in fact, with nature's own brambles and the other seductively falling on her cheek. Other signs of this regression to nature are visible in the following expressions: "le cotillon un peu *retroussé par mégarde*," "elle s'était *délacée*," "la manche *avalée jusques sous le coude*," la coiffure ... *détachée*," "*négligemment.*" The tightness of her skirt is an indirect reference to the exposed silhouette. The parts of the body which attract the voyeur's im-mediate attention are the thigh, the leg, "le sein," and "la gorge," which is the seventeenth century meant the breasts, the arm and the passage of its veins, the elbows, the hand, the hair, and the cheek. None of these, with the exception of the breasts, which is an erotogenic zone, is intrinsically erotic but rather acquires erotic value by associa-tion with the lovemaking process. The whiteness, daintiness, and roundness of the body, however, are constant attributes of erotic

beauty ("blancheur," "blanc," "délicatesse," "potelé," and elsewhere "embonpoint.")[35] Celadon's ecstasy reaches such propor-
tions at the beautiful sight of his beloved that he momentarily
loses life, recalling the love/death motif:

... il demeura immobile sans pouls, et sans haleine, et n'y avait en lui autre signe
de vie que le battement de coeur et la vue ... (p. 178)

The last and perhaps most overt sublimation is the pleasure both
Astrée and Celadon derive from fetichism, a perversion literally
defined in a description by D'Urfé:

Amour qui fait trouver des contentements extrêmes à ceux qui le suivent en des
choses que d'autres mépriseraient, représenta à cette feinte Alexis un si grand
plaisir d'être dans la robe qui soulait toucher le corps de sa belle bergère, qui ne
pouvant la dépouiller si tôt, elle commença à la baiser et à la presser chèrement
contre son estomac, et regardant sur la table, elle vit sa coiffure et le reste de
son habit. Transporté alors d'affection, elle les prend et les baise, se les met
dessus, et peu à peu s'en accommode, de sorte qu'il n'y eut personne qui ne
l'eut prise pour une bergère. Etant vêtue de cette sorte, elle s'approche du lit
où Astrée reposait, et se mettant à genoux devant elle, commença de l'idolâtrer.
(p. 229)

The reciprocity of the lovers, who simulate the love act through the
donning of each other's clothes, is translated linguistically by the
placement of the names Alexis and Astrée alternately at the initial
and final positions of two extended periodic sentences that delay
time and prolong the ecstasy of wish fulfillment:

Alexis mourait d'envie de posséder tout le jour cet habit, lui semblant que le
bonheur de toucher cette robe qui soulait être sur le corps de sa belle maîtresse,
ne se pouvait égaler. *Astrée*, qui aimait passionément cette feinte druide, et qui
désirait de laisser tout à fait l'habit de bergère pour prendre celui de druide,
afin de pouvoir demeurer le reste de sa vie auprès d'elle, avait un désir extrême
de porter les habits *d'Alexis*.

IV. TRANSGRESSION

Interdiction, rejection, taboo, social stigma – this is the etiology of
guilt which naturally, and perhaps necessarily, accompanies eroticism.
As in the hedonist tradition, guilt motivates the avoidance of pain,
and the pleasures of transgression stimulate approach behavior. Thus

eroticism is characterized by a constant alternation of repulsion and attraction, interdiction and transgression.[36] *Astrée* reflects this alternation which could not be perpetuated without Celadon's self-inflicted guilt feelings:

Combien de fois faillit-elle, cette feinte druide, de laisser le personnage de fille pour reprendre celui de berger et combien de fois se reprit-elle de *cette outrecuidance*! (p. 22)

Like the temptations of forbidden fruit, the taste of love is sweeter when it is denied:

... mais quelle devint-elle quand elle jeta les yeux sur son visage. Et quelle devint Alexis, quand elle vit venir Astrée vers elle pour la baiser. Mais enfin, ô Amour! en quel état les mis-tu toutes deux quand elles se baisèrent! (p. 205)

Erotic acts in *Astrée* are suggested, symbolized, and muted perhaps by literary censure but more surely by the natural inhibitions of the characters. Acting in a seventeenth-century fictional world where the "bienséances," reserve, and what Leo Spitzer so aptly called the "Klassische Dämpfung" are, if not yet codified officially, at least present in the air. The kiss, often on the hand, constitutes fulfillment of the lovers' desires:

Et lors toutes trois s'approchèrent de son lit. Léonide s'assit en un siège au chevet, et Astrée sur le lit, cependant que Diane allait portant sur la table ce que Léonide posait. Quant à Alexis, s'étant un peu relevée sur le lit, elle aidait à Astrée, lui ôtant tantôt un noeud, et tantôt une épingle, et si quelquefois sa main passait près de la bouche d'Astrée, elle la lui baisait, et Alexis, feignant de ne vouloir qu'elle lui fît cette faveur, rebaisait incontinent le lieu où sa bouche avait touché, si ravie de contentement que Léonide prenait un plaisir extrême de la voir en cet excès de bonheur. (p. 219)

The kiss, which is described euphemistically as "une faveur," is the vehicle for Celadon's coy flirtations ("feignant de ne vouloir qu'elle lui fît cette faveur"). Prolonged delay in the description is the key to the erotic effect of this passage. Time is extended by the use of postposition, gerundives, participles and dependent clauses that elongate the sentence into the typical classical period with a rather untypical effect here of eroticism. Preceded by the seductively slow stripping way of convention ("tantôt ... tantôt), the innocent kiss is encased in an erotic context whose intensity is established by the suggestion of grave taboos like exhibitionism, orgy ("toutes trois

s'approchèrent ... Léonide prenait un plaisir extrême de la voir"),
and rape ("Alexis, s'étant un peu relevée sur le lit"). The kiss
becomes the symbol of the erotic act itself, a happening confirmed
by the subsequent triple reference to ecstatic fulfillment ("ravie de
contentement," "plaisir extrême," "excès de bonheur"). The muted
form of lovemaking continues in Book III during the great nocturnal
scene containing a convergence of erotic signs: suggested partial
nudity; presence of the bed; relaxation of inhibition; simulated
strip-tease; mention of erogenic zones; whiteness and roundness of
the naked body; cruelty and kindness of love.

Une grande partie du reste de la nuit se passa de cette sorte ... Astrée qui étant
presque toute déshabillée sur le pied de son lit laissait quelque fois nonchalam-
ment tomber sa chemise jusques sous le coude, quand elle relevait le bras pour se
décoiffer ... Mais lorsque se décrochant, elle ouvrait son sein, et que son collet
à moitié glissé d'un côté laissait en partie à nu sa gorge, ô belle druide! Jamais
la neige n'égala la blancheur du tétin, jamais pomme ne se vit plus belle dans
les vergers d'amour, et jamais amour ne fit de si profondes blessures dans le
coeur de Céladon qu'à cette fois dans celui d'Alexis. (p. 220)

Night is a perfect backdrop for love. In its blackness, secrecy and
absence of routine activities, night depicts the intrinsic evil in love's
transgression. Like Baudelaire who cultivated the benefits of evil –
"la volupté unique et suprême de l'amour gît dans la certitude de
faire le Mal." – D'Urfé too links beauty, evil and love in the magic of
poetic prose.[37] The sacred pleasures of Eros are encoded in that
emotive apostrophe to Alexis ("O Belle druide"). The apostrophe
is a vocative, rhetorical figure which in its simplicity assumes a
conative function in the Jakobsonian sense. It stops the flow of the
extended sentence fragment, by a sudden turning away from the
previous audience to address oneself directly to the new audience or
object. It poeticizes the context, and rivets the readers' attention to
the uniqueness of the normally absent or abstract or imaginary object
being represented. It is the seme of absence implicit in the apostrophe
which conveys the erotic message in the same manner that silence,
separation and their extensions in Death signify the unobtainable,
the restricted, the forbidden. The apostrophe, with its intrinsic
urgency and stop value, is a sign of differentiation, of newness, and,
as Barthes so aptly observed in Le Plaisir du texte, it is the new in
contrast to the sameness of repetitive language which is pleasure,
bliss, Eros. On the psychoanalytic plane Freud, too, observed that in
the adult novelty always constituted the condition for orgasm. And

as early as 1920 the Russian formalist Victor Shklovski characterized the poetic itself as a process of "making strange."[38] The intensity of the erotic setting of D'Urfé's passage reaches a climax in the final periodic sentence. Tensions of delay stem stylistically from the build-up in the tricolon with each of the members increasing in length. The hyperboles, the anaphoras, the postpositions that hold back the kernel of each clause to the final position ("Jamais ... jamais ... jamais"), form a kind of repetitive, incantatory language which Barthes admits despite himself is as intrinsically erotic as the excesses of obsessive rhythms, litanies, and spiritual rituals. The prose is poetic. The proliferation of colorful comparisons and metaphors derived from codes of nature (*neige: blancheur du tétin*), agriculture (*pomme: vergers d'amour*), and chivalry (*blessures dans le coeur*) raise the level of D'Urfé's prose discourse to a poetic semiosis, the sign language of Eros. Unable to achieve the concision and density that poetry accorded Baudelaire, D'Urfé's eminently classical prose does capture the profound, dynamic ambivalence of Eros through the seductive, suggestive flashes of taboo and its ever-threatening disappearance. Surely *Astrée* has been neglected far too long as a valuable contribution to the annals of erotic literature. As Freud put it in that famous essay "On the Poet and Day-dreaming": "the aesthetic pleasure we gain from the works of imaginative writers is of the same type as 'fore-pleasure' and ... the true enjoyment of literature proceeds from the release of tensions in our minds."[39]

NOTES

[1] George Bataille, *Erotisme* (Paris: Editions de Minuit, 1957), p. 278: "Je pars essentiellement du principe que l'érotisme laisse dans la solitude ... l'érotisme est défini par le secret. Il ne peut être public ... l'expérience érotique se situe en dehors de la vie ordinaire."

[2] Philip Rieff, *Freud, The Mind of the Moralist* (New York: Viking Press, 1959), p. 28. Cf. Herbert Marcuse, *Eros and Civilization: A Philosophical Inquiry into Freud* (New York: Vantage Books, 1962), p. 11: "The uncontrolled Eros (life instinct) is just as fatal as his deadly counterpart, the death instinct ... they strive for a gratification which culture (repression, civilization, restraint) cannot grant."

[3] "Et toi, dit-il, symbole d'une entière et parfaite amitié." (p. 30) All references to *Astrée* will be from the Gérard Genette edition (Paris: 10/18, 1964).

[4] Oswald Ducrot and Tzvetan Todorov, *Dictionnaire encyclopédique des sciences du langage* (Paris: Seuil, 1972), pp. 134-135.

[5] Havelock Ellis, *Studies in the Psychology of Sex* (New York: Random House, 1906), p. 1.

[6] Philip Rieff, *Freud, The Mind of the Moralist*, p. 119.

[7] Stanley Hall, *Adolescence*, Vol. 1, p. 470, cited by Ellis, p. 8.

[8] Gilles Deleuze, in *Logique du Sens*, Collection "Critique" (Paris: Editions de Minuit, 1969) suggests the arbitrariness of erotic signs when he refers to the inseparability of all parts of the body and their relation to the erogenic zones. "Notre corps sexué est d'abord un habit d'Arlequin. Chaque zone est donc inséparable d'un ou plusieurs points singuliers: d'un développement sériel défini autour de la singularité: d'une pulsion investissant ce territoire; d'un objet partiel 'projeté' sur le territoire comme objet de satisfaction (image): d'un observateur ou d'un moi lié au territoire, et éprouvant la satisfaction! d'un mode de raccordement avec les autres zones." (p. 229).

[9] Charles Peirce, in distinguishing between icon, index, and symbol, sees metaphor as a subdivision of an icon or that sign which by its very nature bears a relationship to the object.

[10] See Marcuse for the development of this theme.

[11] Merleau-Ponty, *Signes* (Paris: Gallimard, 1960), p. 386. With regard to the effects of a recent relaxation of morality on eroticism see Violette Morin's, *Un Mythe Moderne: l'Erotisme* (Paris: Casterman, 1964), p. 41.

[12] Michael Riffaterre, "Paragramme et Signifiance," *Semiotexte* II (Spring, 1975), 25-31.

[13] M. Riffaterre's "Modeles de la phrase littéraire" in *Problems of Textual Analysis*, eds. P. R. Leon, H. Mitterand, P. Nesselroth, and P. Robert (Montreal: Didier, 1971), pp. 133-151. See especially Riffaterre's application of generative stylistics to a text by the Marquis de Sade in *Diacritics*: "The Self-Sufficient Text" (3/1973).

[14] Ludwig Wittgenstein, *Philosophical Investigations* (New York, Oxford: 1953), Section 129, 415.

[15] Sigmund Freud, *Civilization and Its Discontent*, ed. Ernest Jones (London: Hogart Press, 1949), p. 39: "Beauty and attraction are first of all the attributes of a sexual object ... the quality of beauty seems, on the other hand, to attach to certain secondary sexual characters."

[16] Bataille, p. 22.

[17] *Astrée*, p. 321: "Belle Astrée, a repris Celadon, il n'est plus temps que je sois appelé votre maitresse, j'ai trop de *gloire* à porter le nom de votre très humble serviteur."

"Adamas loua dans son âme *le courage* du berger, et fut bien aise de voir en lui cette marque de *la générosité* de ses ancêtres (p. 295).

[18] See Ellis, p. 52 for a discussion of the magic power of urine. Ellis insists on the role of wetness in eroticism on p. 57.

[19] Cf. Jean Starobinski's *L'Oeil Vivant* (Paris: Gallimard, 1961) for a fascinating thematic study of '*le regard*' as a motif in French literature. In an essay on Corneille, whose use of the lightness/darkness symbolism closely resembles D'Urfé's, Starobinski underlines the importance of the stimulating *éblouissement* and the curiosity of its ambivalence. "Et pourtant il est difficile de renoncer aux plaisirs de la lumière: quelle joie à être illuminé par la beauté! Quelle joie plus grande encore d'être source de lumière! D'où la singulière ambivalence de tous les personnages cornéliens à l'égard de l'éblouissement." (p. 36)

[20] *Astrée*, p. 81: "... prendre pitié de ma vie et joindre votre prudence à mon désir, afin de me sortir de cette fâcheuse *prison*."

[21] *Astrée, p. 38, p. 42.*

[22] Cf. *Astrée*, p. 303: "Je n'ai besoin, répondit Alexis (Celadon déguisé), un peu émue, que de *prendre courage.*"

"Belle Astrée, a repris Celadon, il n'est plus temps que je sois appelé votre maîtresse, j'ai trop de gloire à porter le nom de votre *très humble serviteur.*" (p. 321)

[23] Theodore H. Gaster, *The New Golden Bough* (New York: Criterion Books, 1959), pp. 90-91: "Breaches of sexual morality disturb the course of nature, particularly by blighting the fruits of the earth."

[24] Gilles Deleuze, *Logique du Sens*, p. 231: "Les trois pulsions se mélangent en profondeur, dans de telles conditions que la conservation fournit plutôt la pulsion, la sexualité l'objet substitutif, et la destruction le rapport entier réversible."

[25] Bataille, p. 17.

[26] Bataille, p. 30.

[27] *Astrée*, p. 337: A genie persuades Alexis (Celadon) "qu'il ne peut se perdre plus glorieusement qu'en aidant à désenchanter la Fontaine de la Vérité d'Amour."

[28] Meschonnic, *Pour la poétique, II* (Paris: Gallimard, 1973), p. 46.

[29] John Lapp studies the dream as a stylistic device in seventeenth-century French literature in *Aspects of Racinian Tragedy* (Toronto: University of Toronto Press, 1955), pp. 179-186.

[30] Cf. Rieff (see note 2): "Freud thought his concept of Eros and Plato's were identical" (p. 153).

[31] *Astrée*, p. 263: "Après l'avoir remerciée du *secours* qu'elle m'était venue donner."

[32] Eros and violence have been allied ever since the bachic festivals. Cf. Bataille, p. 23: "Essentiellement le domaine de l'érotisme est le domaine de la violence, le domaine de la violation ... le plus violent pour nous est la mort qui, précisément, nous arrache à l'obstination que nous avons de voir durer l'être discontinu que nous sommes." Moreover, the Marquis de Sade defined violence and murder as the summit of erotic stimulation.

[33] Madame de Lafayette, *La Princesse de Clèves*, Albert Cazes edition (Paris: Société les Belles Lettres, 1934), p. 148: "*Voir*, au milieu de la nuit, dans la plus beau lieu du monde, une personne qu'il adorait; et la *voir* tout occupée de choses qui avoient du rapport à lui et à la passion qu'elle lui cachoit, c'est ce qui n'a jamais été goûté ni imaginé par nul autre amant."

[34] Cf. *La Princesse de Clèves*, p. 147: "Il faisoit chaud, *et elle n'avait rien* sur sa tête et sur sa gorge que les cheveux *confusément* rattachés. Elle était sur un lit de repos. ..." Madame de Lafayette's "confusément" is homologous to Baudelaire's "nonchalemment" and to D'Urfé's "négligemment"; all signs of relaxed taboo.

[35] Proportion and symmetry are stable signs of beauty. Cf. *Astrée*, p. 233: "La première chose qu'elle (Alexis) en vit, ce fut le pied et la jambe, et jusques à la moitié de la cuisse et puis le sein presque tout à nu. La blancheur et la délicatesse du pied, *la juste proportion* de la jambe, la rondeur et l'embonpoint de la cuisse, et la beauté de la gorge ne se pouvaient comparer qu'à eux-mêmes."

[36] Bataille, p. 79: "Ce jeu alternatif est caractéristique du domaine religieux"

[37] The comparison to Baudelaire is not as far-fetched as it may seem. For

example, one of Baudelaire's more common adverbs is "nonchalemment" used similarly by D'Urfé as the semic marker of relaxation. The same effect is noted elsewhere in the adverbs "paresseusement," and "négligemment."

[38] See Victor Erlich, *Russian Formalism*, 2nd rev. ed. (N. Y: Humanities, 1965), pp. 176-77.

[39] Sigmund Freud, "On the Poet and Day-Dreaming" in *Creativity and the Unconscious* (Harper Torch Books, 1958), p. 54.

CHAPTER 3

HIDDEN PATTERNS IN THE FRENCH CLASSICAL NOVEL*

INTRODUCTION

The concept of 'pattern' is not only essential to an understanding of
the nature and scope of structural stylistics, but also constitutes a
primary motivation for the use of computer aids in textual analysis.
This study discusses some of the basic components underlying structural stylistics, and the application of these principles to a computer-
assisted study of the French classical novel.[1]

Structural stylistics is not concerned with the enumeration of
grammatical elements in a text whose style is described as a deviation from a vaguely defined normative grammar.[2] Nor does it focus
on the author's psyche, as in genetic stylistics, where textual supports
are shown to be reflective of the author's particular psychological
state of mind.[3] Structural stylistics is a method for exclusively
intrinsic textual analysis, and its application is dependent upon the
perception of linguistic patterns within a given text. With the use of
information theory and computer technology the nature and functioning of these patterns can be studied more accurately and
efficiently.[4]

Perception is the critical factor here because it distinguishes this
computer analysis from most which profess to be rigorously exhaustive
in the detection of selected categories. Unless a stylistic element
reached my awareness as principal decoder, it remained inoperative
as a variable in the study. Affectivity was determined to a large extent by contextual contrast.[5] Whenever there was a break in a
pattern, an unexpected appearance of a textual anomaly which
momentarily deceived my anticipation and created a mild shock or
surprise effect, it was most frequently a semantic or stylistic component contrasting with the pattern that constituted the source of
textual affectiveness. This deviation from the contextual norm
forced me to re-read the sentence and engage in a more thorough
decoding of the message. In a structural stylistic analysis, whose

purpose is to determine the nature and functioning of intrinsic and underlying mechanisms that impart coherence and multilevel significance to a text, phenomena which are extrinsic and not perceptibly encoded within the text are considered irrelevant. Therefore I disregarded author's intention and diachronic considerations unless they were verbally marked within the text. This study, then, involved a basic confrontation between myself and the text, the receiver and the message, the decoder and the code. I read the text slowly and attentively, decoding it sentence by sentence according to the linguistic principles of convergence, contextual contrast, structural semantics, and well known rhetorical definitions of tropes and figures.

METHODS: STUDY I

The focus in this structural stylistic analysis is on the linguistic phenomena which force the reader into a more thorough decoding and which motivate his subjective responses to the text. This analysis, which searches for the core of the creative process, attempts to determine precisely *how* the written word creates expressive effects on the reader and how these different words fall into recognizable patterns of meaning. It is for this reason that during the preliminary stages of the research readers' opinions from the seventeenth, eighteenth, nineteenth, and twentieth centuries were collected and used both as a control for the analyst's decoding of specific passages and, more importantly, as signals of a stylistically active component in the text. Variables and criteria for stylistic significance were determined more rigorously by the principles of contextual contrast and convergence in which a high frequency of stylistic elements occurs within a small segment of a natural-language string. Such a convergence naturally increases the perceptibility of the stylistic variable and thereby justifies the relevance of this element in the study. Without denying the validity of subjective reader reactions, the approach used here disregards the content of the value judgements and considers their objective capacity as markers of textual affectiveness.[6]

The specific aim of this study is to identify, describe, and classify stylistic and semantic patterns woven intricately within the fabric of a selected seventeenth-century literary work – Madame de Lafayette's *La Princesse de Clèves* (1677). This novel is often cited as lacking in style, impossible to subject to stylistic analysis, and at worst, an example of 'bad style.'[7] And yet, logically irreconcilable with these preconceived value judgements, literary critics frequently cite *La Princesse de Clèves* as the best French classical novel. It is unquestionably the jewel among the proliferation of novels which appeared throughout the seventeenth century. A possible explanation for this incompatibility is a common confusion between criticism and analysis, one being necessarily a judgement and the other a methodical, scientific examination of concrete evidence. It is simply unfair to impose a twentieth-century esthetic on a seventeenth-century novel. The purpose of this study is to present textual evidence in support of the contention that *La Princesse de Clèves* is a stylistically analyzable novel, cohesively constructed on many different levels according to an extensive, dialectical system of alternations. Observed in the form of echoes, reflections, correspondences, and homologues, it is my hypothesis that the chiastic structure is achieved stylistically by various related devices, such as coupling, antithesis, and parallelism, all of which converge toward a global effect of symmetry, balanced recurrence, and 'harmony,' which comprise major elements in the conventional definitions of French classical style.[8]

Unlike several stylistic studies done with the aid of computers — Louis Milic's *A Quantitative Approach to the Style of Jonathan Swift*,[9] Robert Cluett's "Style, Precept, Personality: A Test Case (Thomas Sprat, 1635-1713),"[10] or Patricia Koster's "Words and Numbers: A Quantitative Approach to Swift and Some Understrappers,"[11] — whose stylistic descriptors are limited exclusively to grammatical categories, this study extends the scope of variables to include conventional rhetorical categories of tropes and figures as well as perceptible semantic structures. Milic clearly rejects formal rhetorical devices: "The rhetorical categories are of little use in the classification series. ... They are the consciously adopted elements of composition, as opposed to the heedless output of internal pressures" (p. 86). And yet, the stylistic profile of *La Princesse de Clèves* is so much dependent upon the manipulation of 'antithesis' and 'hyperbole' and a multiplicity of variations on these, that it is virtually inconceivable to exclude these categories from any stylistic analysis of the novel. A grammatical analysis of a literary work generates its grammar, not its style.

The study is, in fact, a dual enterprise involving the progression from an exclusively mechanico-manual approach to one using the computer. Both approaches, however, deal with style and semantics from the point of view of the text and its effects on a reader who, as if peering through a finely-focused microscope, sees infinitely tiny infrastructures which play an integral role in catching and holding that reader's attention without his even being aware of the interplay. The second approach with the computer differs from the first in its degree of fine-focusing.[12] The computer transforms the attentive reader into a micro-reader.

The first study, *A Structural Stylistic Analysis of La Princesse de Clèves*,[13] deals specifically with those stylistic and semantic structures perceived during the course of a close examination of the text. A structure is the relationship of two or more elements; an 'exaggeration,' for example, is a kind of stylistic structure in which a superlative or hyperbolic expression occurs in a neutral context, the two elements of the structure in this case being 'hyperbole' and 'context.' If a designated context is noticeably replete with superlatives, as is often the case in *La Princesse de Clèves*, there will be little if any effect created by an additional superlative; thus, the potential effect of any given stylistic device is directly related to the context in which it occurs. In *La Princesse de Clèves* a generally hyperbolic context is established and maintained by a systematic use of superlatives. The presence of such a heightened backdrop comprising the macro-context makes it difficult, but not impossible, for individual elements of exaggeration (whether they be in the form of a striking character, an extraordinary event, a shocking sentence or word, or a recognizable rhetorical device) to be contrastive enough to reach the perception of the reader. Critics have shortsightedly described the style of *La Princesse de Clèves* as abstract, monotonic, and colorless, refusing to explain the function of the hyperbolic field or even to see the more subtle polarization procedures at work within the descriptive fabric of the text. A heightened backdrop is established, the context becomes saturated with hyperboles, and additional exaggerations integrate smoothly into the context but remain unnoticed. Contrast and integration are two steps of a procedure constantly at work in the novel and eminently functional in the modification of the reader's perceptions of the text with each successive reading. This is one of the many reasons why we can and do enjoy re-reading a literary work.

A semantic structure can be described as the interrelationship of two or more elements of 'meaning' (semes).[14] The two terms can relate by disjunction (opposition) or conjunction (similarity). In *La Princesse de Clèves* structures such as love/hate, absence/presence, or exterior/interior, and multiple variations of these constitute the very core of the novel's semantic fabric. Independently each of the elements takes on several different lexical forms, and it is the multiplicity of these transformations[15] that accounts for the fictional integration and sense of continuity in the novel. Let us consider, for example, the concept of 'escape' and its transformations. The heroine, Mme. de Clèves, disappears; she refuses to speak to her lover for fear of disappointing both her husband and herself; she employs generalities rather than the more precise but incriminating first person, 'I'; she feigns illness to avoid reality; she leaves the Court society for the more solitary country life in Coulommiers. On the other hand, the heroine also exhibits an opposite form of behavior in which she systematically approaches the dangerous male, M. de Nemours. She longs for her lover's presence; she speaks to others specifically about him; she visits the Court salons and partakes in grandiose Court functions where she is forced to be in the presence of her lover. The pattern which results from the interrelationship of 'escape' and 'approach' is a semantic structure familiar to psychologists as the classical 'approach/avoidance' conflict. There are many such structures throughout the novel, and each one of the components constitutes a variable in the analysis. Whenever possible both elements of the binary structure were tagged as one category. Without the use of a computer and because of the extent of the data retrieved, it was impossible within the scope of the first study to perform and report the more subtle cross-correlations within one or more patterns.

In the initial study variables were immediately noted on McBee data-processing cards, as the analyst read the text, typed one sentence on each card (an important stage in slowing down the reading and decoding process), and analyzed the sentence for active stylistic and semantic components.[16] The frequency and distribution of variables were tabulated by hand and calculated in percentages. (See Figure 1 and Figure 2). Results were then analyzed and interpreted. A more detailed study of the chiastic structures functioning in the novel was subsequently undertaken.[17] This kind of approach, while it is tedious and time consuming, reaps both qualitative and quantitative information which can and should be made available to investigators intent on performing more specific analyses of stylistic or semantic origin.[18]

METHODS: STUDY II

The second study involved the following procedures:
(1) The preparation of input (coding and storing of data in a suitable medium for processing).
(2) The conversion of data from McBee data-processing cards to IBM computer cards. An intermediary step included the recording of the McBee system to accommodate the eighty column computer cards.
(3) The development of a program of clearly defined instructions in machine-readable format. This program written in COBOL was designed to determine:
(a) The frequency and distribution of linguistic elements. These data are used to determine precisely which stylistic and semantic tools are present in various contexts and the extent to which these tools are used throughout the novel (tabulation and summaries). Results in study II are somewhat but not appreciably different from those obtained in the first study because the analyst has had the advantage of an additional reading. (See Figure 3.)
(b) The mean and standard deviation of words used in each sentence throughout the novel and in sentences occurring within the first ten pages of each of the four volumes of the work.
(c) The longest and shortest sentences in number of words (standard search subroutine).
(d) Frequency lists of linguistic elements in selected segments of (1) 100 sentences (2) chapters and (3) the entire novel, arranged in descending order of occurrence. (See Figures 4 and 5.)
(e) The fifty consecutive sentences which most accurately represent the structural profile of the novel. The stylistic differential is determined by adding the variance between samples and the entire novel. A search for the sample containing the smallest variance produced the desired fifty consecutive sentences.
(f) The cross-correlation of parameters. These data make it possible to determine the interrelationship of form and content and the manner in which messages of the novel are conveyed. The cross-correlation involves four matrices designed to determine the collocation of (1) stylistic elements in stylistic contexts, (2) stylistic elements in semantic contexts, (3) semantic elements in stylistic contexts and (4) semantic elements in semantic contexts. A list is provided for each linguistic element and the sentence numbers in which this element is located (See figure 6).
(4) Analysis of the retrieval.
(5) Interpretation of the data.

RESULTS

(a) *Frequency and distribution of linguistic elements*
 The first part of the program which provides a sentence-by-sentence explication of the entire novel with regard to stylistic and semantic elements is descriptive and therefore difficult to summarize. A sample of the data is seen in Figure 3, where the numbers in parentheses represent the presence of the figure of speech more than once. Such information constitutes a useful record for the literary scholar and is available for further investigative research. To explain precisely how the record can be utilized, let us consider sentence No. 2:

Ce prince étoit galant, bien fait et amoureux: quoique sa passion pour Diane de Poitiers, duchesse de Valentinois, eût commencé il y avait plus de vingt ans, elle n'en étoit pas moins violente, et il n'en donnoit pas des témoignages moins éclatans. (p. 3)[19]

This long (*44* words) and highly hypotaxic sentence is constructed with a striking effect of *balance* achieved by the apparent equality in the protasis and apodosis (*apodpro*) in the central clause beginning "quoique" and ending "violente." A structural balance is evidenced by the initial *enumeration* of three *adjectives*: "galant," "bien fait," and "amoureux," a configuration which mirrors the global tripartite construction beginning with the intensifying *demonstrative pronoun* ("*ce* prince"), followed by the description of the king's *passion*, a conventional *metonymy* for *love*, and ending with the *negation* and embedded *litotes* "et il n'en donnoit pas des témoignages moins éclatans." The terminal *conjunction* "et" which links the second part of the sequence to the third is homologous and in parallel position to the *punctuation* mark ":" which similarly links the first clause to the second. Internal rhythmic factors which create contrapuntal and contrastual patterns are equally functional in the effects of balance and proportion as evidenced by the *repetition* in final position of the relative and vague *adverb of quantity* "moins," which is set up in contrast to the more *precise* expression of quantity in "plus de vingt ans." On the semantic level the seme "*time*" has a double function; firstly, the age of the king's mistress is implied in her portrait placed effectively in *apposition*, and secondly, the *constancy* of the king's *passion*, in spite of the age of his mistress, is rendered all the more extraordinary. The juxtaposition of 'constancy' and 'love' is a dialectic which is activated throughout the novel, and it is referred to in the computer print-out as 'out/in,' a shorthand notation for the exterior/interior and approach/avoidance structures discussed in detail in the study. The last *adjective*, "éclatans," repeating "éclat" in sentence 1 (which was homologously in final position of the protasis), lexically establishes a tight narrative unity (*continu*) within the very first paragraph of the novel, a unity which, incidentally, will remain operative throughout by the continuous functioning of a system of structural repetitions.

(b) *Words per sentence*

The average number of words in any given sentence of the novel is 36, a figure which is considered comparatively high for the modern literatures, but standard if not appreciably lower for the seventeenth-century novel. These figures reflect what critics consider to be Madame de Lafayette's major contribution to the history and development of the novel: her concern for concision and dislike of tangential and episodic sequences. Although *La Princesse de Clèves* does contain 'digressions,' they are considerably shorter and more cohesively integrated into the mainstream of fictional events than those found, for example, in the novels of Mlle de Scudéry or La Calprenède, or Honoré d'Urfé's *Astrée*.

In the first ten pages of each volume, containing an average of 91 sentences, there is a noticeable evenness of distribution in words per sentence (Vol. I: 41, Vol. II: 43, Vol. III: 38, Vol. IV: 34). The selected segment for the first three volumes is more evenly spread, and consists of an average of 84 sentences. The fourth-volume segment contains 100 sentences, indicating a small decrease in the number of words per sentence. The general evenness of word-number distribution for this sample confirms and explains linguistically in part the motivation of a generally favorable reader response of harmony and balance in the novel.

(c) *Longest and shortest sentences*

The sentence containing the greatest number of words is No. 679, located on pp. 75 and 76 of Vol. II, and consists of the alarming figure of 179 words. This sentence, representative of many in *La Princesse de Clèves*, is constructed hypotaxically with various connecting punctuation marks like the colon, comma, and semicolon to unite long series of enumerations and appositions embedded within a series of clauses in indirect discourse:

L'on fit publier par tout le royaume, qu'en la ville de Paris le pas étoit ouvert au quinzième juin par Sa Majesté Très Chrétienne, et par les princes Alphonse d'Est, duc de Ferrare, François de Lorraine, duc de Guise, et Jacques de Savoie, duc de Nemours, pour être tenu contre tous venans: à commencer le premier combat à cheval en lice, en double pièce, quatre coups de lance et un pour les dames; le deuxième combat, à coups d'épée, un à un, ou deux à deux, à la volonté des maîtres du camp; le troisième combat, à pied, trois coups de pique et six coups d'épée; que les tenans fourniroient de lances, d'épées et de piques, au choix des assaillans, et que, si en courant on donnoit au cheval, on seroit mis hors des rangs; qu'il y auroit quatre maîtres du camp pour donner les ordres, et que ceux des assaillans qui auroient le plus rompu et le mieux fait, auroient un prix dont la valeur seroit à la discrétion des juges; que ... que ... que; qu'autrement, il [sic] n'y seroient point reçus sans le congé des tenans. (p. 75)

The sentence containing the smallest number of words (3) is No. 1476 located predictably in Vol. IV, p. 151, and embedded within a highly emotional interior monologue disguised as a dialogue between Mme. de Clèves and M. de Nemours:

"Que craignez-vous?"

The wide range represented by the number of words in sentence Nos. 679 and 1476 serves to check and clarify the results of even distribution obtained in part b. Clearly these two sentences are atypical in the novel and achieve their affectiveness primarily as deviations from their contextual norm.

(d) *Frequency lists of linguistic elements in selected segments of the novel*

The frequencies in percent distribution of each of the elements by 100 sentence segments was tabulated and an example of the data is shown in Figure 4. One of the more interesting aspects of these data is seen in the relationship between the relatively low (125 or .59% of the total number of elements) frequency of litotes, the rhetorical figure conventionally identified with the restraint and moderation characteristic of the French classical novel, and the unexpectedly high frequency of hyperboles, more often associated with the Baroque (751 or 3.54% of the total number of elements). It should be noted that hyperboles are predictably high (90) in the first 100 sentences of the novel which contain the superlative portrait descriptions of the court personages. As an internal confirmation of the data, it can be seen that portraits reach their highest frequency in the first 100-sentence segment (44), which also contains the largest number of adjectives (89) and corresponding substantives (83).

Another factor tending to contradict conventionally accepted theories in the French classical novel is the presence of metaphor (128 times) in *La Princesse de Clèves*. The classical novel has the undeserved reputation of being colorless, static, without metaphor, and eminently analytical. The validity of this description is threatened by the following findings: (1) the high frequency of adjectives (731), many of which can certainly be categorized as 'colorful' if not highly emotive and intensifying; (2) the internal dynamics of the exterior/ interior pattern and its structural counterparts that are supported rhetorically by a high frequency of hyperboles; (3) the frequency of descriptive sequences as in portraits (66), some dialogues (total number 752), and passages of clearly mimetic function, (157); (4) the high frequency of the seme 'surprise' (446) indicating the use of linguistic shock effects (e.g. lexical insistence on the word "éclat") which are clearly not 'static' either in origin or function. Rather than attempt to explain what literary scholars meant by the relativistic term 'colorless,' it would be more productive and certainly less impressionistic to consider, for example, the unusually high frequency of negatives (759 or 3.58%, and the third most commonly used device) as a functional mechanism motivating reader responses of 'grayness,' 'monotonic pessimism,' and 'colorlessness' in *La Princesse de Clèves*. Negation not only imparts a distinct tonal effect to the novel, but constitutes one of the basic components in the many analytical patterns constructed on the thesis-antithesis-synthesis dialectic.

The distribution of linguistic elements by volumes (see Figure 4) shows a general evenness, with the exception of a few elements such as 'irony' which increases markedly in the second volume containing the structurally polyvalent digression on Mme. de Tournon-Sancerre-Estouteville; the repercussion of the death of Mme. de Clèves' mother and the princess' transference of psychological support to her husband; the delightful · horoscope incident at the Reine Dauphine's place, in which the fate of the court personages is predicted and subsequently rendered true (irony by retroaction); the digression on Henry VIII's love life and obvious homologue to the Vidame's multiple affairs evidenced shortly after in the "lettre." The seme 'woman' decreases characteristically after the first volume and the introductory portraits. The seme 'hesitation' is clearly at its lowest point in Vol. I because the triangular love affair and conflict situation causing the linguistic and psychological hesitations are not yet established. 'Aristocratic values' such as honor, reputation, the "bienséances," marriage, and politics are generally higher in the first Volume containing the description of characters. 'Love' and the semes it engenders ('jealousy,' 'sincerity,' and 'death') remain at a relatively constant frequency throughout (352).

The common use of dialogue (752, the fourth highest frequency on the list) is one of the unique features of La Princesse de Clèves and marks a sharp deviation from earlier seventeenth-century novels constructed primarily in the third person narrative with only occasional long monologues.

(e) *Representative sample*

The search subroutine designed to identify the fifty consecutive sentences that most accurately represent the structural profile of the novel selected sentence numbers 955-1004 situated in Volume III on pp. 103-108. It is not surprising that the selected segment contains the greatest number of developed structures and the most critically controversial episodes in the novel: (1) the end of the scene in which M. de Nemours and Mme. de Clèves secretly rewrite the Vidame's lost letter; (2) the fate of the Vidame (love's end and death); (3) Mme. de Clève's interior monologue in which she awakens as if from a dream and analyzes the significance of her behavior earlier with M. de Nemours;[20] (4) a third person narrative on the inevitability of fatal jealousy in a love affair; (5) another interior monologue on the nature of Mme. de Cleves' will. This sequence is signalled diacritically as a dialogue scene composed of short, poignant questions all beginning significantly with the impassioned "Veux-je ...";[21] (6) Mme. de Clèves' decision to escape to the country; (7) M. de Nemours' visit to his sister in the country (contrapuntal movement) where he is a hidden witness to the famous (8) confession scene between M. and Mme. de Clèves. The lack of verisimilitude in the confession scene evoked more criticism from seventeenth-century readers than any other episode in the novel, and I think that it is both revealing and scientifically satisfying that the computer identified this scene and its preceding context as most representative of La Princesse de Clèves.[22]

The importance of this particular part of the study needs clarification. There has never been, to my knowledge, a computer program in stylistics written specifically for a literary text and designed to search a representative sample. The usefulness of this technique is most clearly evidenced in the classroom where a teacher might want to select a structurally significant passage for explication or in scholarly publication where a researcher might prefer to concentrate his critical attention on the densest kernel of structural elements.

(f) *Cross-correlation of parameters*

The data for the cross-correlation of elements contain various types of information.

It should be noted that I have selected for analysis and interpretation only a few of the many tagged elements in the data. The
usefulness of the data as a repository of concrete and quantifiable
information will most clearly be evidenced in future stylistic or
semantic studies treating particular problems of the novel.

CONCLUSION

In this computer-assisted study of *La Princesse de Clèves* a close
examination and decoding of the text for active linguistic and
rhetorical categories was performed. The computer enables the
stylistician to penetrate patterns hidden under the weight of
cumbersome but essential information. The results obtained have
significant implications for a generic study of the French classical
novel. For example, the effects of concision, harmony, proportion
and unity, which characterize conventional descriptions of the
French classical novel, are borne out quantitatively in *La Princesse
de Clèves*; however, such elusive terms as 'static,' 'colorless,' and
'monotonic' are shown to be clearly false or at best relativistic
and impressionistic. While classical restraint and moderation are
thought to be articulated by the use of generalizations, proverbial
constructions and litotes, a more accurate picture of the genre
should include the counteractive but cohesive functioning of such
intensifying agents as hyperbolic exaggerations, surprise, mimetic
effects and disjunctive interruptions. Hidden deeply within complex
linguistic and literary matrices of La Princesse de Clèves is a smoothly
operating system of interrelated components which, when perceived
by an attentive reader, will produce the esthetically satisfying effects
of classical symmetry associated with great works of art. The purpose
of this study was merely to penetrate this complex system.

FOOTNOTES TO FIGURE 1

[1] Common analytical patterns are cause/effect, effect/cause: implicit/explicit (i.e. No. 16)
and various tripartite developments. Analytical sequences are frequently introduced by a
marker like "Quand elle fut en train de rever," or "Quand elle pensoit que. ..."
[2] Cyclical structure is a developed system composed of several interrelated elements,
notably 'chiasmus,' 'reciprocity,' 'parallelism,' 'balance,' and 'juxtaposition.'
[3] Discordance or linguistic rupture refers to any linguistic element which produces an
effect of disharmony, unevenness, or interruption in the flow of the syntagma. This
category, as others, can be considered both stylistic and semantic depending upon the
nature of causation.
[4] Since several editions of *La Princesse de Clèves* were consulted during the decoding, a
notation was recorded whenever a punctuational discrepancy occurred. It should be noted
that although this element has the highest frequency of occurrences, it is relatively insignificant to the intrinsic analysis of the literary text.
[5] 'Others/I' refers to the multiple forms of insistence on identity conflicts in the Sartrian
sense of "les autres."

FIGURE 1

*Alphabetic List of Stylistic and Semantic Elements
in Study I and II*

Stylistic

1. adjective	11. apostrophe	21. continuity
2. adverb	12. apposition	22. contrast
3. adv. of quantity	13. archaism	23. cyclic struc.[2]
4. ambiguity	14. asyndeton/poly.	24. definition
5. anacoluthon	15. author intrusion	25. demon. pron.
6. analytical sequence[1]	16. balance	26. dialogue
7. anaphora	17. chiasmus	27. discordance[3]
8. anteposition	18. cliche	28. disjunction
9. antithesis	19. comparison	29. ellipsis
10. apodosis/protasis (apodpro)	20. conjunction	30. enumeration

31. euphemism	41. litotes
32. exclamation	42. metaphor
33. familiar lang.	43. metonymy
34. generalization	44. mimesis
35. hyperbole	45. movement (absence/pres.)
36. implicit/explicit	46. negation
37. indirect discourse	47. oxymoron
38. inversion	48. parallelism
39. irony	49. periodic sentence
40. juxtaposition	50. periphrasis

51. plural	61. rhythm
52. portrait	62. substantive
53. preparation, fore-shadowing	63. suspense
54. pronoun ambiguity	64. technical term
55. punctuation[4]	65. time expression
56. proverb	66. unexpected word
57. question	67. unexpected tense
58. reciprocity	68. vague representative of quantity
59. repetition	69. unusual verb
60. rhetorical question	

Semantic

1. age/youth	9. exterior/inter.	17. obstacle/freedom
2. ambition	10. fear/courage	18. others/I[5]
3. aristocratic tradition	11. folly/calm	19. politics
4. beauty	12. hero/weak	20. refusal/acceptance
5. confession/secret	13. hesitation/certitude	21. reputation
6. constancy/temporality	14. jealousy	22. reserve/extreme
7. death	15. love	23. speech/silence
8. diversion	16. marriage	24. sincerity/lie
25. surprise	26. woman	

FIGURE 2. Frequency and Distribution of Stylistic and Semantic Structures in Volumes I-II (in percent)

Structures	Novel Subdivisions*											
	1	2	3	4	5	6	7	8	9	10	11	12
1 adjective	10	8	6	5	5	4	12	3	11	15	14	9
2 anacoluthon	7	0	0	0	2	3	0	0	0	0	0	0
3 anaphora	16	3	9	4	0	0	0	0	0	0	0	0
4 apposition	10	3	9	7	12	3	0	9	8	6	4	0
5 apodosis/protasis	21	6	3	5	2	0	0	0	0	0	0	0
6 ante/postposition	7	9	10	1	2	9	1	0	1	6	1	6
7 antithesis	5	11	9	5	5	14	17	8	11	12	9	4
8 archaism	0	0	0	0	0	4	1	0	0	0	0	0
9 concretization	16	17	12	15	12	10	5	15	8	3	3	4
10 asyndeton/polysyndeton	3	0	4	4	2	3	1	0	0	0	0	2
11 cliché	3	25	12	12	8	8	12	9	5	9	8	6
12 comparison	3	11	7	11	12	16	15	12	12	7	13	7
13 conjunction	38	25	15	4	0	1	7	0	3	12	1	6
14 disjunction	40	22	19	18	8	16	20	12	14	12	12	13
15 analytical sentence	30	30	22	25	20	24	27	21	26	20	22	19
16 euphemism	3	2	0	1	0	1	5	0	1	3	7	4
17 quantity/vague	5	5	9	6	15	4	4	3	4	6	4	7
18 hyperbole	38	42	42	31	30	27	36	24	30	36	35	32
19 inversion	7	5	4	1	0	0	1	0	0	1	0	0
20 cause/effect	31	15	10	13	40	23	19	18	14	12	14	15
21 irony	10	3	17	17	21	32	24	15	24	17	8	6
22 juxtaposition	16	8	7	4	5	3	1	2	3	3	1	0
23 litotes	10	3	17	2	0	7	5	10	6	10	3	7
24 metaphor	2	5	4	4	2	10	1	5	4	9	3	7
25 metonymy	7	8	6	4	0	1	0	3	3	6	1	4

*Each random division contains approximately 70 sentences of text.

FIGURE 3. *Element Description*

Sentence Number	No. of Words										
1	25	apodpro aristoc	dem pron surpris	compare	hyperb. (3)	juxtapo	advqunt	substan (2)	time...	general	balance
2	44	adj.. (5) parall. outin	apposit portrait love	apodpro punctu. enumer.	dempron pronoun	conjunc repeat (2)	vague.. rhythm	litotes time...	metnymy continu	ngation balance	advqunt age...
3	75	adj... period age	apposit repeat outin (2)	antepos technic (2)	compare time	disjunc continu	define balance	hyperb (6) suspens	advqunt (3) mimesis	portrait cyclic	punctu woman
4	8	pronoun	continu	general	woman	aristoc	metnymy				
5	20	adj... rhythm	dempron substan (3)	cliche continu	euphem balance	hyperb (2) chiasm	woman..	parall. age.. period plural	portrait diversi prepar.	punctu enumer repeat	repeat plural. substan
6	44	apposit time.. (2)	apodpro disharm	antepos death	disjunc (2) aristoc (4)	invers. surpris	portrai adverb	metnymy continu	ngation (2) balance	impexp. woman	portrait aristoc
7	71	adj.. (3) punctu (3) ambition	conjunc (2) period outin (2)	disjunc repeat	euphemi substan (4)	invers recipr.	juxtapo unexpect	vague.. time.. (2)	hyperb (2) disharm	litotes balance	metnymy (2) cyclic.
8	57	adj... oxymor (2) woman	apodpro portrai beauty	dempron punctu diversi	cliche (2) pronoun love...	disjunc period.	define recipr.	invers. general	analysi balance	advqunt woman	perphras aristoc (2)
9	44	adj... portrai outin	antepos punctu beauty	cliche period. adverb	conjunc repeat (4) plural (2)	conjunc rhythm	hyperb (5) tenses	hyperb (2) surpris (2)	disjunc (3) repeat	portrai	prepar
10	27	adj. (3) disharm	apposit suspens	apodpro death	antithe woman	dempron outin	disjunc beauty		juxtap	vague balance	
11	64	adj.. analysis age...	apposit juxtapo aristoc	antithe advqunt marriage	cliche portrait politic	compare punctu (2) plural	conjunc period	punctu (2) plural aristoc repeat	define time..	repeat (2)	hyperb (6) woman..
12	55	anaphor (3) continu	antithe balance	define woman	hyperb. diversi	juxtapo love	portrai enumer		period		recipr.
13	23	adj. (4)	antepos	hyperb (3)	invers	rhythm	suspens	aristoc	surpris		
14	18	disjunc	define	hyperb	perphra	pronoun	substan (2)	tenses	suspens	authintru substan	
15	25	conjunc	hyperb	parall.	perphra	portrai	pronoun	repeat	rhythm		surpris aristoc

FIGURE 4. *Frequencies by Entire Text and by Volumes*

	Entire Text	Percent of total	Volume 1 415	Sentences	Volume 2 422	Sentences	Volume 3 493	Sentences	Volume 4 459	Sentences
adj..	731	3.45	241	3.87	159	3.11	167	3.29	164	3.43
anacol.	9	0.04	5	0.00	0	0.00	4	0.08	0	0.00
anaphor	54	0.25	17	0.27	5	0.10	7	0.14	25	0.32
apposit	118	0.55	53	0.83	30	0.59	25	0.49	10	0.21
apodpro	44	0.21	26	0.42	2	0.04	6	0.12	6	0.13
antepos	248	1.17	97	1.56	47	0.92	64	1.26	40	0.84
antithe	226	1.07	32	0.84	53	1.04	49	0.96	72	1.50
archaic	25	0.12	2	0.03	11	0.21	6	0.12	6	0.13
dempron	353	1.66	120	1.93	77	1.50	84	1.65	72	1.50
asynde	64	0.30	24	0.39	6	0.12	14	0.28	20	0.42
cliche	308	1.45	100	1.61	61	1.10	72	1.42	75	1.57
compare	218	1.03	60	0.96	67	1.31	53	1.04	38	0.79
conjunc	301	1.42	99	1.59	81	1.58	56	1.14	63	1.32
disjunc	765	3.51	239	3.84	185	3.62	195	3.84	147	3.07
define	383	1.81	102	1.64	91	1.78	94	1.85	96	2.01
euphemi	73	0.34	18	0.29	19	0.37	13	0.26	23	0.48
vague.	187	0.85	56	0.90	41	0.80	50	0.96	40	0.84
hyperb	751	3.54	222	3.57	203	3.97	170	3.35	156	3.26
invers.	44	0.21	22	0.35	10	0.20	3	0.06	9	0.19
analysis	397	1.87	124	1.98	100	1.93	90	1.77	83	1.73
irony	205	0.98	79	1.27	74	1.45	31	0.61	24	0.50
juxtapo	96	0.45	44	0.71	13	0.25	26	0.51	13	0.27
litotes	125	0.59	34	0.55	38	0.74	29	0.57	24	0.50
metapho	128	0.60	28	0.45	34	0.66	42	0.83	24	0.50
metnymy	128	0.60	58	0.93	23	0.45	22	0.43	25	0.52
negation	759	3.58	179	2.88	177	3.46	209	4.11	194	4.05
advqunt	258	1.24	105	1.70	47	0.92	63	1.24	52	1.09
oxymor	50	0.24	14	0.22	9	0.18	10	0.20	17	0.36
parall	175	0.63	56	0.93	50	0.98	30	0.59	38	0.79
periphras	184	0.63	35	0.56	35	0.08	51	1.00	69	1.44
imp. exp	234	1.10	62	1.00	52	1.02	51	1.00	69	1.44
portrai	65	0.31	57	0.42	4	0.08	3	0.06	2	0.04
punctual	1020	4.81	245	3.94	265	5.16	232	4.57	278	5.61

FIGURE 5. *Stylistic and Semantic Elements in Descending Order or Occurrences*

No.	Stylistic Element	No. of Occurrences	No.	Stylistic Element	No. of Occurrences	No.	Semantic Element	No. of Occurrences
1	punctua.	1020	36	contrast	161	1	outin..	466
2	disjunc	766	37	recipro	158	2	surpris	446
3	negation	759	38	mimesis	157	3	woman	370
4	dialog	752	39	perphras	134	4	love..	352
5	hyperb	751	40	prepar.	132	5	weak. hero	288
6	adj..	731	41	rhythm	129	6	hesitation	252
7	substan	705	42	metnymy	123	7	fear..	220
8	repeat	704	43	metaphor	128	8	reserv	209
9	plural	505	44	litotes	125	9	sincere	199
10	time...	499	45	ambiguity	119	10	aristoc	188
11	analysis	397	46	question	119	11	obstacl	186
12	general	384	47	apposition	118	12	silence. spe	156
13	define	383	48	period	116	13	confess	139
14	continu	353	49	juxtapos.	96	14	marriage	132
15	dempron	393	50	fam. lang.	76	15	politic	120
16	movement	335	51	exclamation	75	16	folly	116
17	balance	333	52	euphemism	73	17	death	110
18	cliche	303	53	portrait	66	18	refuse	104
19	conjunc	301	54	asynde..	64	19	others	99
20	pronoun	294	55	verb...	61	20	constan	65
21	disharm	265	56	anaphor	54	21	beauty	66
22	suspens	284	57	technic	50	22	jealous	60
23	adverb	278	58	oxymoron	50	23	age	56
24	advqunt	268	59	invers.	44	24	ambition	49
25	antepos	248	60	apodpro	44	25	repute	27
26	impexp	234	61	rhet. quest.	43	26	diversi	24
27	antithe	226	62	ellipse	42			
28	compare	218	63	chiasm	28			
29	cyclic	214	64	unexpect	227			
30	irony	208	65	archai	25			
31	vague..	187	66	author int.	23			
32	ind. disc	181	67	apostrophe	22			
33	parall.	176	68	proverb	116			
34	enumer.	171	69	anacolu	9			
35	tenses	168						

FIGURE 6. Hyperbole: A Stylistic Element

Hyperbole is present in the following sentences:

1	3	5	6	7	8	9	10	11	12	13	14	15	16	17	18	19	20	21	23	25	26	27	31	43	44	45
52	55	56	57	63			10	64	65	68	69	70	71	73	74	79	82	84	85	87	88	91	96	99	100	101
102	104	107	108	115		125	126	127	128	129	131	132	136	140	144	148	152	155	157	158	161	162	163	166	167	
171	173	174	179	181	183	184	186	188	190	192	193	194	198	199	201	202	205	207	213	218	221	228	230			
233	234	235	236	244	245	246	248	252	256	259	262	268	270	272	273	283	284	287	292	295	296	298	302			
303	293	307	312	313	314	316	318	319	321	322	323	327	332	333	339	341	354	355	356	363	369	370	372	375		
381	384	389	397	400	402	404	406	409	412	413	417	418	419	421	426	432	435	436	440	445	450	454				
455	458	459	462	463	465	467	468	470	473	475	477	480	481	483	486	487	490	492	504	508	510	511	514			
516	522	524	526	527	531	532	534	536	537	539	540	541	542	545	550	555	556	557	560	561	568	570	571	573		
574	576	577	580	581	582	586	587	590	596	599	600	604	610	611	614	616	618	628	634	641	642	643	646	647		
648	650	657	660	662	663	666	667	674	675	677	679	681	682	684	689	699	700	701	703	704	705	706	709			
711	715	717	721	722	730	736	738	740	741	742	744	747	750	751	753	754	755	757	759	760	770	771	772	774		
775	777	779	780	781	783	784	788	789	793	796	798	801	804	806	808	813	815	817	822	824	828	829	831			
834	835	838	840	843	848	849	850	852	860	861	863	865	867	901	905	906	908	909	914	916	919	925	934	937		
939	944	949	957	958	962	964	965	967	975	976	981	985	992	998	1002	1005	1009	1010	1012	1014	1016	1017	1018	1019	1020	
1028	1030	1036	1037	1041	1042	1046	1050	1053	1055	1057	1058	1059	1063	1065	1071	1075	1076	1079	1080	1084						
1085	1086	1087	1089	1090	1091	1092	1093	1094	1095	1097	1105	1107	1109	1115	1116	1119	1120	1124	1125	1127	1132	1141	1154	1155	1156	
1157	1159	1173	1184	1185	1189	1194	1196	1199	1207	1210	1215	1216	1220	1223	1225	1229	1233	1235	1236	1237	1239	1240	1241	1243		
1246	1251	1252	1255	1258	1260	1261	1263	1267	1272	1273	1285	1286	1291	1296	1298	1299	1302	1305	1312	1315	1319	1320	1326			
1330	1334	1336	1339	1340	1347	1356	1357	1364	1374	1381	1384	1385	1386	1394	1396	1398	1399	1400	1402	1404	1412	1414				
1415	1421	1431	1433	1435	1440	1441	1443	1445	1446	1450	1452	1454	1457	1460	1462	1466	1468	1469	1472	1485	1494	1499	1500	1502		
1504	1509	1512	1513	1516	1520	1535	1543	1549	1551	1552	1556	1558	1567	1583	1590	1592	1595	1602	1603	1607	1608	1609				
1620	1622	1624	1625	1638	1640	1646	1648	1650	1652	1656	1660	1662	1671	1672	1673	1679	1683	1685	1688	1689	1690	1695	1696			
1697	1698	1699	1702	1703	1704	1705	1708	1713	1715	1716	1724	1725	1727	1729	1738	1740	1741	1743	1746	1751	1755	1756	1757	1759		
1761	1763	1766	1771	1776	1779	1780	1782	1785	1786	1787	1788	1790	1791	1792												

"HYPERBOLE" occurs 751 times in 618 sentences in the following stylistic contexts:

Litotes	42	rhythm	63	asynd	32	general	179	rhetques	9
metaphor	59	substan	329	cliche	153	disharm	119	famlang	32
metonymy	65	apostr.	5	compare	109	balance	136	dialog	267
ngation	314	technic	25	conjun	114	suspens	95	ambigu	43
advqunt	110	recipr	56	disjun	300	ellipse	17	enumera	89
oymor	27	unexp.	13	define	157	contrast	82	adverb	180
parall.	86	tenses	71	euphem	26	movemen	106	plural	220
perphra	50	adj..	354	vague	67	verb..	24		
impexp.	75	anacolu.	5	invers	26	proverb	6		
portrai	42	apposit.	16	analys	150	mimesis	45		
punctu.	495	apodpro	16	irony	88	question	19		
pronoun	117	antepos	116	juxtapo	44	indisc	56		
period	61	antithe	101	time..	171	cylic	91		
prepar.	57	archai	12	continul	35	chiasm	19		
repeat	296	dempron	120	exclam	23	autintr	8		

IN THE FOLLOWING SEMANTIC CONTEXTS:

Hesitation	98	surpris	189
refuse	37	jealous	30
age	35	obstacl	61
folly	46	sincere	73
aristoc	83	death	47
ambition	19	confess	54
outin	186	fear	68
beauty	34	woman	159
weakhero	113	others	39
diversi	19	silen/speech	62
marriage	52	constanc	42
love...	159		
reserve	75		
repute	11		
politic	43		

NOTES

* The original version of this study appeared as an article entitled "Quantitative Stylistics in the French Classical Novel" in *Language and Style XI*, 2 (Spring, 1978) 94-115.

[1] I wish to express my appreciation to the American Council of Learned Societies and to the State University of New York for their support of this project. Special thanks to Professor Arjani of Westchester Community College for his programming expertise.

[2] See Michael Riffaterre, *Essais de stylistique structurale* (Paris: Flammarion, 1971), p. 136: "La variabilité des effets montre clairement qu'ils sont régis par le contexte et que, lorsqu'il s'agit de les percevoir, la présence physique du contexte l'emporte sur la conscience que le lecteur peut avoir de la norme générale." For those who, like Charles Muller in his *Essai de statistique lexicale: "l'Illusion Comique" de Pierre Corneille* (Paris: Larousse, 1967), define style as a deviation from the norm, see the complications implicit in this definition in J. Dubois, *et al, Rhétorique générale* (Paris: Larousse, 1970), p. 17: "Le point délicat est, bien sûr, de déterminer la norme à partir de laquelle on définira cet écart qui se résoudra lui-même en norme."

[3] An illustration of genetic stylistics can be found in Leo Spitzer's *Linguistics and Literary History* (New York, 1958).

[4] Sally and Walter Sedelow, "A Preface to Computational Stylistics," in *The Computer and Literary Style*, ed. Jacob Leed (Ohio: Kent State University Press, 1966), p. 1: "Stylistic analysis, the study of patterns found in the process of linguistic encoding of information, is of importance to any major research focused upon or dependent upon the production or analysis of language. Through the use of computers, it should be possible to achieve more accurate detection and delineation of such linguistic patterns than has hitherto been the case."

[5] The importance of contextual contrast, convergence, and perception in structural stylistics is discussed in detail by M. Riffaterre, *Essais de stylistique structurale*, pp. 40-42, 60, 64-94. See Pierre Ducretet, "Quantitative Stylistics: An Essay in Methodology," *CHum, Vol IV*, 3 (January, 1970), 187-191. Mr. Ducretet's insights into the usefulness of 'context' in the preparation of indexes, concordances, and dictionaries are valuable.

[6] I agree completely with the Sedelows who say, "Such patterns also serve to confuse or clarify, bore or interest, persuade and entrance, or repel and disengage them." (*op. cit.*, p. 1). However, see Riffaterre, p. 43: "Dépouillée de sa formulation en termes de valeur, la réponse secondaire devient un critère objectif de l'existence de son stimulus stylistique."

[7] E.g. Daniel Mornet, *Histoire de la littérature francaise* (Paris, n.d.), p. 5. Mornet denies the existence of any style at all in *La Princesse de Clèves*.

[8] *Cf.* René Bray, *La Formation de la doctrine classique en France* (Paris: Hachette, 1927); Will G. Moore, *French Classical Literature: An Essay* (Oxford University Press, 1961); Henri Peyre, *Qu'est-ce que le classicisme?* (Paris: Nizet, 1965); Elbert Borgerhoff, *The Freedom of French Classicism* (Princeton: Princeton University Press, 1950); Yves Gandon, *Du Style classique* (Paris: Editions Albin Michel, 1972).

[9] (The Hague: Mouton, 1967.)

[10] Robert Cluett, *CHum*, V, 5 (May, 1970), 257-276.

[11] Patricia Koster, *CHum,* IV, 5 (May, 1970), 289-302. See also the more recent study by D. Ross Jr. and R. Rasche, "Eyeball: A Computer Program for Description of Style," *CHum* VI, 4 (March, 1972), 213-222.

[12] See Robert S. Wachal's "On Using a Computer" in *The Computer and Literary Style*, (Ohio: Kent State University Press, 1966), pp. 14-37.

[13] (The Hague: Mouton, 1976.

[14] A. J. Greimas, *Sémantique structurale* (Paris: Larousse, 1966), p. 20: "Nous désignerons du nom de *structure élémentaire* un tel type de relation. En effet, puisqu'il est convenu que les termes-objets seuls ne comportent pas de signification, c'est au niveau des structures qu'il faut chercher les unités significatives eleméntaires, et non au niveau des éléments." See also Stephen Ullmann's *Précis de sémantique francaise* (Bern: A. Francke, 1952).

[15] The term 'transformation' is used here in the sense that Piaget defined it in *Le Structuralisme* (Paris: PUF, 1968), p. 6: "... une structure est un système de transformations, qui comporte des lois en tant que système (par opposition aux propriétés des éléments) et qui se conserve ou s'enrichit par le jeu même de ses transformations."

[16] The interrelationship of form and content in stylistic analysis goes back to Saussure's definition of language as a system of signs. He further explained the 'sign' as the relationship of 'le signifiant' (the word, per se) and 'le signifié' (the thing signified by the written word). Charles Bally explained the relation as follows in his *Traité de stylistique francaise*, I (Paris: Klincksieck, 1951), p. 155: "Le côté affectif d'un fait d'expression ne peut être réellement saisi que par contraste avec son contenu intellectuel. ..."

[17] See my article "The Art of Repetition in *La Princesse de Clèves*," *Modern Language Review* 68 (January, 1973), 40-50.

[18] I am in complete agreement with Herbert S. Donow, who states in his article "Concordance and Stylistic Analysis of Six Elizabethan Sonnet Sequences," *CHum* IV, 3 (March, 1969), 205-216: "Although the production of the concordance has occupied the bulk of my time during the past few months, I do not see it as the principal part of my undertaking. Rather, it is a logical outgrowth of and a tool for an analysis of sonnet style."

[19] All references to *La Princesse de Clèves* are taken from the Albert Cazes edition (Paris: Les Belles Lettres, 1934). In the explication above, underlinings refer to the words in the print-out in Figure 3.

[20] This sequence is constructed according to a recurrent contrastual dialectic. The analytical passage is signalled characteristically by an emotive build-up of anaphoric and antepositioned markers of analysis "quand elle pensoit ... et que ... quand elle pensoit encore que. ..." See my "Analytische Dialektik in der *Princesse de Clèves*," *Poetica* (May, 1972), 183-190, for a detailed discussion of patterns within analytical sequences.

[21] This sequence illustrates a recurrent pattern of Will-Reversal-Resolution in which Mme. de Clèves repeatedly violates torturous resolutions imposed on herself by herself.

[22] Cf. Bussy-Rabutin, "Lettre à Madame de Sévigné," 29 june 1768, *La Princesse de Clèves*, Albert Cazes edition (Paris: Les Belles Lettres, 1934). Valincour's *Lettres à Mme. la marquise ... sur le sujet de la Princesse de Clèves* is reproduced with critical annotations in Maurice Laugaa's recent edition (Tours: Université François Rabelais, 1972). Fontenelle, "Lettre sur *La Princesse de Clèves*," in *Le Mercure Galant* (May, 1628).

III

SATIRE

CHAPTER 4

MATHURIN REGNIER'S *MACETTE:*
A SEMIOTIC STUDY IN SATIRE*

Macette disturbs its readers unlike any other Regnier satire. Along with the conventionally searing attack on vice and folly launched in formal verse satire by the forces of ridicule and persuasion, this poem plays linguistic tricks on the reader, and with a masterful display of connotative juggling, manages at the same time to praise and blame evil. The reader, Macette's young and silent protégée, and Regnier's narrator-voyeur all witness with increasing uneasiness the promulgation of a life style of vice disguised as virtue. Confusing Macette with the *dramatis persona*,[1] the reader is constantly questioning the validity of the main speaker's heretical and double-edged pronouncements. In fact, the reader is the victim of what might on the surface appear to be a big joke, especially when at the very end of the satire the hidden narrator reveals himself, brutally unmasks the self-proclaimed Mentor, and exposes the vilainous hypocrite for what she really is, a used-up old prostitute turned pious for convenience and all the more vilainous for corrupting the morals of youth.

From the very beginning of the poem, any reader acquainted with Regnier's satires is immediately aware of its uniqueness. Formally idiosyncratic, it is not in the customary epistolary format[2] but rather like a framed portrait, as the proper name in the title would indicate. This portrait, in a dynamic and disquieting state of constant flux, is produced in three parts and by three distinct manners of discourse: firstly, by an 'omniscient' but unreliable author in third and first person narrative (ll. 1-36, 37-50);[3] then by the confused reader who, incorporating the author's equivocal praise in his judgement, tries to interpret Macette's monologue (disguised as a dialogue in direct discourse (ll. 51-108, 109-273);[4] and, finally, by the unequivocal satirist in a first person invective (ll. 275—end). Relieving the reader's doubts, the now reliable author launches a conclusive and excoriating attack on Macette's vicious folly.

Appearing on the surface to resemble a frame around a self-contained portrait, this tripartite format coexists, on the deeper levels, with a more complex system of bipartite structures. The pattern is discernible on a symbolic level in which the two main characters of the highly dramatic poem represent the satirist and his Adversarius.[5] According to the conventions of formal verse satire, the biparite (A/B) design within the poem consists of Part A, or the exposition of an irrational, ridiculous and vicious form of behavior (Macette's perverted ideology), and Part B, a direct recommendation to virtue. The intricacies of the evil behavior are painstakingly examined in Part A where the many facets of the vice are mercilously exposed by a wide and rather lively variety of dialectical and rhetorical techniques. The long exposition unfolds slowly within a highly disjunctive and suspenseful hypotactical structure which effectively sustains reader interest throughout the poem.[6] Part A, or the expositive, negative portion of the satire, normally outweighs Part B, the positive, scathing invective portion, because of its powerful force of argument by demonstration. It is in the very exposition of the destructive aids of human behavior that the satirist, Regnier, can establish the unquestionable truth of his sincere and passionate plea for virtue.

The underlying bipartite structures are hidden effectively on many levels within the verbal constructs of the poem. Poetic language is, by definition, ambiguous and autoreflective, and this definition is substantiated in Regnier's *Macette* by the literary critics who frequently report but too casually label the ever-present contradictions in the poem as 'irony.' When there is juxtaposition and equation of disparate elements, or when an identity is created between at least two opposed if not contradictory structures, let the resultant incompatibility of this relationship be called an ironic effect. Ironies, like structures, are relational and discernible on several levels: thematic, stylistic, semantic, narrative (plot), character, functional, etc. The reader is an essential factor in the description of this dynamic and dialectical process for unless he perceives the relationship existing between a minimum of two equal and opposite elements of meaning, the incongruity is virtually inoperative, and the ironic effect is absent.

The simultaneity of mutually exclusive oppositions is demonstrated in the very first line of the poem, a strategic ploy which takes the reader off guard right from the beginning and acquaints him most effectively with the rules of the linguistic game:

> La fameuse Macette à la Cour si connue,
> Qui s'est aux lieux d'honneur en crédit maintenue[7] (11.1.2)

The reader's curiosity is initially aroused by the title, Macette, and its intrinsic taboo value as a metonymy for prostitution.[8] Macette appeared in Satire XI as one of the more distinguished members of the bordello, and since Satire XII continues the previous satire the reader can logically assume a relationship between the two characters. With raised eyebrows and a hidden smile, the reader's assumption is confirmed in line one, and his anticipation to learn more about the taboo is pleasantly satisfied in the ensuing portrait. As soon as the laudatory but potentially antiphrastic adjective "fameuse" is incongruously attributed to Macette of known dubious morality, a polarity of 'praise and blame' is immediately activated in the poem. The polarity is sustained throughout by innumerable stylistic devices bearing witness to the poem's diversity and converging toward ironic effect. What makes this poem different from Regnier's other satires is the unnerving effects of an all pervasive simultaneity of praise and blame.[9] In the first two lines, the epithet "fameuse" defines Macette with an unexpectedly positive connotation acquired by symmetrical association with its causative equivalent "connue," and reinforced in line 2 by the esteemed aristocratic values of "honneur" and "crédit." A paradigm of praise is set up on the literal level with "fameuse," "connue," "honneur," "crédit," "Cour," and even "maintenue" (positive value of constancy) as its variants. Stated in generative terms, the two line sequence, generated systematically from the kernel word "Cour," is overdetermined.[10] Each of the elements included within the semantic field of "Cour" ("fameuse," "connue," "honneur," "credit," "maintenue") are themselves interrelated tautologically. Each word, then, is generated in positive conformity with the preceding one, is a component of the semantic system "Cour," and constitutes a redundant equivalence of 'praise.'

But all this praise is incompatible with the metonymic value of the name Macette and its negative connotations. On another level, then, each of the variables of 'praise' can be shown to be oxymoric and diametrically opposed to 'praise.' They blame. "Fameuse" and "connue" taken antiphrastically mean 'infamous,' celebrated for ignominy. "Aux lieux d'honneur" is pure sarcasm, for the referent is 'bordello,' as the note in several editions testify. All the more effective is the potential, homonymic ambiguity of "au lieu de," a prepositional phrase which signals contrast in this case to "honneur" and thus reinforces, once again, a negative connotation. "Crédit" is a euphemism in the context of love-making expertise, and prepares the complex system of financial metaphors to be developed later in

the poem.[11] "Maintenue" is all the more ironic as it implies a recurrence of love-making displays. In this short sequence, then, both
positive and negative connotative poles of praise and blame are
activated simultaneously in what can only be interpreted as a mind-
boggling verbal gymnastics.

In order to penetrate the underlying, linguistic mechanisms at
work in this poem of ingenious autodestruction, I shall examine the
component parts of its system, namely (1) the techniques which
establish general statements of truth or universalizable givens; (2)
the techniques of contradiction which lead to the destruction of
these givens, and finally (3) the synthesis of these contrastive structures in the ironies of the satire. In an attempt to respect the order
and arrangement of the poem and, in particular, its effects on the
reader, the analysis will necessarily be sequential.

The narrator's conscientious valorization of Macette is one of the
tricks which takes the reader off guard and sustains his doubts until
the satirist's outburst at the end of the poem. Achieved by a systematic use of laudatory hyperboles, this valorization establishes the
reader's confidence in Macette and, by extension, in her advice.
When she speaks, the reader considers the words of the Mentor to be
signs of wisdom. But the hyperbolized language carries the seeds of
its own destruction for hyperbole is one of the most common stylistic markers of irony:[12]

> Et *n'a plus autre objet que* la voute etheree;   (10)
> Elle qui *n'eust*, avant que plorer son delit,   (11)
> *Autre ciel pour objet que* le ciel de son lict,   (12)

The repetition of the hyperbolic comparisons "n'a plus autre ... que"
and "n'eust ... autre que" in ll. 10, 11, and 12 enhances Macette's
intrinsic value as a moral model. The main portion of her description
is transcribed in an equally hyperbolic religious code:[13] "la voute
etheree" is a religious cliché and a periphrastic metonymy for God;
"delit" is a theological term for sin; "ciel," which recalls the earlier
"voute etheree" rendering it more explicit, is also a periphrastic
metonymy for heaven and, thus, God. But the spirituality implicit
in the religious code is almost immediately juxtaposed with a contrastively materialistic sign expressed in line 10 by the concrete
lexeme "objet." Taken on a figurative level, "objet" means 'goal,'
but in line 12 it acquires a negative connotation by collocation with
"lict," a metonymy for the sex act.[14] The two codes, spiritual and

material, are perfectly fused in a stinging comic effect when "ciel"
is recalled metaphorically in line 12 to mean either the canopy of a
typical French 'baldaquin' bed or, perhaps, by extension, the ceiling
of the bedroom. Looking at the entire sequence retroactively, with
the end of the poem clearly in mind, it becomes obvious that the
initial hyperboles are sarcastic, false exaggerations containing rudi-
ments of perverted truth. Macette, then, is both praised and blamed
simultaneously, and it is only on the very surface level that her
valorization is activated.

Macette's unbelievable transformation[15] from champion prostitute
to exemplary saint is rendered believable very early in the poem by a
dynamic accumulation of hyperbolic descriptors. But when these
rhetorical signs are perceived by the reader as symbols of irony, the
demonstration stops at the credibility gap. Victim of an ingenious
tour de force played on him by an unreliable *persona,* the reader is
almost convinced of Macette's sincerity even before he hears her
personal account. As a prostitute, Macette is characterized most
nobly, an incongruity which results in a vivid comic effect. The
narrator expresses her life style by the linguistic vehicles of fencing,
aristocratic games, and military metaphors:

A soutenu le prix en *l'escrime d'amours,* (4)
Lasse enfin de *servir* au peuple *de quintaine,* (5)
N'estant *passe-volant, soldat* ni *capitaine,* (6)
Depuis les plus *chetifs* jusques aux plus *fendans* (7)
Qu'elle n'ait desconfit et mis dessus les dents, (8)
Lasse, di-je, et non soule enfin s'est retiree (9)

"Soutenu le prix" remains hyperbolically laudatory until the comic
metaphor "l'escrime d'amours" annuls the praise by interference
with a pejorative connotation in the plural form of "amours," a
subtle indication of love's recurrence. The aristocratic game metaphor continues in line 5 by "quintaine," and is analogously deprecia-
ted by the verb "servir de," implying a widely-ranged ("au peuple")
self-debasement which increases proportionally as the accumulation
of Macette's men piles higher in the following lines six and seven.
Adding to the comic effect is the reversal of male-female roles implicit in the use of "servir," a verb traditionally associated in the
"courtois" code with the subservient male who renders undying
service to his "dame." "N'estant passe-volant, soldat, ni capitaine"
is a hyperbolic display of military fakes ("passe-volant") and figures
in linear array. The accumulation is reinforced in line 7 by the

superlative antithesis "les plus chetifs" and "les plus fendans," recalling both the military and game metaphors. "Fendans" continues the fencing metaphor metonymically. The general effect of this grandiose accumulation of plurals is to affirm the already implicit recurrence of Macette's love-making expertise. In short, the narrator sees Macette as a woman worldly wise who has clearly 'been around!'

The predicate adjective "lasse" in initial and emphatic position in lines 5 and 9 takes on added significance by association with three different codes and contexts: (1) literal fatigue resulting from physical games ("escrime," "quintaine") (2) comic exhaustion resulting from burlesque military victories ("soldat," "capitaine," "desconfit" and its figurative synonym "mis dessus les dents," all of which are components of a military code); (3) boredom and fatigue resulting from too frequent acts of love. The multiple levels implicit in "lasse" are confirmed not only by its repetition in line 9, mimetic of recurrence, but also in the narrator's emphatic insistence, "di-je," drawing the reader's attention to the antepositioned word "lasse." Moreover, the use of the descriptive adjective "soule," which often appears in love contexts (e.g. sated lover),[16] functions as an additional effect of insistent repetition. All this introductory apparatus, like an encomiastic exordium, prepares the reader for Macette's sudden transformation ("s'est retiree") from body to soul.

Convincing the reader more subtly of Macette's sincerity, the narrator paints a rather clever portrait of himself as a skeptic. He is not a man to be led around by the nose, in contrast to his most obvious literary analogue, Orgon, who like the narrator ("tapi dans un recoin") is hidden under a table to witness the unmasking of an abominable religious hypocrite.[17]

> Moy mesme qui ne croy de leger aux merveilles,   (37)
> Qui reproche souvent mes yeux et mes oreilles,   (38)
> La voyant si changée en un temps si subit,   (39)
> Je creu qu'elle l'estoit d'ame comme d'habit,   (40)

The constant, hidden, authorial presence, establishing a titillating voyeur setting within the poem, is one of its major sources of dramatic irony.[18] While the reader is shocked by the moral implications of Macette's blasphemy, the voyeur is doubly shocked for he sees his pragmatic interests threatened. The narrator's chance for success with the silent interlocutor, "une fille où j'ay ma fantasie," diminishes as Macette's persuasion strengthens:

> Quand par arrest du Ciel qui hait l'hypocrisie, (45)
> Au logis d'une fille où j'ay ma fantasie, (46)
> N'ayant pas tout à fait mis fin à ses vieux tours (47)
> La vieille me rendit tesmoin de ses discours. (48)

But the overblown preparation for Macette, "par arrest du Ciel," recalling the earlier reference to miracles "Moy-mesme ne croy de leger aux merveilles" (37), and the exaggerated intensification achieved by the repetition of adverbs "si ... si" in line 39 cast a shadow of doubt on Macette's sincerity. Confirmed explicitly only at the very end of the poem, this doubt is manifested as if unconsciously on a verbal level in "qui hait l'hypocrisie" (45) and the purposely oblique and understated euphemism "n'ayant pas tout à fait mis fin à mes vieux tours" (47). Act I, then, is over; the suspenseful introduction of the star actor is complete; and the main character finally appears before her fictional/nonfictional audience of hidden satirist and impatient readers.

Macette has mastered the art of persuasion. Her direct discourse, rhetorically geared to convince the interlocutor of its universal truth, is a study in verbal magic. Quickly and subtly she establishes herself as a respectable authority figure by the frequent and patronizing use of the interjection "Ma fille," which not only suggests an age difference between the two women, but initates the intentionally personal idiolect of the clergy.[19] Her speech is flourished with religious clichés, "Dieu vous garde et vous veuille benir" (1.51), high-toned optatives and exclamations "qu'il me puisse advenir!" (1.52), "Qu'eussiez-vous tout le bien dont le ciel vous êtes chiche" (1.53), and a series of strong negations:

> L'ayant je n'en seroy plus pauvre ny plus riche; (54)
> Car n'estant plus du monde au bien je ne pretens, (55)
>
> D'autre chose icy-bas le bon Dieu je ne prie: (57)

all of which are designed to capture the confidence of the young girl who is about to receive her sentimental initiation and education.

Macette's authority is alternately confirmed and undermined by a play on the word "savoir":

> A propos, *sçavez*-vous? on dit qu'on vous marie; (58)
> *Je sçay* bien votre cas: un homme grand, adroit, (59)
> Riche et *Dieu sçait* s'il a tout ce qu'il vous faudroit! (60)

Line 58 marks a transition between Macette's pompous introduction of herself and her more direct, didactic, but 'down-to-earth' stance. The conversational use of "savoir" ("A propos, sçavez-vous?") is effective in signaling the tonal contrast. "Je sçay bien votre cas" (1.59) establishes the speaker's position of authority,[20] but in view of Macette's earlier avowal of societal isolation ("N'estant plus du monde au bien je ne prétens" (1.55) the implicit contradiction in her acquired court gossip creates an ironic effect. A further comic effect is achieved by the following popular cliché "Dieu sçait," which vulgarizes and practically annuls the seriousness of the preceding religious jargon. Macette's artificiality is reinforced more directly in her obvious use of false flattery, a technique commonly associated with hyperbolized, courtly language:

> ... vous estes *si* gentille,   (62)
> *Si* mignonne et *si* belle et d'un regard *si* doux   (63)
> Que la beauté plus grande est laide auprès de vous.   (64)

Commanding the respect of an authority in the match-making field, Macette resorts to a myriad of rhetorical devices designed to under-line the universal truth of her teachings.[21] She employs modal verbs of imperative value, and alternates direct concretizations ("satin," "perles," "rubis") with evasive euphemisms ("ce qui peut en amour satisfaire ...") which attenuate the shock effect of her 'realistic' language:

> Vous *devriez*, estant belle, avoir de beaux habits,   (67)
> Esclater de satin, de perles, de rubis.   (68)
>
> Mais pour moi je *voudroy* que vous eussiez au moins   (71)
> Ce qui peut en amour satisfaire à vos soins,   (72)

Sweeping generalizations abound, imparting Macette with an aura of cynical expertise and acquired wisdom.[22] They are formed diversely by the use of abstractions, impersonal expressions, hyperboles, the anonymous and generalizing pronoun "on," plurals, etc.:

> Mais| *tout* ne respond pas au traict de ce visage   (65)
>
> *On a beau* s'agencer et faire les doux yeux,   (75)
> Quand *on* est bien paré, *on* en est tousjours mieux: (76)

Plural substantives also occur in proverbial sequences which, by definition, are comprised of wise sayings and hidden truths pithily expressed and current among the common folk.[23] Macette's speech is characteristically spotted with popular expressions imparting a tonal informality which is in comic contrast to her high-toned theological and courtly stances:[24]

> Ma foy, les beaux habits servent bien à la mine; (74)
>
> Fille qui sçait son monde a saison oportune. (93)
>
> Qui sçait vivre icy bas n'a jamais pauvreté. (148)

Maxims, or well-turned short sequences with a didactic purpose, are functionally similar to proverbs and structurally similar to standard definitions. A fundamentally antithetical pattern and a high frequency of plural forms (especially the first person plural) are characteristics of the maxim:

> Nos biens comme nos maux sont en nostre pouvoir, (92)
>
> Chacun est artisan de sa bonne fortune, (94)
> Le malheur par conduite au bonheur cedera. (95)
>
> Il faut faire vertu de la necessité:" (147)

Definitions in the conventional format of an equation are created with the verb "être" and intensified by hyperboles in the immediate stylistic context:

> Ces vieux contes d'honneur dont on repaist les dames (81)
> Ne sont que des appas pour les debiles ames (82)

The reductive "ne ... que" construction, the pejorative metaphor "vieux contes" associated blasphemously with "honneur," and the agricultural metaphor "repaist" inappropriately juxtaposed to the aristocratic appellation "dames" clearly diminish the positive value of "honneur" in the first part of the equation. The resultant 'depoetization' of a conventionally esteemed value is continued by the minimizing attributive "appas," signifying magical charm, and "debiles," an epithet whose negative connotative value is intensified all the more by its inversion.

An example of an internally dialectical definition which carries within it the simultaneous confirmation and destruction of a truth is the much cited maxim "L'honneur est un vieux sainct que l'on ne chomme plus" (94). No sooner is the positive identity between "honneur" and "saint" established by the verb "être" than the personification is simultaneously minimized by collocation with the pejorative adjective "vieux." The dependent clause "que l'on ... chomme," whose kernel word is "chomme," is generated tautologically from "vieux," repeats it semantically, and exhibits a conventional cause/effect relationship. "Ne ... plus" is negative but oppositional with respect to the present. It intensifies as well as nullifies the negativity already implicit in "chomme" so that the original equation is now totally and doubly reversed. The *tour de force* achieved here by an oxymoric and eminently dynamic verbal process is quite standard for maxims, especially those written by La Rochefoucauld, who later perfected the format with distinction.

Macette's generalizations are characteristically terse, direct and rarely metaphoric. She has mastered the empirical method to perfection. After a series of concrete examples, and in good rhetorical form, Macette cones in on the essential point of her lesson in one pithy, inductive truism:[25]

> Combien, pour avoir mis leur honneur en sequestre,   (97)
> Ont-elles aux atours eschangé le limestre   (98)
> Et dans les plus hauts rangs eslevé leurs maris?   (99)
> *Ma fille, c'est ainsi que l'on vit à Paris,*   (100)

The brutality of the reductive truth announced in line 100 is both softened and strengthened by the personal interjection "Ma fille" which also establishes a psychological distance between the two women by recalling their status and age difference.[26] The force of the blunt truism is generated from its stylistic contrast to the preceding, descriptive and effusive language. Line 97 ("mis leur honneur en sequestre") contains a nobly stated, evasive euphemism. Line 98 ("aux atours eschangé le limestre") represents a descriptive metaphor of acquired wealth in which an effect of concretization is achieved in the antithetical naming of intensely beautiful and ugly fabrics. Lines 97 and 98 taken separately are internally contrastive, one exhibiting linguistic evasiveness and the other an effect of extreme precision. But taken as a unit lines 97 and 98 are directly contrastive in form to the bluntness of the final comic line: "Ma fille, c'est ainsi que l'on vit à Paris."[27] Line 99 ("les plus hauts rangs"), continuing the heightened tone of the two preceding lines, is equally descriptive and hyperbolic. This contextual flamboyance is sharply reduced in line 100 by a convergence of reductive devices. The verse is atypically homogeneous, consisting of uniformly short, hammering syllables united by a strident assonance in [1]. The relief-producing neutral construction "c'est" calls special attention to whatever follows;[28] "ainsi" is an inductive conjunction which summarizes; "l'on" generalizes; "Paris" is not only a metonymy for city life but constitutes the conventionally symbolic representation of 'life.' This contrastively logical, 'down-to-earth' language is mimetic of Macette's ideological pragmatism and is appropriately suited to her earthy character portrayal.

Like her pessimistic reevaluation of honor, Macette also minimizes chastity and its traditionally esteemed value:

> Et la vefve aussi bien comme la mariee,   (101)
> Celle est chaste, sans plus, qui n'en est point priee   (102)
> Toutes au fait d'amour se chaussent en un poinct,   (103)

The negative sting at the end of line 102 ("qui n'en est point priee"), acting like a sententious "pointe," reiterates and extends the negativity of the preceding disjunction "sans plus" (meaning "aucune autre"). The sequence ends with an inductive generalization, reproducing the same pattern as the one noted in the passage on honor, which ended inductively with "Ma fille, c'est ainsi que l'on vit à Paris" (100). The procedures are remarkably identical, and the empirical method using inductive reasoning can be considered a stylistic marker of Macette's particular pattern of logic. Chastity, minimized and ironically reduced to the sad state of a woman's simply not being courted, is qualified as illusive. Macette proves her point effectively by citing additional examples:

> Et Jeanne que-tu-sçais, dont on ne parle point,   (104)
> Qui fait si doucement la simple et la discrete,   (105)
> Elle n'est pas plus chaste, ains elle est plus secrete,   (106)

It is significantly Macette, the champion mask-bearer, who brutally unmasks "Jeanne que-tu-sçais" and all self-proclaimed saints by juxtaposing popular, if not vulgar, terminology with their identity:[29]

> Toutes au fait d'amour se chaussent en un poinct.   (103)

Macette is the supreme, moral leveler who strips us all ("toutes") of presumptuous and pretentious self-satisfaction, exposing man's universal hypocrisy when it comes to the basic question of love. This Montaigne-like uniformity among men is expressed in a characteristically positive/negative fashion:

On trouve bien la cour dedans un monastere   (118)
Et après maint essay enfin j'ay reconnu   (119)
Qu'un homme comme un autre est un moine tout nu   (120)

In line 120 the equation between man and monk is clearly appreciative until the taboo attributive "tout nu" ironically reduces the
identity to what can only be considered a burlesque metaphor.

Sin, too, is redefined in line 128 to conform to Macette's prag-
matist ideology. In the form of a maxim, this heretical pronouncement on sin summarizes a series of mask metaphors (cf. "desguisant,"
"envelopant," "caché"). The irony in the example below is due to
the ambiguity of "double entendre," actualized by the superimposure of two contrastive codes: religious ("ame," "flame") and
sensual ("ame," "flame," "plaisirs," "bouillons"):

C'est pourquoy *desguisant* les bouillons de mon ame,   (125)
D'un long habit de cendre *envelopant* ma flame,   (126)
Je cache mon dessein aux plaisirs adonné;   (127)
Le peché que l'on *cache* est demi pardonné,   (128)

There is an interesting effect of concretization established by the
use of plurals ("les bouillons," "plaisirs") appropriately occurring
only with the lexical components of the sensual code, and reminding
the reader once again of Macette's wide experience in love affairs.
The comic generalization in line 128 is another example of Macette's
empirical, inductive reasoning which parodies the logic of an author-
itative expert in the field of morality.

Physical love, the sin committed more frequently and easily in
youth is transformed linguistically into virtue by the aging and
defensively nostalgic Macette. This transformation is achieved by
the dexterous manipulation of double-entendre resulting from a
fusion of the religious and sensual codes in the word "passion":[30]

*Pourveu qu'*on ne le sçache il n'importe comment,   (131)
Qui peut dire que non ne peche nullement   (132)
Puis la bonté du Ciel nos offences surpasse: (133)
*Pourveu qu'*on se confesse on a tousjours sa grace;   (134)
Il donne quelque chose à nostre passion: (135)
Et qui jeune n'a pas grande devotion   (136)
Il faut que pour le monde à la feindre il s'exerce: (137)

The repetition of the concessive conjunctions "pourveu que" are
indicative of Macette's relativist, pragmatic philosophy of morality.

Relativity implies a willingness to make exceptions ("pourvu que …") within the sanctioned, universal doctrines. The irony in the passage is actualized not only by the unexpectedly reductive and blasphemous conclusions in lines 131 and 134, all the more blasphemous as they are couched in a context of religiosity, but by the hyperbolic "tousjours" which signals impossible exaggeration. The ironic effect is intensified by the inappropriate verb "s'exercer," normally associated with legitimate professions, and here incongruously attributed to the pretense of religious devotion.

Vanity and excessive displays are valued highly in Macette's perverted system. This transformation of church-sanctioned modesty and self-denial is achieved primarily by a clever play on the word "bien," a lexeme of positive connotation when used as an adverb, and equally positive in both the religious ("le bien" meaning "le salut") and economic senses ("le bien" meaning "l'argent"). From line 152 to line 210 there is a sustained ironic effect created by the incompatible superimposure of a financial code, stressing the profit motive, and its structural opposite, a religious code sanctioning self-denial and a search for salvation:

> *Se voir du bien*, ma fille, il n'est rien de si doux, (151)
> S'enrichir de bonne heure est une grand'sagesse, (152)

> Où lorsqu'on a *du bien*, il n'est si decrepite (157)
> Qui ne trouve (en donnant) couvercle à sa marmite. (158)

> Il n'est que d'en avoir, *le bien* est tousjours *bien,* (191)

> Je ne juge pour moy les gens sur ce qu'ils sont, (199)
> Mais selon le profit et *le bien* qu'ils me font. (200)

> Il faut suivre de près *le bien* que l'on differe (209)
> Et ne le differer qu'en tant que l'on le peut, (210)

Lines 209 and 210 are developments of an extended, financial metaphor involving complicated debt protocols. The metaphoric passage is didactic in purpose and suggests that rituals respected between debtor and creditor should be similarly respected between lovers. Macette draws an equation between love and finance, once again, by the superimposure of codes, a technique which has a strong potential for double-entendre and, therefore, ironic effect:

> Que *le plus* ou *le moins* y mette difference (205)
> Et tienne seullement la partie en souffrance, (206)
> Que vous *restablirez* du jour au lendemain; (207)

Et tousjours retenez le bon bout à la main,   (208)
De crainte que le temps ne destruise *l'affaire*   (209)
Il faut suivre de près *le bien* que l'on *differe*   (210)
Et ne le *differer* qu'en tant que l'on le peut,   (211)
On se puisse aisement *restablir* quand on veut.   (212)

Lexical components belonging clearly to the field of debt protocols are underlined above, with the exception of "le bien" and "l'affaire", which are equally associable with 'sensuality.' The entire sequence embodies a double-level irony of provocative, taboo connotation which is crystallized strikingly in "le bon bout à la main" (208).

As Macette's arguments for the profit motive become more persuasive, her language becomes stronger, and she switches from abstract generalizations to an accumulation of direct imperatives. This forward thrust is accompanied by negations and their corresponding, backward pull on the rhythmic development:

Vendez ces doux regards, ces attraicts, ces appas,   (163)
Vous mesme *vendez-vous*, mais *ne vous livrez pas*;   (164)
Conservez vous l'esprit, *gardez* vostre franchise,   (165)
Prenez tous s'il se peut, *ne soyez jamais prise*.   (166)

Surtout *soyez* de vous la maistresse et la dame;   (173)
Faites, s'il est possible, un miroir de vostre ame,   (174)

Fuyez ce qui vous nuit, *aymez* ce qui vous sert,   (176)
Faites profit de tout et mesme de vos pertes;   (177)

Ne faites, s'il se peut, *jamais* present *ni* don,   (179)

Not constant but alternating, the positive/negative polarity is created by a convergence of parallel antitheses ("Vendez-ne vous livrez pas"; "prenez-ne soyez jamais prise"; "Fuyez-aymez"; "Faites-ne faites jamais"). The parallelism is reinforced by the redundance "s'il se peut," "s'il est possible," and "s'il se peut" in analogous position. The connotative development is equally alternating: l. 163 is affirmative; l. 164 affirmative and negative; l. 165 affirmative; l. 166 affirmative and hyperbolically negative ("jamais"); lines 173 and 174, 176 and 177 are affirmative; line 178 reaches a crescendo of negativity ("jamais ... ni"). As the pointed imperatives continue, the metaphors grow increasingly concrete, and the profit motive is firmly established within an intricate system of financial metaphors. This materialistic, descriptive field is in direct contrast to the earlier religious code and pervading atmosphere of spirituality created by the contextual saturation of virtues like honor, simplicity, discretion, glory, and their structural counterpart, sin.

Just as these traditionally esteemed virtues are mercilously reduced
to the statute of illusion and, in that, depoeticized, the act of love (cf.
"l'envie" below) is similarly depoeticized, vulgarized by association
with terms of financial gain:

> L'envie en est bien *moindre* et *le gain* plus *contant.*   (172)
>
> *Faites profit* de tout et mesme de *vos pertes*;   (177)

And just as Macette equated saints and sinners alike by their natural
desire for passion, she similarly democratizes society, equating all
manner of men by their passion for money:

> Que *le gain* a bon goust, de quelque endroit qu'il vienne; (194)
>
> *Estimez* vos amans selon *le revenu*:   (195)
> Qui *donnera le plus*, qu'il soit le mieux venu;   (196)
> Laissez la mine à part, prenez garde à *la somme*;   (197)
> *Riche* vilain vaut mieux que *pauvre* gentilhomme: (198)
> Je ne juge pour moy les gens sur ce qu'ils sont,   (199)
> Mais selon *le profit et le bien* qu'ils me font.   (200)
> Quand *l'argent* est meslé, l'on ne peut reconnoistre   (201)
> Celuy du serviteur d'avec celuy du maistre;   (202)
> *L'argent* d'un cordon bleu n'est pas d'autre façon   (203)
> Que celuy d'un fripier ou d'un aide à maçon.   (204)

The societal democratization is brought about semiotically by an
intersection of codes: courtly ("le gentilhomme," "bon goust,"
"serviteur ... maistre"); religious ("cordon bleu," which is a
"chevalier de l'ordre du St. Esprit"); popular ("pauvre," "vilain,"
"fripier," "aide à maçon"). When these lexical signs, which correspond respectively to three different social classes, intersect in a financial code, the equation between social class and money is drawn. The
comic aspect of this maliciously materialistic system of criteria, "Je
ne *juge* pour moy les gens sur ce qu'ils sont" (199), is crystallized in
the sententious verse:

> Qui donnera le plus, qu'il soit le mieux venu   (196)

whose internal rhyme ("plus ... venu") and thematic compactness
are truly memorable. Love and money are identities; they are one
and the same means of exchange in Macette's reconstructed socio-
economic system:

En amour autrement c'est imbecilité;   (240)
Qui le fait à credit n'a pas grande resource,   (241)
On y fait des amis mais peu d'argent en bourse.   (242)

Here as before there is a juxtaposition of the sensual code ("amour," "amis") and a more highly developed financial code ("fait à credit," "grande resource," "peu," "argent en bourse"), which actualizes a detestable identity between love and money.

The dangers implicit in norm reversals and the revolutionary rejection of accepted mores are reflected in Macette's frequent but often unexpected use of strong, defensive negations and oxymorons like "douce peine," "vertu criminelle," and "sainte pecheresse." As if to translate her own internal conflicts and hesitations resulting from an awareness of the inherent dangers, she contradicts her silent conscience, shrieks out "NON," for no apparent reason, and alarms the reader who can not see or hear any opposition emanating from the silent interlocutor:

Non, non, faites l'amour, et vendez aux amans   (159)
Vos accueils, vos baisers et vos embrassemens;   (160)
C'est gloire et *non pas* honte, en ceste *douce peine,*   (161)

Non, si j'estoy de vous, je le planteroy là.   (228)

Mais non, ma fille, *non*: qui veut vivre à son aise,   (237)
Il *ne* faut simplement un amy qui vous plaise,   (238)
Mais qui puisse au plaisir joindre l'utilité;   (239)

The effect of sustained dialectic and self-contradiction is reinforced by Macette's use of the contrastive conjunction "Mais" (cf. 1. 239 above), which signals an abrupt transition. In the section of the poem devoted to the minimization and destruction of conventionally esteemed 'types,' the use of "mais" is particularly effective in underlining the reversal.

pos./neg.	"Tous ces beaux suffisans, dont la cour est sémee,	
neg.	Ne sont que triacleurs et vendeurs de fumee,	(214)
pos./neg.	Ils sont beaux, bien peignez, belle barbe au menton	
neg.	*Mais* quand il faut payer, au diantre le teston!	(216)
pos./neg.	Et faisant des mourans et de l'ame saisie,	(217)
neg.	Ils croyent qu'on leur doit pour rien la courtoisie	
neg.	*Mais* c'est pour leur beau nez! Le puits n'est pas commun	(219)
neg.	Si j'en avois un cent, ils n'en auroient pas un.	(220)

The last two verses, "Mais c'est pour leur beau nez ...," reach a high peak of oblique invective by the dripping sarcasm in "leur beau nez!," the comic metonymy "nez," and the exaggerated proverb "Le puits n'est pas commun, Si j'en avois un cent, ils n'en auroient pas un." Macette's total rejection of the court dandy is delicately foreshadowed in the beginning of the sequence by the antiphrastic and ironic use of "beaux suffisans" (213); the agricultural, reductive metaphor "semee" placed inappropriately in association with "Cour"; the minimization of the character achieved by "ne ... que," and the pejorative connotation in "triacleur" (or charlatan) and "vendeur de fumee," a metaphor for insignificance. Moreover, the comic alliteration in voiced and devoiced plosives "Ils sont beaux, bien peignez, belle barbe au menton" (215) renders the caricature all the more burlesque. All this stylistic artillery prepares the contrastive conjunctions "Mais" (ll. 216 and 219) and 'overdetermines' the sequence. What appeared on the surface to be a verse alternation of positivity and negativity is really, on the deeper levels, an internal alternation of incongruous oppositions with a higher frequency of negativity and resultant blame. Satire, which is classified rhetorically as *laus et vituperatio* (or 'praise and blame') involves a combination of both, and a masterful distortion of blame into praise.

Other archetypal figures are presented, equalized or universalized, and immediately denigrated. "Le poète croté" or "l'homme à satyre" is described as a grotesquely comic character, but not any different from all other men:

> *Mais* Dieu sçait, c'est un homme aussi bien que les autres: (225)

The satirist's aim is to attack, "mesdire," and his tool is invective, described by Macette metaphorically as "le feu":

> Ces hommes mesdisans ont le feu sous la levre,   (233)

When Macette recommends that her protegée choose an "abbé" for a lover, there is a supremely ironic and multi-level fusion of the three mainstreams of the poem: religious/spiritual, sensual, and material. Moreover, there is an abrupt and unexpected transition from the negative depiction of the "poète croté" ("Ils sont matelineurs, prompts à prendre la chevre" (234)[31] to the positive but ironic depiction of the "abbez":

> Prenez moy ces abbez, ces fils de financiers,   (243)
> Dont depuis cinquante ans les peres usuriers,   (244)
> Volans à toutes mains, ont mis en leur famille   (245)
> Plus d'argent que le Roy n'en a dans la Bastille;   (246)

The reader is taken off guard by Macette's rapid switch to praise
and by the heretical associations of wealth and/or sexual liaison
with members of the clergy. Macette militantly convinces the young
girl that a rich abbot is the prime target:

> C'est là que vostre main peut faire de beaux coups. (247)

Macette characteristically pays the clergy a left-handed compliment,
simultaneously praising and blaming them in a perfectly ironic spirit:

> Ayez dessein aux dieux; pour de moindres beautez (267)
> Ils ont laissé jadis les cieux des-habitez. (268)

Although the shock effect of these hyperbolic and seemingly incompatible associations is intense, the reader should find Macette's
teaching perfectly logical and coherent within her own distorted
system. In fact, she practices what she preaches:

> Jour et nuict elle va de convent en convent, (23)
> Visite les saincts lieux, se confesse souvent, (24)
> A des cas reservez grandes intelligences, (25)
> Sçait du nom de Jesus toutes les indulgences, (26)

She is a reputed scholar, adept at handling the newest of jargon, and
Regnier takes advantage of the comic, phonetic effects of these
neologisms:

> Elle lit saint Bernard, la Guide des Pecheurs, (20)
> Les Meditations de la mere Therese, (21)
> Sçait que c'est que *hypostase* avecque *synderese*; (22)

Understandably Macette wants her young protegée to be just as
worldly wise as she is, to understand 'innocence' for what it is, a
powerful ("donnant vie et trespas") deceptive mask, never to be
confused with chastity. In the sequence below Macette defines
innocence inductively by the circular procedure of stating a generalization, clarifying it by specific examples, and restating another
similar generalization in oxymoric terms:

> *En amour l'innocence est un scavant mystere* (257)
> Pourveu que ce ne soit une innocence austere (258)
> Mais qui sçache par art, donnant vie et trespas, (259)
> Feindre avecques douceur qu'elle ne le sçait pas; (260)

Il faut aider ainsi la beauté naturelle,   (261)
L'innocence autrement est vertu criminelle,   (262)

It is at the conclusion of Macette's teachings, as the circle closes,[32] that her real motivation for haunting churches is fully revealed. When the poet stated earlier:

Elle a mis son amour à la devotion. (16)

the reader appreciates finally by retroaction the dripping irony of the implication. The double-level meanings are created not only from the superimposure of the sensual, religious, and courtly codes ("amour," "dévotion"), but from an interplay of literal and figurative significance. Now re-reading the first part of the poem, and armed with an understanding of Macette's own peculiar ideology, the reader experiences an entirely different reaction. He becomes aware of an irony of antiphrasis:

Pour beate partout le peuple la renomme,   (33)
Et la Gazette mesme a déjà dit à Rome,   (34)
La voyant aymer Dieu et la chair maistriser   (35)
Qu'on n'attend que sa mort pour la canoniser.   (36)

The poem ends with the satirist's expected invectives, curses, and sarcastic rhetorical questions:

Ha, *vieille*, dy-je lors, qu'en mon coeur *je maudis*,   (275)
Est-ce là le chemin pour gaigner Paradis?   (276)

He must appropriately condemns her to a life of eternal old age to be spent in dire poverty and in suffering. The satirist's virtuosity is vividly displayed in a series of dialectically contrived tortures:

Dieu te doint pour guerdon de tes ceuvres si sainctes(277)
Que soient avant ta mort tes prunelles esteintes,   (278)
Ta maison descouverte et sans feu tout l'hyver,   (279)
Avecque tes voisins jour et nuict estriver   (280)
Et trainer sans confort, triste et desesperee,   (281)
Une *pauvre vieillesse* et tousjours alteree.   (282)

What motivated this barrage of diabolical inventions?[33] Apart from Macette's abominably Machiavellian system which she promulgates as a life style of virtue, her denunciation of sanctioned values, and her destruction of archetypal heroes, the poet, echoing the reader, reacts with virulent horror to the very last words of the impostor. In her parting promise, uttered in a characteristically cool, matter-of-fact manner, the reader pauses to reflect upon the poetic and stunning convergence of ironies in the pun on "A Dieu":

> Je vous verray domain. A Dieu, bon soir, ma fille.   (273)

The satirist's cathartic outburst, which is anticlimactic after Macette's theatrical exit, can not destroy the reader's cynical suspicions of external hypocrisy, the recurrence ("demain") of more spectacular, linguistic trickery, the procreation and fiendish regeneration of Macette's folly in another innocent victim.

NOTES

* This article appeared in *Semiotica* 13:2 (1975), 131-153.
[1] See Maynard Mack, "The Muse of Satire," *The Yale Review* 41: (1951), 80-92. Commenting on the satiric effects created by author and speaker differentiation, Mack cites Jonathan Swift's *Modest Proposal* ("where the relation of the speaker to the author is extremely oblique not to say antithetical" (p. 83). Macette's antithetical relationship to the author is implicit throughout and suspended to the end of the poem to allow for a grandiose unmasking, and invective apotheosis.
[2] Joseph Vianey, *Mathurin Regnier* (1896, rpt. Slatkin, 1969), p. 110. "Il ne faut donc pas s'étonner qu'il ait conçu la satire, comme il l'avait conçue l'Arioste, à l'imitation d'Horace. Il en fit une sorte d'épître familière, adressée à un ami. ..." For additional sources see J. Cordens Lyons, "Notes on M. Regnier's *Macette*," *Studies in Philology* 28 (1931), 301-305.
[3] See l. 37: "Moi-même qui ne croy de leger aux merveilles." This line is in direct contrast to the preceding thirty-six lines which in view of their third person narrative in indirect discourse, are more general and far less personal. The sudden switch to the first person (emphasized by the pronoun "Moi-même," the abundance of first person pronouns (ll. 38, 40, 42, 46, 48, 50) and the resultant increase in explicitness mark a contrastive break in this introductory section. The break, confirmed graphemically when the line is indented, is a representative example of the bipartite structures in the poem.
[4] See l. 109: "Moy-mesme, croiriez-vous, pour estre plus agee." This line is similarly in contrast to the preceding lines 51-108 which are more general, and consequently display less personal involvement or sincerity. The numerous maxims, proverbs, false flattery, and minimization of abstract concepts like 'honor,' 'reknown,' 'discretion,' 'simplicity,' etc. bear witness to an effect of generality and contingent insincerity. This section is less direct than the following (ll. 109-273) containing imperatives and negations, a destruction of conventional types (people more often than concepts). The bipartite structure mani-

fested here is homologous, then, to that described above in note 3.

[5] See Mary Claire Randolph's brilliant essay entitled "Structural Design of Formal Verse Satire," *Philological Quarterly* 21 (1942), 368-84. Miss Randolph claims that the usual structure of formal verse satire consists of an outer shell-like framework enclosing the entire piece. Within the frame there is a combative hollowman or interlocutor called an Adversarius who, in Macette's case, is a pessimistic hard-headed Mentor. Miss Randolph rightfully insists on the dramatic elements of the formal verse satire consisting of two actors, a Satirist and his Adversarius, a setting of sorts (the narrator's girlfriend's house), and a thesis to be argued. She also confirms the underlying bipartite patterns of satire.

[6] Benoist, "Des Anacoluthes et de la phrase poétique de Regnier," *Annales de la Faculté des lettres de Bordeaux* (1879), 325-336. Regnier's poetry is characterized by subordination, many interruptive anacoluthons, and a convergence of disjunctive techniques. Lines 1-19, for example, contain symmetrical dependent clauses with initial relative pronouns "qui ... qui" which interrupt the steady flow of the syntagma; two participial clauses "lasse ... lasse"; two gerundive clauses "N'estant ... donnant" each of which interrupts the flow, extending the description into a sustained enjambment. Beneath a surface, then, of verbal simplicity there is a development of persuasive, dialectical argumentation.

[7] All textual references are taken from the Raibaud edition, *Oeuvres Complètes* (Paris, 1958). A recommended edition is Viollet le Duc's 1853 *Oeuvres Complètes* only for its "Histoire de la Satire en France" and Brossette's annotations. See also Jean Plattard's *Oeuvres Complètes* (Paris, 1930) for annotational supplements to Raibaud's very complete edition.

[8] The name Macette appeared in the *Muse Folastre (Proverbes d'amours*, 1st edition, 1603) and according to Raibaud's note Macette designated "une dame experte en trafic d'amours."

[9] 'Praise and blame,' better known as *laus et vituperatio*, is the rhetorical category in which satire has conventionally been placed.

[10] See M. Riffaterre's "Modèles de la phrase littéraire" in *Problems of Textual Analysis*, eds. P. R. Leon, H. Mitterand, P. Nesselroth, and P. Robert (Montreal; Didier, 1971), pp. 133-151, for a discussion of textual overdetermination, oxymoric and tautological sequences, and descriptive systems in generative stylistics.

[11] See pp. 19-22 for a discussion of financial metaphors and the establishment of a materialist code.

[12] See David Worcester, *The Art of Satire* (New York: Morton & Co, 1940) and the roles that invective, burlesque, and irony play in the creation of satire (p. 75). Worcester correctly distinguishes verbal irony (the puzzle of inversion, understatement, exaggeration, etc) and dramatic irony (an irony of fate or "when the field of observation is enlarged from words or personalities to life as a whole and the ways of Providence, the sense of esoteric knowledge is conveyed through dramatic irony" (p. 11).

[13] A code is a linguistic tool consisting of lexical variants that actualize a structure. One can appropriately speak of a 'religious code' referring to words in the text that are normally associated with diverse aspects of religion.

[14] See an interesting use of the word "objet" in D'Urfé's *Astrée*, II, 311-314 ("Tables des lois d'amour"):

Qu'il n'aime jamais qu'en un lieu
Et que cet Amour soit un Dieu
Qu'il adore pour toute chose;
Et n'ayant jamais qu'*un objet*,
Tous les bonheurs qu'il se propose
Soient pour cet unique sujet.

In D'Urfé's poem 'platonic' love and religious love are compatible, both inter-
secting in their spirituality. In Regnier's *Macette* physical love, implicit in "lict,"
interferes and creates an ironic effect by its incompatibility with Macette's professed spirituality.

[15] See Robert C. Elliott, "The Satirist and Society," *A Journal of English
Literary History* 21 (Sept. 1954), 237-48. Elliott discusses the notion of artist
as magician, and presents rather interesting evidence for an early connection of
satire and magic. The magic motif is not absent from *Macette*. Apart from the
most obvious and rather conventional interplay of appearance and reality,
Macette pronounces what sound like magic formulas, miraculous transformations
of reality:

Il faut faire vertu de la necessité   (179)
Il faut que les brillants soient en vostre visage   (150)

Moreover, the theatricality of demasking and sudden surprise in the revelation of
identity are compatible with a magic motif. Cf. the transformation of the
innocent woman "Et Jeanne que-tu-sçais, dont on ne parle point, Qui fait si
doucement la simple et la discrete" (ll. 105-106) into the original 'femme fatale'
endowed with magical, superhuman powers: "Mais qui scache par art, *donnant
vie et trespas*, Feindre avecques douceur qu'elle ne le sçait pas." (ll. 259-260)
This portrait is reminiscent of the deified woman in courtly love romances. See
lines 248-252 in which the militant 'femme fatale' ("coups", "blessez") is
transformed into a goddess of supernatural power ("il nous faut et blesser et
garir; Et parmi les plaisirs faire vivre et mourir." (263-264)).

[16] Cf. Cayrou, *Le Français classique* (Paris: Didier, 1948): N.B. il "se dit aussi
de ce qui rassasie l'esprit. ... Un amant n'est jamais soûl de regarder sa maîtresse."
(Furetière, *Dictionnaire universel*, 1690).

[17] See Molière's analogous depiction of Orante, a "fausse dévote," in *Tartuffe*
(Garnier, II, pp. 640-641):   '

Madame Pernelle:	Tous ces raisonnements ne font rien à l'affaire.
	On sait qu'Orante mène une vie exemplaire:
l. 119	Tous ses soins vont au Ciel; et j'ai su par des gens
	Qu'elle condamne fort le train qui vient céans.
Dorine:	L'exemple est admirable, et cette dame est bonne
	Il est vrai qu'elle vit en austère personne;
	Mais l'âge dans son âme a mis ce zèle ardent
	Et l'on sait qu'elle est prude à son corps défendant.
l. 125	Tant qu'elle a pu des coeurs attirer les hommages
	Elle a fort bien joui de tous ses avantages:

[18] Northrup Frye, "The Mythos of Winter: Irony and Satire," in *Anatomy
of Criticism* (Princeton University Press, 1957), pp. 223-239: "The chief dis-

tinction between irony and satire is that satire is militant irony: its moral norms are relatively clear and it assumes standards against which the grotesque and absurd are measured ... *whenever a reader is not sure what the author's attitude is or what his own is supposed to be, we have irony with relatively little satire*" (italics my own).

[19] See Molière's parody of Macette's language in *l'Ecole des Femmes* (Garnier, I, p. 428)

Agnès: Le lendemain étant sur notre porte
Une vieille m'aborde, en parlant de la sorte:
Mon enfant, le bon Dieu puisse-t-il vous bénir
Et dans tous vos attraits longtemps vous maintenir."

(II, 5: 303-506)

A similar use of the interjection "Ma fille" is represented by "mon enfant." The insistence on beauty and the use of optative sequences in a religious code are clearly reminiscent of Macette's speech patterns.

[20] See Ronald Paulson, *The Fictions of Satire* (Baltimore: Johns Hopkins Press, 1967). "To a greater extent than any of the ancient satirists except Petronius, Lucian lets the evil or folly speak for itself ... we are simply presented with the pseudo-wise exposing his folly" (p. 38). Lucian, like Regnier, often introduced the satire himself "to make sure there are no misunderstandings."

[21] Maynard Mack, "The Muse of Satire, *"op. cit,* p. 83:" [Satire] aims, like all poetry ... to achieve 'that delightful teaching which must be the right describing note to know a Poet by.' And it has, of course, its own distinctive means to do this. Prominent among them to a casual eye is the *exemplum* in the form of portrait ... and the middle style, which stresses conversational speech (more than passion or grandiloquence) along with aphoristic phrasings, witty turns, and ironical indirections."

[22] cf. Northrup Frye p. 280. "Cynicism is a little closer [than skepticism] to the satiric norm." He goes on to explain the latent cynicism of the Menippean satire.

[23] Alex Preminger, *Encyclopedia of Poetry and Poetics* (Princeton University Press, 1965), p. 680. "Proverbial subjects favor customs, superstitions, legal maxims, 'blasons populaires,' weather and medical lore, conventional phrases, and prophecies." Almost all of these occur in *Macette*.

[24] See Joseph Vianey's critical remark on Regnier's use of proverbs: "Regnier abuse des proverbes et ... il trempe trop souvent son pinceau dans la boue ..." (p. 222). Vianey does see the mimetic effects of Macette's popular idiolect ("le langage du personnage est admirablement approprié à son caractère," p. 221), but he completely neglects to explain the effective contrasts at work within her speech. Conversational, popular language coexists with high-toned religious clichés and courtly language, imparting a dynamic quality to the poetic language.

[25] See Alvin B. Kernan's *The Cankered Muse: Satire of the English Renaissance Renaissance* (Yale University Press, 1959) pp. 1-36: "Every satirist is something of a Jekyll and Hyde; he has both a public and a private personality. For the public personality ... the satirist always presents himself as a blunt, honest man with no nonsense about him ... *preference for plain terms which express plain truth*" (p. 171). This "matter of fact", reductive language, is not only discernible in

Macette's speech patterns but is especially characteristic of the satirist-author's invective outburst at the end of the poem.
[26] The age difference is confirmed explicitly in the poem. Notice that the same interjection "Ma fille" as well as the modal verb "devoir" and the epistemological insistence in "savoir" recur in a similar context:

> Je sçay bien que vostre age, encore jeune et tendre,
> Ne peut ainsi que moy ces mysteres comprendre:
> Mais vous devriez, ma fille, en l'age où je vous voy,
> Estre riche, content, avoir fort bien de quoy,
>   (pp. 141-44)

[27] See Gilbert Highet, *The Anatomy of Satire* (Princeton University Press, 1962), p. 5: "... the characteristic features of satire: it is topical, it claims to be realistic (although it is usually exaggerated or distorted); it is shocking; it is informal; and (although often in a grotesque or painful manner) it is funny."
[28] See lines 88 and 89 for another variant of the oxymoric sequence structured on a "c'est" identity:

> Il est bon en discours pour se faire estimer
> Mais au fonds c'est abus: sans excepter personne,

[29] A variant of the use of common names like "Jeanne-que-tu-sçais" and its effect of realism is manifested in line 189:

> Au reste, n'epargnez ni Gaultier ni Garguille;

The alliteration in (g) enhances the comic effect.
[30] The superimposure of the religious and courtly codes in the word "grace" contains a similar, double-entendre and creates ironic effect:

> Il faut que les brillants soient en vostre visage   (150)
> Que vostre bonne grace en acquiere pour vous: (151)

[31] "Prendre la chevre" is a popular expression meaning "se fâcher, s'emporter." "Matelineurs" is a metonymy for "fou" and by homonymic association with "Mathurin" it establishes an identity with Regnier. ("On prononçoit, et même on écrivoit *matelineus*, mot formé de Matelin, dit par corruption de Maturin, saint auquel, par allusion à *matto*, l'on a coutume de vouer les fous." Note by Brossette, 1853, Viollet le Duc's edition.)
[32] See Alvin Kernen, *op. cit*, p. 34: "We seem at the conclusion of satire to be always at very nearly the same point where we began."
[33] See David Worcester, *op. cit*, p. 20: "When an invective piece is sublime in utterance, when it reflects the thwarted passion of a great soul for the good, when it is sincere, and when wrath is not too-long sustained, it is satire."

CHAPTER 5

BOILEAU AND HIS FRIENDLY ENEMY: A POETICS OF SATIRIC CRITICISM*

The time has come to resurrect Boileau. Deposed from his long-term office as legislator of classical doctrine, and shaken abruptly off the high pillars of Parnassus at the end of the nineteenth century, Boileau's poetic talents and techniques need to be re-examined now. Whether his decline in status was due to the iconoclastic effects of Revillout's critical breakthrough in 1890, or to a natural development of changing esthetics, is a difficult question to answer.[1] But surely one cannot disregard even among some of Boileau's most sympathetic critics that a subtle whisper of hesitant suspicion has been in the air – implicating suspicion about his poetic talent and outright condemnation for lack of originality in style and content.[2] I hope to reopen the case for Boileau's poetic affectivity by taking a closer look at the structural complex of his *Satires* – a rich corpus consisting of a prose *Preface*, thirteen poems and two prose *Discours* – with special attention to its unity of form and thought.[3] The particular focus of this study is on the structural relationships between Boileau the lyric poet divided against himself, and Boileau the satiric critic at odds with a multifarious Enemy, the hydra of hypocrisy.[4]

Within Boileau's *Satires* and because of the nature of satire itself, a conflict between the satirist and his critical targets is comically sustained by ambivalent verbal combat. This satiric criticism is characterized formally by an interplay of contrasts which I shall refer to as the poetics of opposition. The targets move in two directions: inwardly, towards the poet himself, his very own enemy, and outwardly towards the Other, that complex of mutable forms which are sometimes more friendly than foul. The enemy takes various shapes – the king, ambiguity, satire, poets, poetry itself, the public, society in general, women in particular, human folly, false nobility and honor, and evil incarnate or *l'Equivoque*. The poet's ambivalent perception of himself naturally affects the poetic expression of his subject and his critical perception of others. Through a systematic investigation into the transformations of the enemy and the network of oppositional relationships between these forms and the poet's own dual self-image, I hope to stimulate a re-assessment of poetic values and at least promote the reinstatement which Boileau truly deserves.

Despite the essentially imitative forms of French classical poetry, Boileau's *Satires* are created within a system of alterity. Throughout the collection and in perfect rhetorical compliance with the satiric genre as simultaneous *laus et vituperatio*, Boileau launches a brutal and ironic invective against his Enemy, that network of changing agressors which is sometimes more friendly than foul. Boileau's foremost friendly enemy is his own ambivalent self-image mirrored in the many faces of his *persona*. This delicate construct of autoperception is laid bare in its dynamic state in the very first text of the *Satires*, the *Discours au Roy*. The structural arrangement of the poem in multiple contrastive patterns of praise and blame is an iconic representation of the poet's inner conflict. The *Discours au Roy* is built on a symmetrical tripartite system of parallel reversals[5] through which the narrator relentlessly portrays himself as the alienated outcast, striving desperately to reunite himself with the archetypal Other, a friendly enemy, here the king. In the first and third panegyric sections of the poem,[6] Boileau's *persona* extends initially hyperbolic praise to the king, and then offers incompatible explanations for what he humbly calls an inability to praise:

> Jeune et vaillant Heros, dont la haute sagesse
> N'est point le fruit tardif d'une lente vieillesse,
> Et qui seul, sans Ministre, à l'exemple des Dieux,
> Soûtiens tout par Toi-mesme, et vois tout par Tes yeux,
> Grand Roi ...
> Mais je sçai peu loüer, et ma Muse tremblante
> Fuit d'un si grand fardeau la charge trop pesante (*Disc.*, 1-10)

Stated more emphatically:

> Pour chanter un Auguste, il faut estre un Virgile. (*Disc.*, 58)

On one level the flattering allusion to the king's absolute rule, accomplished expressively by alliterative repetition in "seul, sans Ministre," and "tout par Toi-mesme et ... tout par Tes yeux," is indisputable, temporal truth referring to the death of Mazarin and the birth of a divine monarch. But Boileau's satiric duplicity masks an undertone of sarcasm directed against the king retroactively in

Satire I and against Chapelain and Colbert in *Satire VII*. In the satire which begins "Muse, changeons de stile ...," the subject of monarchical pensions denied the poet in 1663 by Colbert and Chapelain is more explicity the target of attack. In *Satire I* the king's alleged power is rapidly reversed and cynically displaced by the power of his agents represented metonymically by "Mecenas":

> On doit tout esperer d'un Monarque si juste.
> Mais sans un Mecenas, à quoi sert un Auguste? (I, 85-86)

Moreover, the narrator in the *Discours au Roy* intimates to his own advantage that other poets threaten the king's status of untouchable divinity when they audaciously attribute his immortality to their verses:

> Et Ton nom du Midi jusqu'à l'Ourse vanté,
> Ne devra qu'à leurs vers son immortalité. (*Disc.*, 40-41)

Comparing himself to other poets, the enemy, "ces hardis Mortels," "sans force," "enflés d'audace," and sarcastically "l'autre ... un esprit sans pareil!," Boileau's narrator paints a vivid portrait of himself as an eminently free satirist restrained by only one subject — the king, too exalted a figure for his young and inexperienced hand.[8] But in direct contradiction to the apologetic, self-effacing language in Part I of the poem ("Moi ... demeuré dans un humble silence," "Ma Muse tremblante," "Mon faible genie," "plus sage en mon respect," "ma plume injuste et temeraire"), the poet's self-image is transformed appreciably in Part II, where semes of sincerity, rigor, independent freedom, and bold confidence dominate the semantic field.[9]

> Moi, la plume à la main, je gourmande les vices,
> Et gardant pour moi-mesme une juste rigueur,
> Je confie au papier des secrets de mon coeur. (Disc., 70-73)

> Je vais de toutes parts où me guide ma veine,
> Sans tenir en marchant une route certaine,
> Et, sans gesner ma plume en ce libre metier,
> Je la laisse au hazard courir sur le papier. (*Disc.*, 77-80)

In a hammering accumulation of negations and in utter defiance of others' hypocrisy, Boileau's *persona* flatly refuses to pay false homage to the king:[10]

Il n'est espoir de biens, ni raison, ni maxime,
Qui pust en Ta faveur m'arracher une rime. (*Disc.*, 113-114)

At this the impassioned peak of his rudeness, and signaled by the contrastive conjunction "Mais," the poet quickly reverses his threatening stance only to pay long and obsequious homage to his unrivaled king (V. 115-130):

Mais lorsque je Te voi, d'une si noble ardeur,
T'appliquer sans relâche aux soins de Ta grandeur (*Disc.*, 115-11)

But the exalted and potentially sarcastic praise in Part III stops suddenly once again in line 131 by means of the same contrastive conjunction "Mais." Then in *da capo* format, the poet's modesty, fear of reprisal, and duty to sincerity elucidated initially in Part I are finally recalled in a characteristically circular scheme. In the closing verses of the satire, the narrator concretizes the nature of his conflict in an extended comparison. By attributing qualities of the endangered seaman to the satirist, the narrator calls attention to implicit threats plaguing the poet and his coveted sense of freedom, a threat which developed naturally as soon as he compromisingly entered the ranks of the flattering poets:

Comme un Pilote en mer, qu'épouvante l'orage,
Dès que le bord paroist, sans songer où je sais,
Je me sauve à la nage, et j'aborde où je puis. (*Disc.*, 133-140)

What heightens the irony of his tortured capitulation is the certitude of the satirist's conviction, the dogmatic and aphoristic manner in which his moral position against hypocrisy and equivocation are expressed.[11] And when he lies, he does so in a similarly assertive fashion by means of forceful metonymic identities:

Puisque vous le voulez, je vais changer de stile.
Je le déclare donc. *Quinaut est un Virgile*. (IX, 287-288)

To prove a point and refine a definition Boileau invariably has his satirist engage in a dazzling dialectic of demonstration according to standard antithetical patterning. First a generalized abstraction (1) appears which automatically engenders (2) interrogations about specification and qualification. Then (3) particulars are rendered contrastively in the form of a negation which in turn engenders its contrast in a (4) strong affirmation. The final statement of the demonstration is frequently in a memorable aphoristic formula – the kind of verse which won Boileau fame as a poet. Boileau's prose in the *Preface* illustrates this dialectic in a compact form:

(2) *Qu'est-ce qu'*une pensée neuve, brillante, extraordinaire?

(3) *Ce n'est point*, comme se le persuadent les Ignorans, une pensée que personne n'a jamais euë, ni dû avoir. *C'est au contraire* une pensée qui a dû venir à tout le monde, et que quelqu'un s'avise le premier d'exprimer.

(4) Un bon mot n'est bon mot qu'en ce qu'il dit une chose que chacun pensoit, et qu'il la dit d'une maniere vive, fine et nouvelle (Preface, p. 4)

Numerous variations on this dialectic are noticeable throughout the *Satires*, especially in *Satire VIII*, constructed as a forensic debate with rebuttals and proofs for the paradox that man with his Reason is "le plus sot animal." Other stylistic signals for demonstration in the *Satires* are the predominance of dialogue forms, debates, rhetorical and literal questions, antithetical and oxymoric structures.

While Boileau's frequent recourse to abstraction, *lieux communs*, and the proverbial maxim is functional in reinforcing the strength of his convictions, the satirist does not disregard the effectiveness of concretization, precision and target name-calling:

Le mal est, qu'en rimant, ma Muse un peu legere
Nomme tout par son nom, et ne sçauroit rien taire.
(*Disc.*, 81-82)

There is no doubt, especially after reading *Satire XII*, probably the most poetic and personal of Boileau's poems, that ambiguity is his fiercest enemy. Yet he, too, must resort to an effect of ambiguity, that is of imprecision, when in his *Preface* he attempts with obvious frustration to define literary excellence by the ineffable:

Un ouvrage a beau estre approuvé d'un petit nombre de Connoisseurs, s'il n'est plein d'*un certain* agrément et d'*un certain* sel propre à piquer le goust general des Hommes ... Que si on me demande ce que c'est que cet agrément et ce sel, Je répondray que c'est *un je ne scay quoy* qu'on peut beaucoup mieux sentir, que dire.
(Preface, p. 3)

Satire, itself, that floating form of necessary contradiction and ambivalence, is the quintessence of friendly enemies, a "monstre" the poet calls it, death itself, "un méchant métier," "A l'auteur qui l'embrasse il est toujours fatal" (VII, 3), a senseless, involuntary torrent of will that propels the satirist despite himself. The purpose-lessness of satire, in the face of its tradition of beneficial reform, is repeated so often by the poet that its leitmotif reaches the propor-tions of an obsession:

> Ainsi, sans m'aveugler d'une *vaine* manie (*Disc.*, 13)
>
> Muse, c'est donc *envain* que la main vous demange (VII, 21)
>
> . Mais à ce grand effort *envain* je vous anime: (VII, 25)
>
> *J'ay beau* frotter mon front, *j'ay beau* mordre mes doigts (VII, 27)
>
> C'est *envain* qu'au milieu de ma fureur extrême
> Je me fais quelquefois des leçons à moi-mesme.
> *Envain* je veux *au moins* faire grace à quelqu'un
> Ma plume auroit regret d'en épargner aucun; (VII, 49-52)
>
> Enfin sans perdre temps en de si *vains* propos (VII, 59)

The poet's periodic but futile attempts to abandon satire are mirrored by the cyclical ironies of the *da capo* structure seen both in the *Discours au Roy* and in *Satire VII*, which begins with a friendly invitation to leave satire and ends on a pathetic resignation to resume its inanity:

> Muse, changeons de stile, et quittons la Satire: (VII, 1)
>
> Finissons, Mais demain, Muse, à recommencer. (VII, 96)

The parallel positioning of the initial first person plural imperatives, "changeons," "quittons," "finissons," effects an authorial intimacy and significant depreciation in strength of conviction. But the dic-tatorial impulse to resume once again the "métier funeste"[12] is ex-pressed appropriately by the forceful infinitival imperative, "Muse, à recommencer." Although inspiration is clearly a gift from God, or a similar outside agent like a Muse, the poet, perhaps unknowingly, attributes personal responsibility for his inspiration by associating its effects to a natural phenomenon:

Mes vers, comme un torrent, coulent sur le papier. (VII, 43)[13]

The satirist, who sees himself rather pathetically as a worthless poet, cannot resist a natural instinct for pleasure, a gratifying impulse to rhyme which in itself bestows merit and value on him:

> Souvent j'habille en vers une maligne prose:
> C'est par là que je vaux, *si je vaux quelque chose.* (VII, 61-62)

Despite the deleterious if not fatal effects of his two-faced friend, satire, the poet is driven by a hedonistic and uncontrollable urge to write:

> Enfin c'est mon *plaisir*, je veux me satisfaire. (VII, 89)

He describes his ambivalent state of mind by means of the hypothetical subjunctive, expressing fear and doubt, as well as an accumulation of parallel antitheses representative of his splitting internal conflict:

> Ainsi, soit que bien-tost, par une dure loi,
> La Mort d'un vol affreux vienne fondre sur moi;
> Soit que le Ciel me garde un cours long et tranquille,
> A Rome ou dans Paris, aux champs ou dans la ville,
> Deust ma Muse par là choquer tout l'Univers,
> Riche, gueux, triste ou gay, *je veux faire des vers.* (VII, 63-68)

Like the Cornelian hero caught between the onrushing will and his suppressing Reason, the poet's passionate pleas for freedom to write satiric poetry reach the heights of lyrical intensity in *Satire IX.* Modern psychological theorists investigating the role of freedom in the creative process have found that the creative individual, who is invariably involved in changing the status quo, must necessarily experience different kinds of freedom in order to create effectively.[14] He must have the freedom for study and preparation, the freedom for unlimited exploration and inquiry, the freedom of expression, and the freedom to perform without excessive evaluation from others. Satire is the art form of reform, the poem of restraint. And Boileau, then, is ironically limiting the freedom of all poets by engaging in creative criticism. The poet's duality of emotion towards the satiric genre is appropriately represented in *Satire IX* by a bipartite arrangement in which the poet and "Son Esprit" dialogue about the dubious merits of satiric criticism. Boileau uses the word "esprit" in this satire in much the same way he interchanged it with "nature" in the *Traité du Sublime.*[15] But the term "esprit" has multiple meanings in Boileau's works, meanings which sometimes contradict each other and contrast intuitive creative power or "puissance" (in Descartes' terms) with judgment and restraint. Nowhere in Boileau's works is the complex duality of this term more expressively rendered than in *Satire IX* where the two aspects of the creative mind are actually severed, personified, and dialogue realistically in classical Freudian patterns of ego and superego interaction. Not unlike Mallarmé's paralysis before the whiteness of his blank page, Boileau's restraining superego, tempted by silence, is painfully aware of his sterile power as a poet and social critic. He describes this empty stillness, in contrast to the fertile rushes of energy from his other self, through a dense concentration of imagery in which his mind is frozen and his inspiration petrified. He laughs pathetically at his own impotence:

> On croiroit à vous voir dans vos libres caprices,
> ...
> Qu'estant seul à couvert des traits de la Satire,
> Vous avez tout pouvoir de parler et d'écrire.
> Mais moi, qui dans le fond sçais bien ce que j'en crois,
> Qui compte tous les jours vos defaux par mes doigts;
> Je ris, quand je vous vois, si foible et si stérile,
> Prendre sur vous le soin de reformer la ville, (IX, 7-16)

His tortured mind wavers incessantly between renunciation of this purposeless vocation and defiant determination to defend his *raison d'être*. In a grandiose but finally unsuccessful campaign of rationalization, the satirist tries to convince himself that his chosen genre is unique in its edifying and didactic purpose:[16]

> La Satire en leçons, en nouveautez fertile,
> Sçait *seule* assaisonner le plaisant et l'utile,
> Et d'un vers qu'elle épure aux rayons du bon sens,
> Détrompe les Esprits des erreurs de leur temps.
> Elle *seule* bravant l'orgueil et l'injustice,
> Va jusques sous le dais faire paslir le vice; (IX, 267-272)

Satire *is* his inspiration, his guidepost along the path of poetic creation, his courage and force, his Mentor – a fatal teacher who encourages unsociable propensities to criticize others:

> C'est Elle [la Satire] qui m'ouvrant *le chemin* qu'il faut suivre,
> M'inspira dés quinze ans la haine d'un sot livre,
> Et sur ce mont fameux où *j'osay* la chercher,
> *Fortifia* mes pas, et m'apprit à *marcher*.
> C'est pour elle, en un mot, que j'ay fait voeu d'écrire. (IX, 279-283)

And who are those others who constitute the very substance of Boileau's poetic creation? In the *Discours sur la Satire*, which serves as a defensive preface to *Satire IX*, the poet describes his literary enemies metaphorically by the expressive vehicle of a volatile nation:

> Je sçavois que la nation des Poëtes, et sur tout
> des mauvais Poëtes, est une nation farouche qui
> prend feu aisément, et que ces Esprits avides
> de loüanges ne digereroient pas facilement une
> raillerie, quelque douce qu'elle put estre. (Disc. S., p. 77)

The poet's overseer and querulous superego in a seemingly endless scourge of masochistic retribution cites specific names on an impressively long list of literary enemies:

> Et qu'ont fait tant d'Auteurs pour remuer leur cendre?
> Que vous ont fait Pervin, Bardin, Pradon, Haynaut,
> Colletet, Pelletier, Titreville, Quinaut,
> Dont les noms en cent lieux, placez comme en leurs niches
> Vont de vos vers malins remplir les hemistiches? (IX, 97-100)

In a sarcastic attack on Cotin, and not without latent fear of monarchical reprisals, the more cautious poet explains to his rash and intuitive *Esprit* the contingent dangers of implication by insinuation:

> Vous aurez beau vanter le Roy dans vos ouvrages,
> Et de ce nom sacré sanctifier vos pages.
> Qui méprise Cotin, n'estime point son Roi,
> Et n'a, selon Cotin, ni Dieu, ni foi, ni loi. (IX, 303-306)

The poet's furtive suspicion of "ces flots d'Ennemis" motivates periodic paranoiac outbursts against other defensive poets who cannot, themselves, tolerate the slightest nuance of negative criticism.[17] It is they, in turn, who condemn the poet Boileau and who overestimate his destructively critical intention:

> Traiter en vos écrits chaque vers d'attentat,
> Et d'un mot innocent faire un crime d'Etat. (IX, 301-302)

Despite his own personal desires for acceptance, *en masse* and through the comic force of parody Boileau's swift and courageous *Esprit*-ego mocks "les poètes doucereux" who write Odes "en phrases de Malherbe"[17] and Eclogues "entouré[s] de troupeaux, Au milieux [sic] de Paris. ..." More specifically he condemns the literary tyranny of Chapelain whose personal and political vendetta had serious repercussions for the poet Boileau:[18]

> Mais que pour un modele, on montre ses écrits,
> Qu'il soit le mieux renté de tous les beaux Esprits:
> Comme Roi des Auteurs, qu'on l'éleve à l'Empire:
> Ma bile alors s'échauffe, et je brûle d'écrire: (IX, 217-220)

No more talk of poetic sterility, no "vers froids" when Boileau's *Esprit*-ego finally succombs to his satiric bent. In a satire dedicated to his idol Molière, who was like Boileau "dans les combats d'esprit sçavant Maistre d'escrime" ((II, 5), the poet parodies what he calls the 'cold epithets' of court poets and their practice of hyperbolization:

> Si je loüois Philis, *En miracles feconde,*
> Je trouverois bientost, *A nulle autre seconde.*
> Si je voulois vanter *un objet Nonpareil;*
> Je mettrois à l'instant, *Plus beau que le Soleil.*
> Enfin parlant toûjours *d'Astres et de Merveilles,*
> De *Chef-d'oeuvres des Cieux,* de *Beautez sans pareilles;* (II, 37-42;
> italics are Boileau's)

Parodic literary debates and vehement quarrels are depicted realistically also in *Satire III,*[19] a less personal poem displaying Boileau's skill in mimetic description of the traditional "Dîner Ridicule." It is in *Satire III* that we find a good example of intertextuality, the stylistic marker of conscious poetic integration. *Satires II* and *III* are interconnected explicitly by the sarcastic allusion to a common satirist termed evasively "on" then "un jeune homme":

> Les Heros chez Quinaut parlent bien autrement,
> Et jusqu'à *je vous hais,* tout s'y dit tendrement.
> On dit qu'on l'a drapé dans certaine satire,
> Qu'un jeune homme ..." – "Ah! je sçai ce que vous voulez dire,"
> (III, 187-190: italics are Boileau's)

Unlike the easy, unimaginative rimesters represented by Quinaut, the Abbé de Pure, Pelletier, and above all "Bienheureux Scudéri" and Ménage, whom the satirist associates ironically in *Satire II* with Malherbe, Boileau's *persona* is frustrated by an inability to find rhymes. His inspiration is described as a self-destructive cleavage, an anguished trembling, an imprisonment of wills. He is split between

his will to rhyme freely and the divisive influence of his controlling
mind. In a hate-filled curse directed at the other poets' ease with
rhyme, the satirist displays a profound envy which can probably be
extended to Molière himself:[20]

> Maudit soit le premier dont la verve insensée
> Dans les bornes d'un vers renferma sa pensée,
> Et donnant à ses mots une étroite prison,
> Voulut avec la rime enchaîner la raison. (II, 53-56)

The structure of comparison in *Satire II*, in which Molière's facility
for rhyme is contrasted to the satirist's search for spontaneity, is
an iconic representation of the poet's contrasting self-appraisal.
But Boileau's torment of conflicting wills, which is expressed implicitly through manifold forms of opposition, is hidden throughout
by satiric humor, by a constant ebb and flow of sometimes false,
sometimes true praise and blame.[21] As Jules Brody put it, there is a
"complex connivance of the natural and the intellectual, vitality and
restraint,"[22] reflected memorably in the concluding verses which
stress through affirmation and negation the futility of teaching the
art of genius:

> Toi donc, qui vois les maux où ma Muse s'abîme
> De grace, enseigne-moi l'art de trouver la rime:
> Ou, puisqu'enfin tes soins y seroient superflus,
> Molière, enseigne-moi l'art de ne rimer plus. (II, 97-101)

Poetry is slavery for Boileau's satirist in *Satire II*, "un triste métier,"
"un rude métier," "fatal au repos," a "Démon" in fact, who has
come to pay him back for his sins:

> Mais moi qu'un vain caprice, une bizarre humeur,
> Pour mes pechez, je croi, fit devenir Rimeur: (II, 11-12)

And this Baudelairian infatuation with demonic powers of
poetry is encoded throughout Boileau's satires in religious clichés
("contentement," "*cloüé sur* un ouvrage"):

> Mais depuis le moment que cette frenesie
> De ses *noires vapeurs* troubla ma fantaisie,
> Et qu'*un Démon jaloux* de mon contentement,
> M'inspira le dessein d'écrire poliment:
> Tous les jours malgré moi, cloüé sur un ouvrage,
> Retouchant un endroit, effaçant une page,
> Enfin passant ma vie en ce triste métier,
> J'envie en écrivant le sort de Pelletier. (II, 79-76)

By means of light/dark metaphors in *Satire XII*, his most religious poem, Boileau develops an extended association of the devil with one aspect of poetic creation, *l'Equivoque*, or the frustrating inability to find the appropriate expression for a thought:

> Et ne viens point ici de *ton ombre grossière*
> Enveloper mon style *ami de la lumiere*. (XII, 13-14)

As in Baudelaire's sonnets, Boileau's devil is both coveted caressingly and rejected harshly in characteristically schizoid fashion – a pattern which is wholly compatible with the many variants of ambivalent 'approach/avoidance' evidenced throughout Boileau's *Satires*. Interestingly enough, the quotation below reveals the interplay of light/dark and cold/heat metaphors in an integrated religious structure of the devil as inspiration:

> Fui donc. Mais non, demeure; *un Demon* qui m'inspire
> Veut qu'encore une utile et derniere Satire,
> De ce pas, en mon livre, exprimant *tes noirceurs,*
> Se vienne en nombre pair, joindre à ses Onze Soeurs;
> Et je sens que ta vûë *échauffe* mon audace.
> Viens, approche: Voyons, malgré l'âge et sa *glace,*
> Si ma Muse aujourd'hui sortant de sa langueur,
> Pourra trouver encore un reste de vigueur. (XII, 17-24)

And not less anticipatory of Baudelaire's "hypocrite lecteur" is Boileau's ambivalent hate and love for his reading public who perceives him as the diabolical critic:

> Et Tel en vous lisant admire chaque trait,
> Qui dans le fond de l'ame, et vous craint et vous hait. (VII, 19-20)

Their hypocrisy is encoded in the traditional antitheses of white/black and exterior/interior semiosis:

> C'est là ce qui fait peur aux Esprits de ce temps,
> Qui tout blancs au dehors, sont tout noirs au dedans.
> Ils tremblent qu'un Censeur, que sa verve encourage,
> Ne vienne en ses écrits démasquer leur visage (*Disc.*, 83-86)

With unrelenting anaphoric insistence, Boileau cracks the whips of satire on his two-faced public:

> *Ce sont eux* que l'on voit, d'un discours insensé,
> Publier dans Paris, que tout est renversé,
> Au moindre bruit qui court, qu'un Auteur les menace
> De joür des Bigots la trompeuse grimace,
> *Pour eux* un tel ouvrage est un monstre odieux;
> C'est offenser les loix, c'est s'attaquer aux Cieux: (*Disc*, 21-26)

And, yet, the public is identified beneficently with the poet, not explicitly as "son semblable," but implicitly as the ultimate and just Judge of lasting literature:

> Envain contre le Cid un Ministre se ligue,
> Tout Paris pour Chimene a les yeux de Rodrigue.
> L'Academie en corps a beau le censurer,
> Le Public revolté s'obstine à l'admirer. (IX, 231-234)

> On a beau se farder aux yeux de l'Univers;
> A la fin sur quelqu'un de nos vices couverts
> Le Public malin jette un oeil inévitable;
> Et bien-tost la Censure, au regard formidable,
> Sçait, le crayon en main, marquer nos endroits faux
> Et nous developper avec tous nos defaux. (XI, 27-32)

Even in his less lyrical poems like *Satire I, Contre les Moeurs de la ville de Paris*, Boileau's narrator paints an intimate portrait of himself as the naively candid observer in conflict with his false friends. By an accumulation of negations and semantic reversals supported stylistically by proximal antitheses, the poet contrasts his genuine sincerity to the hypocrisy of his contemporaries:

> Je ne sçai ni tromper, ni feindre, ni mentir,
> Et quand je le pourois, je n'y puis consentir,
> Je ne sçai point en lâche essuyer les outrages
> D'un Faquin orgueilleux qui vous tient à ses gages:

> Pour un si bas emploi ma Muse est trop altiere.
> Je suis rustique et fier, et j'ai l'ame grossiere. (I, 43-50)

Like the proverbial satirist who is traditionally earthy and realistic in his brutal reform of society's wicked ways, Boileau's "rustique" describes his quality of candor with the aid of animal metaphors:

> Je ne puis rien nommer, si ce n'est par son nom.
> J'appelle un chat un chat, et Rolet un fripon. (I, 51-52)

In *Les Embarras de Paris*, or *Satire VI*, which is associated thematically with the first satire although relatively less personal, the satirist's
lively portrayal of the demonic Parisian society is achieved primarily
through the staccato rhythms of short sentence fragments, exclamations, anacoluthons, short questions imitative of conversational
dialogue, and frequent verbs of rapid motion. To simulate the city
sounds, Boileau's *persona* resorts once again to the mimesis of
animal similes with special preference, it seems, for cats:

> Et quel fâcheux Demon durant les nuits entieres,
> Rassemble ici *les chats* de toutes les goutieres?
> J'ai beau sauter du lit plein de trouble et d'effroi,
> Je pense qu'avec eux tout l'Enfer est chez moi,
> L'un *miaule* en grondant comme un *tigre* en furie:
> L'autre roule sa voix comme un enfant qui crie.
> Ce n'est pas tout encore. Les souris et les rats
> Semblent, pour m'éveiller, s'entendre avec les *chats* (VI, 3-10)

The whole city like a vibrant Breughel painting is depicted dramatically from two contrasting audio-visual perspectives, sights and
sounds seen and heard from inside (V. 1-30) and the same but
worse experienced on the outside (V. 31 – end); the temporal level
is transformed gradually from early morning to night when "le poete
gueux," in a brief moment of personal appraisal, contemplates
his sense of limited freedom:

> Mais moi, grace au destin, qui n'ai ni feu ni lieux,
> Je me loge où je puis, et comme il plaist à Dieu. (VI, 125-126)

While the subject of the first and sixth satires appears a mere 'sterile'
transformation of Juvenal's Umbricius leaving Rome[23] into the
poet's evasion from contemporary Parisian vices, the oxymoric
structures of the poems, that is, the reversals, alternatives, questions
and answers, and constant antithetical positioning of the narrator
against 'the others' is a poetic complex characteristic of Boileau's
style. In *Satire I*, however, there is more personal involvement in
the particular torments of the poet, crystallized in the portrait of
Saint-Amant, that unfortunate plaything of fate and the king's
ministers. Not wanting to undergo Saint-Amant's cyclical circuit
from poverty to courtly fame and back to shame and dishonor,
Damon, the *persona*, momentarily contemplates law as an alternative
to poetry. He describes this profession in one of Boileau's most
mellifluous metaphors:

Moi? que j'aille crier dans ce païs barbare,
Où l'on voit tous les jours l'Innocence aux abois
Errer dans les détours d'un Dédale de lois, (I, 117-120)

To reinforce the absurdity of the legal profession and the horrors of
city dwelling, Damon encodes the hypothetical alternatives in
forceful adynatons,' a figure intrinsically related to reversals and
appropriate for Boileau's view of contemporary society as a world
turned upside down:

Avant qu'un tel dessein m'entre dans la pensée,
On pourra voir la Seine à la Saint-Jean glacée,
Arnauld à Charenton devenir huguenot,
Saint-Sorlin janseniste, et Saint-Pavin bigot. (I, 125-128)

A sense of freedom, freedom to shun the debased morality of Paris,
freedom to write poetry, freedom to criticize, freedom to choose —
this is what the satirist holds dear in that "siècle de fer" in which the
wheel of Fortune, "le sort burlesque," plays havoc with mortals'
lives. It is precisely this futile search for total liberation and contingent resignation to sincerity which restrain the poet from love and
eventual marriage, an institution which he describes in terms of
enslavement:

De *servir* un Amant, je n'en ai pas l'adresse.
J'ignore ce grand art qui gagne une maîtresse, (I, 54-55)

In *Satire X*, Boileau's *persona* plays the role of a scornful and sceptical preacher who, in a dialogue with Alcippe, paints vivid portraits
of demonic women, each one more horrible than the other. Boileau's
satiric virtuosity is unmatched in this impressive display of female
types. First there is "la femme sans honneur," then "la coquette,"
"l'avare," "la coléreuse," or the woman changed into Satan, "la
malade imaginaire," "la précieuse," and finally "la dévote hypocrite
et bigotte," with reference to nine others whom the satirist could
potentially develop in this already long and extensive poem. All of
these universalizable female portraits have one thing in common:
the enslavement trap and the marriage yoke. *Satire X* presents a
colorful panorama of court society, offering brutal attacks not only
on women as the enemy but on men like "le mari trompeur et trompé,"
the salon poet, and the tyrannical "directeur de conscience." In a
rather touching account of his loneliness, Alcippe espouses familiar
Jansenist principles of the paradox of freedom, to which the satirist
will counter with a sarcastic riposte:

> L'Hymenée est un joug, et c'est ce qui m'en plaist.
> L'homme en ses passions toûjours errant sans guide,
> A besoin qu'on lui mette et le mors et la bride.
> Son pouvoir malheureux ne sert qu'à le gesner,
> Et pour le rendre libre, il le faut enchaîner.
> C'est ainsi que souvent la main de Dieu l'assiste.
> — Ha bon! voila parler en docte Janseniste. (X, 112-118)

The poem ends on a high crescendo of threatening negative epithets — a descriptive prelude to the reversal of fate and prophecy of eternal enslavement with the devil herself:

> Sous le faix des procez abbatu, consterné,
> Triste, à pié, sans Laquais, maigre, sec, ruiné,
> Vingt fois dans ton malheur resolu de te pendre,
> Et, pour comble de maux, reduit à la reprendre. (X, 735-738)

Not wishing to restrict the depiction of his Enemy to females alone, Boileau's satirist directs his sceptical invective in *Satire IV* against man in general and, later, in *Satire VIII*, against human folly. Like his satire on women, *Satire IV* contains a relatively impersonal series of stereotyped portraits sprinkled with abundant proverbialisms and universalizing maxims designed to support the paradoxical contrast and *rapprochement* between human wisdom and folly. Representative portraits of human folly like the pedant, the "galant," the bigot, the "libertin," and the charlatan are alternated systematically with a plethora of abstractions, aphorisms and *lieux communs*:

> Chacun veut en sagesse ériger sa folie, (IV, 50)

> Le plus sage est celui qui ne pense point l'estre. (IV, 54)

> Mais chacun pour soi-mesme est toûjours indulgent. (IV, 59)

Consistent with the poetics of opposition, Boileau presents a series of contrasting portraits in which the miser is compared to the spend-thrift; the cool and calculating gambler who considers fate his personal science is then followed by the furious fanatic whom a priest exorcises. And in contrast to this enumeration of general types, the picturesque and brutally incriminating portrait of Chapelain in particular, "montez sur deux grands mots, comme sur deux échasses" looms to the foreground:

> Chapelain veut rimer, et c'est là sa folie." (IV, 90)

Satire VIII, like *Satire IV*, develops within an overriding and extended comparison of man to the lowest form of animal, the ass:

> Quoi? me prouverez-vous par ce discours profâne,
> Que l'Homme, qu'un Docteur est au dessous d'un asne?
> Un Asne, le joûet de tous les animaux,
> Un stupide Animal, sujet à mille maux;
> Dont le nom seul en soi comprend une satire?" (VIII, 275-279)

But the structural arrangement of *Satire VIII* in the form of an intellectual demonstration is more intricate than the earlier fourth satire. Man's weaknesses, according to the Doctor's interlocutor, are ambition, avarice and inconstancy, traits which are demonstrated through multiple examples to be clearly absent from the animal kingdom:

> *Jamais* contre un Renard chicanant un poulet,
> Un Renard de son sac n'alla charger Rolet.
> *Jamais* la Biche en rut, n'a pour fait d'impuissance,
> Trâiné du fond des bois un Cerf à l'Audiance,
> *Et jamais* Juge entr'eux ordonnant le congrés,
> De ce burlesque mot n'a sali ses arrests.
> ...
> *L'Homme seul, l'Homme seul* en sa fureur extrême,
> Met un brutal honneur à s'égorger soi-même. (VIII, 141-152)

Debate procedures predominate in *Satire VIII*, and when strict dialogue is absent, a hypothetical dialogue is parodied subtly by verb tense manipulation:

> "Qui pouroit le nier?" poursuis-tu. Moi peut-estre. (VIII, 60)

> "Tout beau," *dira* quelqu'un, "raillez plus à propos:
> Ce vice fut toûjours la vertu des Heros." (VIII, 97-98)

The satirist's adversary, identified as a poet, then elucidates a false and wickedly anti-Christian morality in the guise of wisdom. Below surface structures of philosophical demonstration, *Satire VIII* contains not only many of Boileau's most intensely moving verses but some of his more unusual rhymes:

> Mais sans examiner si, vers les antres sourds,
> L'Ours a peur du Passant, ou le Passant de l'Ours: (VIII, 61-62)

Even more exotic is the following sonorous combination:

> Chercher jusqu'au Japon la porcelaine et l'ambre,
> Rapporter de Goa le poivre et le gingembre. (VIII, 75-76)

Arranged oppositionally on a grandiose comparison of true and false nobility, Boileau's fifth satire, linked structurally to the fourth and eighth, appears similarly impersonal and more immediately involved with the universal, philosophical and moral issues of the times. These three poems interrelate thematically when Boileau's satirist defines nobility as the essence of true virtue, approaching divinity:

> La Noblesse, Dangeau, n'est pas une chimere
> Quand sous l' étroite loi d'une vertu severe,
> Un homme issu d'un sang fecond en Demi-Dieux,
> Suit, comme toi, la trace où marchoient ses ayeux. (V, 1-4)

As we have seen in many of his satires, Boileau concretizes his definitional demonstration of true and false nobility through allegory and an extended comparison in animal code of "Le Coursier" and "Le Jument":

> On fait cas d'un Coursier, qui fier et plein de coeur,
> Fait paroistre en courant sa boüillante vigueur:
> Qui jamais ne se lasse, et qui dans la carriere
> S'est couvert mille fois d'une noble poussiere:
> Mais la posterité d'Alfane et de Bayard,
> Quand ce n'est qu'une rosse, est venduë au hazard,
> Sans respect des Ayeux dont elle est descenduë,
> Et va porter la malle, ou tirer la charuë, (V. 27-34)

Nobility for the poet is a symbol of truth, a sign of his professed sincerity. Truth is the essence of Boileau's esthetics, his criterion of excellence, the unattainable other side of his ever-encroaching Enemy, hypocrisy. He expressed his esthetics of truth in the 1701 *Preface* to his *Satires* and earlier in the ninth *Epître:*

L'Esprit de l'Homme est naturellement plein d'un nombre infini d'idées confuses du Vrai, que souvent il n'entrevoit qu'à demi; et *rien ne lui est plus agréable* que lors qu'on lui offre quelqu'une de ces idées bien éclaircie, et mise dans un beau jour. (p. 4)

> Rien n'est beau que le vrai. Le vrai seul est aimable. (*Epître* 9, v. 43)

While in 1664 a historical inquiry into the validity of titles of nobility actually occurred and can be considered of potential relevance to *Satires V, VIII,* and *XI,* the poet's obsessive search for truth, personal identity, and fear of exposure before peers and authority are mirrored in this seemingly general inquiry into nobility. Moreover, the structural relation of the semic variant of truth (i.e. 'nobility') to Boileau's more lyrical satires, especially *Satire IX* and his last *Satire XII,* is of particular interest in the deeper understanding of the poet's internal frustrations and anguish. What the poet hates most in himself, he senses deeply in others and criticizes creatively through satire. When, in accordance with classical principles of *honnêteté, bienséance,* and the rigorous control of passion, the poet contrasts the true noble's restraint with the excesses of false nobility, he defensively associates the faults of others with his own patterns of poetic behavior:

> Je m'emporte peut-estre, et ma Muse en fureur
> Verse dans ses discours trop de fiel et d'aigreur.
> Il faut avec les Grands un peu de retenuë.
> Hé bien, je m'adoucis. Vostre race est connuë. (V, 67-70)

This projection mechanism and Boileau's particular sensitivity to his ignoble excesses as satirist were perceived in *Satire IX* as a function of the satiric genre itself. He also evidenced awareness of a shamefully anti-Christian tendency which has, perhaps, partially motivated the poet's recurrent feelings of guilt:

> Est-ce donc là médire, ou parler franchement?
> Non, non, la Médisance y va plus doucement. (IX, 157-158)

> Mais deussiez-vous en l'air voir vos aîles fonduës,
> Ne valoit-il pas mieux vous perdre dans les nuës,
> Que d'aller sans raison, d'*un stile peu Chrestien,*
> Faire insulte en rimant à qui ne vous dit rien, (IX, 55-58)

In the *Discours sur la Satire,* which is Boileau's personal justification for his poetic brutality and ungenerous revenge on his enemies, he cleverly underplays his animosity and insists on his Christian instinct toward forgiveness:

Quelques calomnies dont on ait voulu me noircir; quelques faux bruits qu'on ait semez de ma personne, *j'ai pardonné* sans peine ces *petites vengeances,* au déplaisir d'un Auteur irrité, qui se voyoit attaqué par l'endroit le plus sensible d'un Poëte, je veux dire, par ses ouvrages. (*Disc. Satire,* p. 77)

Satire XI, written much later than *Satire V* and imbued with a distinctively religious tone, deals with the related subject of real honor as the equivalent of truth. The poem is structured on a similarly contrastive scheme. An aphoristic description of honor is juxtaposed to a portrait of the contemporary dishonorable society where hypocrisy and false devotion persist. The poet supports his definition of honor by a fable of the king, but digresses appreciably when he paints an obvious self-portrait of the Censor as seeker of ultimate truth:

> Il rompt tout, perce tout, et trouve enfin passage.
> Mais loin de mon projet je sens que je m'engage
> Revenons de ce pas à mon texte égaré. (XI, 45-47)

Ironically it is from this short but powerful digression that the satire's *tour de force* is executed. Boileau's *persona* suggests that he alone is inspired by God and, therefore, has true honor, since honor is with God alone:

> Et peut-estre est-ce luy qui m'a dicté ces vers.
> Mais en fust-il l'Auteur, je conclus de sa Fable;
> Que ce n'est qu'en Dieu seul qu'est l'Honneur veritable.
> (XI, 204-206)

Satire XII, on *l'Equivoque* is the poetic culmination of Boileau's *Satires* in which the three mainstreams of his philosophical, religious, and literary criticism blend while a dynamic metamorphosis of the friendly enemy Incarnate unfolds allegorically. Because of an extensive system of poetization by concretization observable throughout this satire in multiple forms of comparison, metaphor, metonymy, personification, and allegory, the precise nature of the *Equivoque* is significantly difficult to determine much less describe objectively. First we see *l'Equivoque* as a mere word whose gender is ambiguous:

> Du langage François bizarre Hermaphrodite,
> De quel genre te faire, Equivoque maudite?
> Ou maudit: (XII, 1-3)

This ironic play on the distinction between word and concept is what initially throws the reader off guard especially when the ensuing brutal name-calling appears grossly overstated for such a relatively insignificant linguistic problem:

... Sors d'ici Fourbe insigne,
Mâle aussi dangereux que femelle maligne,
...
Tourment des Ecrivains, juste effroi des Lecteurs; (XII, 5-8)

When *l'Equivoque* is subsequently raised to the level of concept, the reader is immediately reminded of its polysemic value which Boileau, himself, suggested in his apologetic *Discours de l'Auteur*:

... en attaquant l'Equivoque, je n'ai pas pris ce mot dans toute l'étroite rigueur de sa signification grammaticale; le mot d'Equivoque, en ce sens-là, ne voulant dire qu'une ambiguité de paroles, mais que je l'ai pris, comme le prend ordinairement le commun des hommes, pour toutes sortes d'ambiguitez de sens, de pensées, d'expressions, et enfin pour tous ces abus et ces méprises de l'esprit humain qui font qu'il prend souvent une chose pour une autre. (*Disc. A.*, p. 116)

Shunned initially as a suspicious friend of cold and dark shadows, l'Equivoque is then invited as the heat-filled demon of mystery and inspiration to accompany the poet in his last of twelve satires:

Laisse-moi, va charmer de tes vains agrémens
Les yeux faux et gâtez de tes *louches* amans,
...
Fui donc. Mais non demeure; *un Demon qui m'inspire*
Veut qu'encore une utile et derniere Satire,
De ces pas en mon livre, exprimant *tes noirceurs*,
Se vienne en nombre pair, joindre à ses Onze Soeurs. (XII, 11-20)

The problem here and throughout this satire on human error is that the poet talks to and about the *Equivoque* simultaneously in an effective attempt to fathom its ambivalences. Thus the equation between the *Equivoque* and the friendly enemy is established only metonymically, never explicitly. Amidst the poet's doubts as to the purpose of this fantastic and historic inquiry, the *Equivoque* is subsequently generalized metonymically into any form of poetic trickery practised by the frivolous bards of the earlier literary fashion:

Je ferois mieux, j'entends, d'imiter Benserade.
C'est par lui qu'autrefois, mise en ton plus beau jour.,
Tu sûs, trompant les yeux du peuple et de la Cour,
Leur faire à la faveur de tes bluettes folles,
Coûter comme bons mots tes quolibets frivoles.
Mais ce n'est plus le temps ... (XII, 30-35)

Magnified to the highest degree of Evil incarnate, *l'Equivoque*, "sens de travers" and "source de toute erreur," is then traced historically in a biblical context through its varied manifestations as man's pride, idolatry, superstition, and polytheism. Finally it is personified as the false god of fables, dreams and lies, reigning in a topsy-turvy world where vice is revered as virtue and where candor is perceived as rudeness:

> Bien-tôt te signalant par mille faux miracles,
> Ce fut toi qui par-tout fis parler les Oracles.
> C'est par ton double sens, dans leurs discours jeté,
> Qu'ils sçûrent en mentant dire la vérité, (XII, 102-104)

While some vain hope prevailed during the period in which poets expressed an optimistic cult of Reason, the satirist debunks this myth with austere Jansenist scepticism in a provocative allusion to Socrates, the archetypal philosopher-king:

> Et Socrate, l'honneur de la profane Grece,
> Qu'étoit-il en effet, de près examiné,
> Qu'un mortel, par lui-même au seul mal entraîné;
> Et malgré la vertu dont il faisoit parade,
> Très-équivoque ami du jeune Alcibiade? (XII, 146-150)

The implicit reference to Jansenist philosophy automatically engenders its opposition, the heresy of Jesuit casuistry and its inimical relaxed morality. The abhorrent total reversal of universal values is expressed in gripping metaphors of the devil, a monster, and the poisons of the plague:

> Alors, pour seconder ta triste frénésie,
> Arriva de l'enfer ta fille l'Hérésie.
> Ce monstre dès l'enfance à ton école instruit,
> De tes leçons bien-tôt te fit goûter le fruit.
> Par lui l'erreur, toûjours finement apprêtée,
> Sortant pleine d'attraits de sa bouche empestée,
> De son mortel poison tout courut s'abreuver,
> Et l'Eglise elle-même eut peine à s'en sauver. (XII, 189-195)

All the dynamics of Pascal's *Provinciales* are re-enacted as the poet transforms the *Equivoque* into the preacher Lucifer, who disseminates wicked deceptions of probabilism and the vicious system of 'attrition' by which fear alone, without the love of God, can bring false salvation:

Qu'aussi-tôt tu posas l'énorme fondement
De la plus dangereuse et terrible Morale,
Que *Lucifer*, assis dans la Chaire infernale,
Vomissant contre Dieu ses monstrueux sermons
Ait jamais enseignée aux Novices Demons, (XII, 274-276)

As soon as the Jansenist-Jesuit split is established and the narrator's particular allegiance confirmed, the experienced satirist anticipates repercussions from those who, like himself, live in a reign where Jansenism is dying and Le Tellier has usurped the religious throne from the now quiet Madame de Maintenon:

J'entends déja d'ici tes Docteurs frenetiques
Hautement me compter au rang des heretiques;
M'appeller scelerat, traître, fourbe, imposteur,
Froid plaisant, faux boufon, vrai calomniateur,
De Pascal, de Wendrock, copiste miserable,
Et, pour tout dire enfin, janseniste execrable, (XII, 321-326)

The poem, which marks a triumphant finale to Boileau's literary career, ends appropriately on an imperative note of renunciation from Satire, that foul and friendly enemy whose formal contradictions ally it intrinsically to the fatal *Equivoque*. And for the pleasure of his regenerating public Boileau immortalizes the poet's pathetic sense of defiant purposelessness in the memorable creation of these few sonorous and remarkably classical verses:

Concluons, l'homme enfin perdit toute lumiere,
Et par tes yeux trompeurs se figurant tout voir,
Ne vit, ne sût plus rien, ne pût plus rien savoir! (XII, 138-140)

NOTES

* This article appeared in *Modern Language Notes* 91 (1976), 672-697.
  [1] For the origin of this critical breakthrough refer to Revillout's "La Légende de Boileau," *Revue des Langues Romanes* 34 (1980), 449-502; 35 (1891), 548-96; 36 (1892), 524-72; 37 (1894), 59-114, 149-81, 197-215, 374-82, 443-56, 552-65; 38 (1895), 75-83, 127-34, 221-31, 255-68, 316-29. See Boudhors' introduction to his edition of the *Satires* (Paris: Belles Lettres, 1934) for a discussion of the legend. "Régent du Parnasse, législateur de la Raison, grand-maître de l'École classique: c'est dans cette attitude, sous ces insignes et à ces titres que s'est dressée la gloire de Boileau – et qu'elle s'est écroulée. Le Romantisme a jeté à bas cette statue." (p. XIV) All citations in this chapter will be from Boudhors' edition.

[2] See Bernard Beugnot and Roger Zuber, *Boileau visages anciens, visages nouveaux* (Montreal: Presses de l'Université de Montréal, 1973) for a survey of Boileau's reputation in France and abroad from 1665-1970. Antoine Adam's introduction to the *Oeuvres complètes* (Paris: Gallimard, 1966) starts in the following provocative manner: "Nous ne songerions plus à voir en Boileau l'un des très grands noms de notre littérature *Le Lutrin* ne nous fait plus rire. *Les Satires* et *les Epîtres* nous semblent simplement des oeuvres intéressantes et vigoureuses, mais non pas des oeuvres de génie. *L'Art Poétique* n'est plus pour nous le code de l'éternelle Raison, et nous savons maintenant que Molière ni Racine n'ont eu besoin de Boileau pour écrire leurs chef d'oeuvres." (p. IX) Daniel Mornet, *Nicolas Boileau* (Paris: Calmann Lévy, n.d.): "Il est trop évident que Boileau n'est jamais un penseur. Ce qu'il pense ... il le pense avec Juvénal, avec la Mothe le Vayer, avec une douzaine de Satiriques, avec tout le monde." (p. 43) René Bray, *Boileau, l'homme et l'oeuvre* (Paris: Boivin, 1942): "[Boileau] C'est un fantôme verbal, en compagnie duquel il faut que tous nos écoliers vivent pendant des années et à qui ils vouent dès lors une haine solide. Boileau mérite un autre sort." (p. 4) Even as early as 1890 in *Le Grand siècle: Boileau* (Paris), M. Richard writes: "Ouvrez les maîtres, les grands critiques, même les plus dévoués à la gloire de Boileau, les manuels et les traités|d'histoire littéraire, c'est à qui s'évertuera à chercher une excuse pour les imperfections et les imitations par trop serviles qu'il est de bon ton de confesser et de reconnaître dans les premières satires du jeune imitateur de Juvénal et d'Horace." (p. 109) Emile Deschanel in *Le Romantisme des classiques: Boileau, Charles Perrault* (Paris: Calmann Lévy, 1891): "Despréaux était enfermé dans ce cercle restraint [de la satire.] C'est une circonstance atténuante pour excuser son peu de fécondité." (p. 61)

[3] While publication dates from 1665-1711 are easily verifiable, there is a discrepancy as to the precise year in which Boileau actually created the individual satires, not to mention when, how, and why he edited them. Le Verrier's edition with Boileau's annotations is a valuable reference. René Bray simplifies the problem by grouping the creation of the satires into three periods: *Satires I-VIII* in 1666, *Satires VIII* and *IX* in 1668, and *Satires X-XII* in 1694. The chronology of these satires is more delicate than this categorization indicates. Antoine Adam and René Bray disagree, for example, on the dates of *Satires I* and *VI*; cf. *Histoire de la littérature française au XVIIe siècle* (Paris: Del Duca, 1962), III, 94.

[4] Although E. B. O, Borgerhoff in his excellent article entitled "Boileau Satirist: *Animi Gratia*," *Romanic Review* 43 (1952), 241-255, has few compunctions about identifying Boileau, the man, with the poet's *persona*, narrator, adversary and satirist, I endeavored to maintain these distinctions. Any interpretative references to personality traits and behavioral patterns are therefore relegated strictly to the poetic creation which is that elusive and constantly transforming voice of the poet.

[5] The important role which reversals play in Boileau's philosophical and moral thinking is evidenced in *Le Discours au Roy*, v. 91-92:

> Ce sont eux que l'on voit, d'un discours insensé
> Publier dans Paris que tout est renversé.

Cf. *Satire II*, v. 21-22:

Enfin quoi que je fasse ou que je veuille faire
La bizarre toujoûrs vient m'offrir le contraire.

[6] One of the many possible structural divisions is I, v. 1-62: Praise; II, v. 63-114: Transition, Boileau vs. the Other poets; III, v. 115-end: Strong Praise.

[7] Boileau's pretended inability to praise is a *leitmotif* throughout the *Satires* (e.g. I, 42-47; II, 19-20, and VII, 26). The structural and metrical similarity of *Satires I* and *II* to the *Discours au Roy* is noteworthy in their parallel openings:

Damon ce grand Auteur, dont la Muse fertile
Amusa si longtemps, et la Cour et la Ville. (I, 1-2)

Rare et fameux Esprit dont la fertile veine
Ignore en écrivant le travail et la peine. (II, 1-2)

Jeune et vaillant Heros, dont la haute sagesse
N'est point le fruit tardif d'une lente vieillesse. (*Disc.*, 1-2)

[8] This rationalization is repeated in *Satire IX*: "L'honneur de le louer [Le Roi] m'est un trop digne prix." (v. 314)

[9] Boileau's ambivalent self-confidence in the *Discours au Roy* is transformed into superiority in *Satire VII*: "Je sens que mon esprit travaille de génie." (v. 41)

[10] Indirect undercutting of the king is evidenced in *Satire VII* whose thematic structures parallel many of those found in the *Discours au Roy*:

S'il faut rimer ici, rimons quelque loüange,
Et cherchons un Heros parmi cet univers,
Digne de nostre encens et digne de nos vers. (VII, 22-24)

[11] See Nathan Edelman's stunning article entitled "*L'Art Poétique*: 'Long-temps Plaire et Jamais ne Lasser" in *French Classicism*, ed. Jules Brody (New Jersey: Prentice-Hall, 1966) for an insightful and sensitive look at Boileau's poetic skill. In a slightly different context, Professor Edelman comments on Boileau's certitude: "If his style waxes imperative, to the point of sounding dogmatic to us at times, this comes from the certitude of strong personal faith in his experience of beauty and art, but not out of any concern with official regulations." (p. 209)

[12] See *Satire IX*, v. 243 for other semes of death. Cf. v. 137 "noyé," v. 26 "tombé."

[13] *Satires VII* and *II* contradict each other on the question of personal poetic freedom. In *Satire II* the poet describes the paralyzing inability to rhyme his thoughts, which, as Brody puts it (p. 70) is "less an ability to *find* rhymes than ... absence of method to guide his search. "*Boileau and Longinus* (Geneva: Droz, 1958).

[14] Morris I. Stein's book entitled *Stimulating Creativity* (New York: Academic Press, in preparation) promises an informed discussion of this subject. See his "Creativity in a Free Society" in *Graduate Comment* V, 1 (Oct. 1961), 26 pp. Frank Barron in *Creativity and Personal Freedom*, as well as in "Psychology of Imagination," *Scientific American* 199 (1958), 151-166, was a

pioneer investigator in the subtle psychological relationships between freedom and creativity. Cf. Jacques Barzun, "Each Age Picks its Literary Greats," in the *New York Times Book Review* of March 6, 1955.

[15] See Jules Brody's discussion of the term "esprit" in his *Boileau and Longinus* (Geneva: Droz, 1958), pp. 58-59. Brody's work on Boileau is indispensable. He is one of the few critics who restored originality and unity of thought to the poet Boileau.

[16] See Borgerhoff's detailed analysis of *Satire IX, op. cit*, pp. 245-253, where he makes reference to the structures of inversion in both halves of the poem. He discusses the implicit cyclical return to the beginning of the satire.

[17] See *Satire IX*, v. 250-266, for a developed parody of these poets.

[18] In the introduction to Emile Magne's *Bibliographie générale des oeuvres de Nicolas de Boileau Despréaux*, 2 vols. (Paris, 1929), the argument between Gilles and Nicolas is explained. Ironically, and *a propos* of the validity of biographical criticism, it is entertaining to note that Boileau's father said of him, "Colin est un bon garçon qui ne dira jamais de mal de personne." (p. 4)

[19] *Satire III*, 221-222:

> Aussitost sous leurs pieds les tables renversées
> Font voir un long débris de bouteilles cassées:

[20] Borgerhoff, p. 244, discusses Boileau's backhanded attack and simultaneous compliment to Molière.

[21] For a detailed analysis of simultaneous opposition in satire and the resultant effects of irony, see Chapter 4 entitled "Mathurin Regnier's *Macette*: A Semiotic Study in Satire," pp. 91-114.

[22] Brody, p. 59

[23] Otto Benicke, *Boileau imitateur d'Horace et de Juvénal* (Paris, 1864).

IV

FABLE

CHAPTER 6

SIGNS OF IRONY IN LA FONTAINE'S *FABLES**

> Il y a autant de registres dans
> l'ironie que de systèmes de signes
> dans la vie intellectuelle: par
> exemple, la pantomime ironique,
> qui s'exprime par gestes, l'ironie
> plastique qui dessine des caricatures,
> enfin et surtout l'ironie du langage,
> écrit ou parlé, la plus nuancée et la
> plus maniable de toutes les ironies ...
> Jankélévitch, *L'Ironie*, p. 44

The symbolic discourse of La Fontaine's fables is constructed on an illogical assumption of animal communication in imitation of humans, an incongruity which renders the readings highly ironic. The disparity between statement and intention, theory and practice, authorial promise and literary delivery is signalled at the start of the collection by a parodic epic dedication − "Je chante les héros dont Esope est le père" − whose heightened tone runs counter to the familiarity of the humble characters in this comedy of symbolic animals. Irony, as we observe it in literature, is a surface phenomenon, a fused entity of harmonious uniformity, and the perfect illustration of the Hegelian dialectic which hides a deeper schism of incompatible contrasts. The purpose of this study is to penetrate the hidden by identifying signs of irony in the fable, signs which work imperceptibly to create and expand meaning in the poetic discourse. The scope of the analysis is the first book of the *Fables* beginning with *La Cigale et la Fourmi* and ending majestically with *Le Chêne et le Roseau*. As is true of most well-written beginnings, this first book of fables contains the structural elements of the whole and acts as a miniature model. Although more could and should be said about the illuminating and representative qualities of literary beginnings as a form in general, and about the design of this first book of fables in particular, its extraordinary symmetry and complex orchestration of simple con-

trapuntal structures, that is not my purpose. Since the primary focus
is the notion of the sign, that is, the relationship between the signifier
and signified, the expression and content, this analysis will necessarily
involve the interrelationship of stylistic and semantic features in the
establishment of ironies.

Irony has achieved the status of an ism and as such is a naughty
word. Some of us even teach our students to avoid it in critical
writings because of its ambiguity. It is my feeling that this is a
disservice performed in the face of ignorance and a failure to distinguish simple structural elements underlying irony's complex function. And this simple structural element is, ironically, ambiguity
itself.[1] A key to the hidden design of irony is found in classical
rhetoric. Irony (*eironeia*) from the Greek originally meant 'dissimulation' especially through understatement. Irony involves the
art of the hidden, the elusive, the oblique. The *eiron* of Greek
comedy was the underdog, the weak but sneaky trickster who
triumphed over the boastful and stupid *alazon*. Classical rhetoricians
distinguished several varieties of irony which I prefer to call signs of
the one technique whose structural model involves the simultaneous
juxtaposition of mutually exclusive oppositions, a synthesis of
dissonances, and the surface fusion of disquieting contrasts. Double
or multiple meaning and the disparity between statement and intention normally associated with irony are results of this synthesis and
interplay of connotations, more accurately described in semiotic
terms as an intersection of metaphoric codes. Sarcasm involves
double meanings in which both parties, the speaker and the hearer,
the dupe and the duper, are conscious of a double meaning, and where
what is said is the exact opposite of what is meant. In *La Cigale et
la Fourmi* when the ant says "vous chantiez! J'en suis fort aise"
the sarcasm implied in the emotional response is mordant; its ironic
effect acts as a foreshadowing of the ensuing word play "Eh bien!
dansez maintenant." "Dansez" signifies by extension the graceful
extrication of onself from a difficult situation and the continuation
of the same fruitless act as "chanter." Both verbs *chanter* and *danser*
belong to a paradigm of artistic and spiritual endeavor which is in
characteristic opposition to the mundane and materialist ethic of
the industrious laborer symbolized by the ant. The calculated indifference of the ant bears the seeds of ironic disinvolvement which
resembles the classical naiveté of Socratic dialogue. The verb *danser*
has a history of extended meaning and appears in its metaphoric
sense in many proverbial and figurative expressions such as *entrer en
danse* for 'to participate in some activity'; *donner une danse à*

quelqu'un for 'to reprimand'; *ne pas savoir sur quel pied danser* or *quand le chat n'est pas là les souris dansent*. The effectiveness of this verb in the fable is precisely the contrastive play on the literal significance of *chanter* and the figuration extensions of *danser*.

The litotes or understatement, whose signs say less than they signify, is the essence of irony. Its rhetorical counterpart is the hyperbole whose amplified signs say more than they actually signify. Euphemism, which is a subset of the understatement, involves the attenuation of an unpleasant idea. La Fontaine draws humorous effects from the contrast between the implied meaning and the stated words. Frequently this transposition carries a sarcastic tone:

> La fourmi n'est pas prêteuse:
> C'est là son moindre défaut.

The latter of these two verses has caused considerable debate because of the seeming contradiction in the euphemism "son moindre défaut." Maurice Grammont has offered the most convincing linguistic explanation for this misunderstanding.[2] Apparently in the sixteenth and seventeenth centuries a subordinating clause did not necessarily refer to the entire main clause but only to the most important word in that clause ("prêteuse"). Thus, the verse really means "son défaut est d'être prêteuse" – and since the ant is not a lender, the statement acts as an antiphrastic sarcasm. La Fontaine says the opposite of what he means and thereby creates not only the ambiguity of irony but the extension of meaning characteristic of evocative poetic discourse.

When the fabulist in *Le Corbeau et le Renard* understates the absurdity of animal communication:

> Maître renard, par l'odeur alléché,
> Lui tint *à peu près* ce langage:

all the weight of satiric mockery falls on the seemingly insignificant words "à peu près" which function as a subtle sign of ironic nonchalance with regard to verbal animal communication. Hyperbole or overstatement, antiphrasis and contrast, asteism and charientism (or forms of the joke called punning and reparti) are other traditional signs of irony mentioned by classical rhetoricians.[3] But in order for an ironic effect to be actualized in the narrative discourse, these figures must undergo a reversal process with elements in their context, a dynamic dialectic which results in the awareness of a disturbing surface incongruity. A disparity between what is stated and what 'is', or what is meant, is the necessary contrastive mechanism underlying irony. Thus all hyperboles or litotes are not automatically ironic; the classification system is more complex. An identification of a structural mechanism of contradiction must precede for the typology to be justified. For example, the amplification technique in Fable II which involves a three-fold allusion to nobility – *Maître corbeau*, (*Maître renard*), becoming the exaggerated *Monsieur du corbeau* – refers to the bird whose ranking on the scale of beauty and voice is probably of the lowest. This reversal of expectation and contradiction of nature have the ironic effect of antiphrasis. The reversal model is particularly effective in the expression "Maître l'Ane" because of the negative valuative associations of the donkey (*Les Voleurs et l'Ane*). The technique is echoed by variant forms such as *compère le renard* and *commère la cigogne*. The ternary structure and concomitant crescendo effect observed in *La Cigale et la Fourmi* are repeated in the fox's flattery:

> Que vous êtes *joli*! que vous me semblez *beau*!

> Vous êtes *le phénix* des hôtes de ces bois.

The contradiction implicit in this continued hyperbole depends on a destruction of our image of the crow as ugly and of loud, shrill voice. The antithetical intention of the dissimulation is rendered most obvious by sarcasm:

> *Sans mentir*, si votre ramage
> Se rapporte à votre plumage,
> Vous êtes le phénix des hôtes de ces bois.

Mockery, sneering, imitation for the sake of ridicule, conscious naiveté, and parody can similarly be ironic signs provided they are embedded within the oppositional structure described. Truth becomes falsehood, blame becomes praise through the reverting force of ironic duplicity. Thus the courteous replies of the reed to the oak which convey implications of conscious naiveté involve a fundamental antiphrasis:

> Votre compassion...
> Part d'un bon naturel.

This false flattery simultaneously evokes and masks the oak's symbolic value of compassion which is really "orgueil" and "générosité" in the classical sense. The oak is endowed with the positive and negative traits of the *généreux* whose self-love, egotism, and exemplary nobility make of him the prototyped hero in contrast to the weak reed who becomes, by virtue of ironic reversal, a strong and respectable hero in the fable. It is this antiphrastic model and reversal principle resulting in contradiction at the deeper base of surface statements that actualize verbal irony. Even La Fontaine's contemporaries revealed an awareness of this interplay in their choice of critical vocabulary. Bouhours observed:

> On peut tout dire en riant, et même si vous y prenez garde, le faux devient vrai à la faveur de l'ironie: c'est elle qui a introduit ce que nous appelons contre-vérités. (*La Manière de bien penser dans les oeuvrages d'esprit*, Paris: L. Lucas, 1691, p. 29)

La Fontaine's language itself represents a serious deviation from the expected, and Ferdinant Brunot even called it the contrary of poetic language of his time.[4] La Fontaine manifests the oppositional model on the surface of his poetic text through rhythmic contrasts.[5] Consider, for example, the first four verses of *Le Corbeau et le Renard*:

> Maître corbeau, sur un arbre perché,
> Tenoit en son bec un fromage.
> Maître renard, par l'odeur alléché,
> Lui tint à peu près ce langage:

Two verses of ten syllables are contrasted with two verses of eight. The ten syllable verses are perfectly symmetrical with two contrastive hemistichs alternating four syllables with six, and with the first hemistich of each containing the animal type with title (*Maître corbeau, maître renard*), and the second hemistich acting as an epithet which describes the physical and emotional states of the animal. The two verses of eight syllables reproduce the effect of symmetry through verbal repetitions (*tenoit ... tint*) and act as a rhythmic prelude to the verbal meeting of the minds that is to take place between the two protagonists. In contrast to these even syllable verses is the one seven syllable verse which, by nature of its formal difference, draws special attention to its moralizing content:

> Apprenez que tout flatteur

Pivotal contrast is the structural principle underlying the generic definition and contrapuntal composition of the fable, and La Fontaine states this openly as fabulist in *Le Bûcheron et Mercure* (V, 1)

> Tantôt je peins en un récit
> La sotte vanité jointe avecque l'envie,
> Deux pivots sur qui roule aujourd'hui notre vie:
> ...
> J'oppose quelquefois, par une double image,
> Le vice à la vertu, la sottise au bon sens,
> Les agneaux aux loups ravissants,
> La mouche à la fourmi...

Opposition, reversal, and contradiction are variant manifestations of one and the same basic binary pattern which has been observed by other critics such as Gohin[6] and especially Collinet (whose discussion of "les fables doubles" in *Le Monde littéraire de la Fontaine*[7] is a perfect illustration of the pattern). What Collinet and others did not see is the all-inclusiveness of this structure, its manifestation on multiple levels of the text and in particular its vital role in the establishment of ironies within the comic framework of the satiric fables – ironies which by nature of their duality switch comedy to cruelty and add a touch of the bittersweet to the predominant atmosphere of gaiety. The fables constitute a complex orchestration in counterpoint, a smooth mixture of the epic and the familiar, the lyric and the eloquent. Duality is illustrated thematically by the doublets *La Besace* and *L'Homme et son image* which develop the same idea in opposite forms: man's propensity to find fault in *others* and his refusal to recognize faults in *himself*. The complementary themes are just another manifestation of the leitmotif of alterity and resemblance which is generically inherent to the fable. The two fables which overtly display the doubling feature in Book I are *La Mort et le Malheureux* and *La Mort et le Bûcheron* whose effectiveness depend on the interplay of contrast and symmetry. Contrary to these two fables which are based on opposition such that the same idea is presented in two different tones, *Le Coq et la Perle* represents a doubling pattern based on resemblance. Two slightly different stories are told but both in the same tone creating a disparity of expression and content that bespeaks irony.

Since irony involves the simultaneous expression of two meanings, it is the perfect vehicle for the depiction of nature's paradoxical reality. It is no surprise, then, that the oxymoron and paradox *per se* are common rhetorical signs of ironic intention. And whenever the writer creates an illusion, especially of beauty, and suddenly destroys that illusion by a change of tone involving a reversal and contradiction, a surprising ironic effect is achieved. The faster the switch, the greater the surprise which forces the reader into a re-examination of the ideas presented. The most effective figure for this rapid reversal is the *rejet*:

> Même il m'est arrivé quelquefois de manger
> Le berger. (VII, 1)

But the reversal may occur as a structural pattern over a longer period. When the benefits of the sumptuous city life and the peaceful but meager country life are compared and contrasted on the basis of culinary criteria in *Le Rat de Ville et Le Rat des Champs*, La Fontaine suddenly destroys the illusion of urban paradise by the intrusion of frightful noises. The same pattern occurs in Fable V, *Le Loup et le Chien*. The domesticated dog eulogizes the padded life of court hunting in contrast to the wild life of the wolf in a double-level language which alternates and superimposes animal and courtly metaphors. Through the associative properties of words and their semantic fields, this fused language achieves the spiritual heights of satiric persuasion:

> Le loup déjà se forge une *félicité*
> Qui le fait pleurer de tendresse.

Suddenly the entire argument is turned about by the unexpected sight of the dog's peeled back. At this point of ironic reversal the fable pivots on the opposite direction away from the enslavement of court security toward the qualified merits of political and social freedom.

Above and beyond these hidden mechanisms of opposition and resemblance, modern criticism has identified two major forms of irony: verbal and dramatic. Verbal irony is a form of speech in which one meaning is stated and a different one intended. We have shown how a myriad of techniques such as hyperbole, litotes, euphemism, sarcasm, and paradox are employed by satiric writers such as La Fontaine to create a disparity between statement and intention. Naiveté is a form half way between verbal and dramatic irony and approaches the understatement in structural design. Foreshadowing, which sets the stage for a semantic turn about, is an important sign of irony that can only be determined by retroaction.

Dramatic irony is a plot device in which the spectator and reader know more than the protagonist, as for example when the reader realizes in advance the absurdity of the frog's intention to blow himself up to the cow's size. When a character in a narrative reacts in a way contrary to expectation, an ironic effect is actualized. Every time noble language is put in the mouth of an animal, an ironic incongruity creates dramatic effects for two reasons: firstly, because of the generally accepted impossibility of verbal animal communication, and secondly, because of the contradiction implicit in the equation of animality and baseness which runs counter to man's nobility. Moreover, there may be a contrast between how the character conceives of himself and what the play demonstrates about this character. This gap, illustrated by the unjustified flattery of the crow by the fox, creates a deep-seated irony and resembles the components of hypocrisy. Lastly, characters or situations are often compared or contrasted with parodic effects. Thus, whenever an animal imitates human behavior by using language or expressing emotions normally attributable to humans, like the frog who expresses envy, this disparity is ironic. When the cicada says: "Je vous paierai ... foi'd'animal, Intérêt et principal," the use of a sophisticated system of monetary exchange in the linguistic medium of an economic code by one of earth's smallest creatures is an absurdity which culminates aptly in the pun on *foi de gentilhomme*. "Intérêt," "principal," and even "crier famine" are terms which in the mouth of an animal take on the comic characteristics of a technicism. We laugh at the verbal animal communication for the same reason that we laugh at the unexpectedly sophisticated vocabulary of a child prodigy. At the sound of "foi d'animal" attention is immediately drawn to the intrinsic antithesis between man and animal, an antithesis which La Fontaine tries simultaneously to evòke and to destroy with the unprecedented success of expanded meaning.

The structural element common to these various signs of irony is contradiction. With this model in mind, irony can be defined as the result of a set of conditions. When there is juxtaposition and equation of disparate elements, or when an identity is created between at least two opposed if not contradictory structures, the resultant incompatibility or contradiction is called an ironic effect. Ironies like structures are relational and oppositional. The reader is an essential factor in the dialectical process for unless he perceives the relationship existing between a minimum of two equal and opposite elements of meaning, the incongruity is virtually inoperative, and the ironic effect is absent. That irony is essentially an oppositional structure is borne out in the fables if we consider merely the titles in the first book. Invariably two speakers, two ideas, two moralities are juxtaposed in a contrastive frame and in a symbolic language of allegory which is, in itself, contrasted to the direct language of the narrator's moral appearing usually at the end or at the beginning of the fable. The moral stands out from the fable's narrative structure like an embossed heading because its direct language is different from the superimposed language of the rest. Consider some of the titles in the first book: *Les Deux Mulets, Le Loup et le Chien, L'Hirondelle et les petits Oiseaux, Le Rat de Ville et le Rat des Champs, Le Loup et l'Agneau, L'Homme et son Image, Le Dragon à plusieurs têtes et le Dragon à plusieurs queues.* These are just a few possible illustrations of the binary pattern. Even when there are three animals mentioned in the fable, they are then contrasted as a unit to another, as in *La Genisse, la Chèvre et la Brebis en société avec le Lion.* The simultaneity of binary and tripartite structures in the fable is a constant. In *La Grenouille qui veut se faire aussi grosse que le Boeuf,* the first fable whose moral is most clearly both universal and topical and as such acts as a social satire, linguistic signs of social intention occur in oppositional pairs *bourgeois* versus *seigneur, petit prince* versus *ambassadeur, marquis* versus *page.* Then, in what is a rather frequently occurring crescendo effect culminating in a global tripartite structure, the narrator pluralizes, hyperbolizes, and universalizes his stated subjects:

> Tout bourgeois veut bâtir comme les grands seigneurs
> Tout petit prince a des ambassadeurs,
> Tout marquis veut avoir des pages.

The fable, which originated in the primitive allegory and has a strong link to the ancient parable,[8] is a legitimate genre which presents animals and plants speaking the language of human beings.[9] The fable is a symbolic form composed of political and social satire, allegory, maxim, and moral. Like allegory, fables involve the dissimulation of one series of incidents under another, and the narrative fiction is usually subordinate to the abstract moral. It is an old form of didactic poetry, and the famous formula *plaire et instruire* are the primary goals of the genre. Since its dual aim is to join the *agréable* and the *utile*, it is no wonder that a contrastive pattern predominates the comedy in which deep-seated seriousness underlies surface light-heartedness. Most critics speak of the fable with disdain declaring that it is a form for children, for the *animae vulgares* or the *ingenia rudia*, a depreciation which runs parallel to that of the formal verse satire, and which makes me wonder just how one can expect so much understanding from the very young. Both the fable and the formal verse satire are structured oppositionally with contrast and contradiction as a basic constituent of their ironic fabric.[10] What is common to the fable, the allegory, and the satire is the necessary presence of hidden elements, messages concealed within a symbolic system that requires decoding and translation. Irony is, like language itself, an allegory for it says one thing and means another, is not meant to be believed but understood, and its symbols require interpretation for successful communication.[11]

A symbol is a motivated sign. In La Fontaine's fables the motivation of the symbolic system is largely archetypal, and ironic effects are derived from a deconstruction of archetypes.[12] A clash between the expected and the represented occurs. When, for example, the crow becomes "Monsieur du corbeau" there is irony by deconstruction of the archetype of the lowly ignoble bird who suddenly acquires exalted human properties of social nobility. In *La Cigale et la Fourmi* the very efficacy of the moral lesson depends on a knowledge of archetypes observed linguistically in the fable by the presence of typing appellations of antonomasias such as *emprunteuse* and *prêteuse*. These substantival forms are rhetorical signs of a structure of categorization. Because of our awareness of the ant as symbol of industriousness and foresight and the cicada as a sap-sucking insect representative of parasitism, the reader suspects the end of the fable way in advance.[13] Thus the poetry of the fable, its particular mind-expanding experience which encourages re-reading and re-thinking, is not a function of the fiction or content, but a product of its expression. The joy and game of the whole poem is in the irony of the ant's punning response to his own key question:

> Que faisiez-vous au temps chaud?
> Dit-elle à cette emprunteuse.
> ...
> Eh bien! dansez maintenant.

I believe that it is the fable's affinity with the primitive allegory that accounts for its fundamentally binary system of alterity and equivalence. Allegory means *allos* or 'other'. Man's self-love, intolerance of others, his resultant bigotry and necessary insularity are leitmotifs most dramatically expressed in the fable *La Besace* by the opposition of symbolic forms. Man is:

Lynx envers nos pareils, et taupes envers nous.

Lynx, a shortened form of the cliché "avoir des yeux de lynx," meaning to be acute-sighted and in this instance hypercritical, is contrasted to the burrowing, small-eyed and hidden-eared mole who lives in dark places. In opposition to the symbolic expression of the moral lesson is the direct, synonymic explanation contained in the next line:

Nous nous pardonnons tout, et rien aux autres hommes.

where *nous* is in chiastic opposition to *autres hommes* and the hyperboles *tout* and *rien* close off the ironic, oppositional symmetry of the verse. Alterity is the essence of irony's deceptive powers by which surface language expresses the exact opposite of its intended meaning. Jankélévitch captured this in his excellent study on *Ironie* when he wrote:

Entre les possibles que l'intelligence lui donne à choisir, l'ironie choisit l'altérité la plus aiguë: elle exprime non pas quelque chose d'autre que ce qu'elle pense, comme n'importe quelle allégorie, mais le contraire, qui est l'autre le plus autre; l'extrêmement-autre. Et elle est *antégorie* en cela. Elle va d'un extrême â l'extrême opposé de cet extrême, c'est-à-dire *a contrario ad contrarium.*[14]

In the allegory characters, events, or ideas are hidden below the surface of other characters, events, or ideas. The historical, political, moral, philosophical, or religious referent is situated beyond allegorical structures which are purportedly described in the narrative fiction. Thus a system of equivalence develops in which A represents B, C represents D, the cicada represents parasitism and the ant industriousness, and so forth with archetypal motivation underlying the system, thus creating a basically symbolic mode of discourse. In La Fontaine's fables animals are symbols of passions, concepts, and morals, and each of the animals is selected because of certain traits normally associated with that animal by mythology and tradition. The fable thus involves the general principle of personification whereby the animal is a form of representation. The use of animals and plants in the fable can only be considered a symbolic, anthropormorphic motif for La Fontaine shows no real scientific knowledge of animal and plant behavior or zoo-semiotics. He has even made some glaring errors like ascribing raisins as food for the fox or a hollow tree as a nest for the eagle.[15] What matters in the fable is the sign value of the animal, its archetypal profile, which enables a system of equivalence to be established between the referent and the symbol, between the representation and its reality. This codal system presupposes a procedure of translation to be performed by the reader wishing to commute intellectually from one code to the other in order to achieve meaningful communication. La Fontaine tells us directly about this system of equivalence in one of his fables in which, ironically enough, there are no animals. In Fable XI, dedicated to la Rochefoucauld, a symbolic system is expressed iconically by the mirror motif and the mythological representation of vanity or Narcissus. The narrator then proceeds to interpret his own symbols:

> On voit bien ou je veux venir.
> Notre âme, c'est cet homme amoureux de lui-même.
> Tant de miroirs, ce sont les sottises d'autrui,
> Miroirs, de nos défauts les peintres légitimes;
>   Et quant au canal, c'est celui
>   Que chacun sait, le livre des Maximes.

At the base of this system of metaphoric equivalence is the dichotomy between the other and the self, alterity and resemblance, observed pronominally in the fable as *notre, nos* versus *autrui, cet homme*, and *chacun*. 'I' is present only as a representation of the absent but omniscient fabulist. The more incriminating *je* is implicit in the distanciation. A multi-level reading of the fable is encouraged because of the system of equivalence whose polysemy constitutes the very essence of irony. In La Fontaine's fables there are at least four levels of meaning: the immediate or literal which is the animal or plant communication, a ridiculous and comic absurdity meant obviously for children; the implied and indirect meaning which is general, involving man in society, politics, and the satiric attack on institutions such as justice, court slavery, plagiary, war, etc. In contrast to the universal is the topical, the social and political attack on institutions of the time; and fourthly, the least obvious target of satiric attack, which is the direct opponent of the 'other,' that is, the absent 'I,' the poet, the fabulist, and, by extension, the reader. The small group of fables written about poetry and the abuses suffered by the poet justify the fourth level reading. In *Simonide Préservé par les Dieux* there is a direct reference to Malherbe, symbol of poetry, which becomes "Parnassus" at the end of the fable. When La Fontaine refers to "mon texte" his subtle authorial intrusion establishes justification for personal involvement in the hermeneutics of the fable.[16]

> Je reviens à mon texte: et dis premièrement
> Qu'on ne sauroit manquer de louer largement
> Les dieux et leurs pareils; ...
> Enfin, qu'on doit tenir *notre* art en quelque prix. (I, 14)

How can these multi-level readings be justified? What signs in the symbolic discourse give us the right to translate a social, political, or personal meaning? Frequently there is one key word whose double or multiple meaning and generalizable potential is so well placed as to draw immediate attention to its signification, as for example the appellation "Le Nord" in *Le Chêne et le Roseau* which identifies Colbert, whose nickname was Le Nord, as a character concealed in the fable by periphrasis. In Fable X, for example, about *Le Loup et l'Agneau*, the reader is programmed dually toward the universal and the literal meanings after reading an introductory and generalizing moral:

> La raison du plus fort est toujours la meilleure :

and subsequently the amplified and highly ironic language of the court spoken parodically by the humble animals:

> Sire, répond l'agneau, que votre Majesté
> Ne se mette pas en colère;
> Mais plutôt qu'elle considère

The third person singular *elle* draws attention to the formality, obsequiousness, and res   ant distanciation established linguistically between members of different rank. But in the very last word of the fable, *procès*, which in its specific meaning pinpoints the target of satiric attack at the judicial system, the whole fable can be re-read as a parody of legal justice:

> Le loup l'emporte, et puis le mange
> Sans autre forme de procès.

Like a *pointe,* the last word invites the reader to reconsider the added significance implied in the semantic fiber of the fable.

The fable which best illustrates these four levels of meaning is

L'Hirondelle et ses petits oiseaux. On the surface, literal level, the prophetic counsel in the form of the swallow suggests that the little birds eat up all the existing grains in order to prevent future catastrophe. The more generalizing and didactic level involves the moral of prevention, and the wisdom of the experienced and traveled. The swallow, a migratory bird and conventional messenger of the Spring, is the symbol of the prophet: *Quiconque a beaucoup vu peut avoir beaucoup retenu.* The third level, in contrast to the universal, is the topical and constitutes the potential reference to a celebrated episode occurring at the time the fable was written: Foucquet's disgrace. Despite frequent warnings from well-informed friends, Foucquet took no precautionary measures to avert his downfall. The fourth and most symbolic level is the personal, the poet as prophet of doom. The poet conceives of himself with respect to his readers as an *autre,* a blind spot in the eyes of his condemned flock, a foreign messenger like the swallow, whose words of wisdom will fall upon deaf ears:

> Nous n'écoutons d'instincts que ceux qui sont les nôtres,
> Et ne voyons le mal que quand il est venu.

Man's frivolity, his presumptuousness, and driven self-love are the causes of his downfall, and La Fontaine advises throughout his fables a decisive control on natural instincts or impulses in order to achieve a conquest of real liberty, the ultimate goal of man.

Multi-level readings are signalled more precisely by the super-position of two or more metaphoric codes creating the impression of a double or multi-level language.[17] In the fable entitled *Les Frelons et les Mouches à Miel* the language of justice alternates inappropriately with terms belonging to the animal metaphor. *Frelons, abeilles, guêpe* and *rayons de miel* (by association) form a coherent metaphoric paradigm in which semes belonging to that paradigm will logically fit, such as *animaux ailés, bourdonnants, une fourmilière, un suc si doux, des cellules si bien baties,* etc. A parallel paradigm of judicial terms develops simultaneously: *réclamèrent, s'opposant, traduisit la cause, les témoins déposaient, Fit enquête nouvelle, le point n'en peut être éclaircit, la cause est pendante, le juge, contredits, interlocutoires, le refus, adjugea ... à leurs parties.* The term 'procès' in the finalizing moral written in a more direct language synthesizes and openly identifies the components of the judicial code. When the two codes coexist simultaneously creating an incongruous metaphoric intersection, the reader is startled by what appears to be a destruction of normal usage called unhappily by some a 'mixed' metaphor. But it is precisely this mixture of metaphors or intersection of codes that creates and expands meaning through the liberties of poetic discourse. This semantic expansion is irony. When in the very first line of the symbolic segment of the fable the fabulist links the term honey to the illogical concept of its master ("Quelques rayons de miel sans maître se trouvèrent"), the reader is immediately jolted into the realization of a sophisticated linguistic game to be continued throughout the poem in parallel symmetry:

> Des *frelons* les réclamèrent;
> Des *abeilles* s'opposant,
> Devant certaine *guêpe* on traduisit la cause.

And when the procedure is reversed and an animal trait with concomitant ironic deflation and ridicule is attributed to a human of high nobility and rank (a judge), the comic and, more precisely, satiric effects can not go unnoticed:

> Il est temps que le juge se hâte:
> N'a-t-il point assez *léché l'ours*?

"Léché l'ours" is a proverbial turn of phrase which implies the illegitimate procedure of elongating cases in order to accrue more profits. The inordinate length of judicial procedures is not only a universal abuse worthy of satiric invective and ridicule but was a topical issue of great debate in 1663. At that time a general inquest was conducted and ended in 1667 with a civil ordonnance reforming justice. It is also worthy of mention that Foucquet's inquest lasted more than two years.[18]

Another level to this fable is announced in the introductory moral which links it thematically to the preceding one, *Le Coq et La Perle*:

> A l'oeuvre on connoît l'artisan.

Imitation in the form of plagiary which is symbolized by the bees was an evil against which the poets of the time were scarcely protected legally. This abuse was a favorite subject of satirists and moralists like Boileau (*Satire I*, v. 93-94) and La Rochefoucauld, and its thematic reference in the fables draws subtle attention to the presence of a hidden but omniscient poet.

In *Le Chêne et Le Roseau* there is not only verbal communication between plants creating ironic disparity but an intersection of plant and human metaphoric codes. Human attributes are imposed on nature and the resultant effect, which is the exact opposite of a technicism, is to create the uncomfortable illusion of a mixed metaphor, of inaccuracy in description, of a destruction of the expected:

> Le moindre vent qui d'aventure
> Fait *rider la face de l'eau*
> Vous oblige à *baisser la tête*
> Cependant que *mon front*, au Caucase pareille,

La Fontaine alternates this superimposed language with direct language in the accustomed metaphoric code of vegetation:

> L'arbre tient bon, le Roseau plie
> Le vent redouble ses efforts
> Et fait si bien qu'il *déracine*

But it is not for this rather flat but functional degree zero style that we remember *Le Chêne et le Roseau*. What gives the reader pause for thought is the poetic refusal of nomenclature, an avoidance of technical precision through the oblique language of periphrasis. The unprecedented dynamic movement of the final enormous antithesis which evokes the comparative size of the oak to the reed is matched only by the poetic powers of a Hugo:

> Celui de qui la tête au ciel était voisine
> Et dont les pieds touchaient à l'empire des morts.

Semantic expansion need not occur through codal intersection alone. Sometimes ironic effects are created by elliptical evocation: a minimum of words are used to express a maximum of ideas. When in *La Mort et le Bûcheron* the poet describes the woodcutter's misery by the mere accumulated mention of highly charged semes, words that carry a history of sociological significance, a wealth of added meaning is implied and left to the contemplation of the informed reader:

> En est-il un plus pauvre en la machine ronde?
> Point de pain quelquefois, et jamais de repos:
> *Sa femme, ses enfants, les soldats, les impôts,*
>   *Le créancier* et *la corvée*,
> Lui font d'un malheureux la peinture achevée.

This technique is the opposite of the periphrasis which avoids the *mot propre* by describing instead of naming. Here the actual term is used, and the concepts underlying it are left unsaid, concepts which would offer explanation for the woodcutter's poverty but which would each take volumes to describe.

But this contrast is in the very nature of irony whose signs themselves fall into oppositional patterns: understated silence carries the same evocative power as exaggeration; sarcasm and euphemism avoid direct truth by oblique and attenuated surface language; periphrasis achieves by abundance what ellipsis effects by absence. Structural signs like rhythmic contrasts and doubling are higher level manifestations of an antithetical state of mind at the very heart of irony. For every sign there is a basic clash between the expected and the represented, a destruction of established patterns, be they archetypal, rhetorical, structural, codal, or other. This destruction which was observed primarily on the level of expression is represented in the content of the fables by the thematics of alterity, the enemy of familiarity and expectation. Signs specific to the fable involve the unusual range of tones from the most serious and didactic carried through the medium of maxim, proverb, and generalizing direct language which runs counter to the childlike gaiety achieved through the symbolic language of animals. The synthesis of these dissonances is in the nature of irony which is unwritten but implicit signification, writing between the lines, whose flashing but nonetheless subtle and almost imperceptible signals like insights light across the mind and force a searching reader to see more than before, to find satisfying and serious intellection amidst the joys of light-hearted comedy.

NOTES

*The original version of this chapter appears in *PFSCL* II (Summer 1979), 51-76.

[1] J. D. Biard, *The Style of La Fontaine* (Oxford: Basil Blackwell, 1966), pp. 105-106: "La Fontaine seems to revel in all forms of ambiguity. ... He is an expert at writing statements which behind the appearance of a straightforward meaning, hide intricate implications or meaningful allusions. The contrast between these various levels of meaning, between the innocuous appearance of the statement and its less obvious suggestions produces a humorous effect involving surprise, hesitation as to which of the possible interpretations was meant by the author, and aesthetic satisfaction at the strict relevance and extreme conciseness of the device." Cf. also Margaret Guiton, *La Fontaine, Poet and Counterpoet* (New Jersey: Rutgers University Press, 1961), p. 35: "La Fontaine deliberately cultivated the ambiguities of language." Cf. Jankélévitch, *l'Ironie* (Paris: Flammarion, 1964), p. 56: "L'ambiguïté de l'Apparence, toujours moyenne entre

l'Etre et le Non-Etre nous inspire une salutaire méfiance qui est, on le verra, l'A B C de l'ironie."

[2] Maurice Grammont, *Essai de psychologie linguistique* (Paris: Delagrave, 1950), p. 200.

[3] J. D. Biard, *The Style of La Fontaine's Fables*, p. 135: "Among all the figures found in the fables, ellipsis, litotes, and euphemism occur far more frequently than they do in any other poetical work of the time."

[4] Ferdinand Brunot, *Histoire de la langue française*, IV, Part I (Paris: Armand Colin, 1930), p. 69: "Aussi sa langue est-elle justement le contraire de la langue poétique de son temps; une grande partie de son charme est fait de toutes les audaces que l'on condamnait."

[5] Ferdinand Gohin, *L'Art de La Fontaine* (Paris: Garnier, 1929), p. 196: "... de même dans la composition rythmique, les effets de contraste sont continuels et merveilleusement adaptés aux oppositions des caractères et des sentiments."

[6] Gohin, p. 123: "... presque toutes les fables opposent le fourbe et la victime, le trompeur et le trompé, l'intelligence et la sottise, les rêves chimériques et la réalité, ou parfois encore un personnage à lui-même, et sa vanité par exemple à son aveuglement ou à sa niaiserie."

[7] Jean-Pierre Collinet, *Le Monde littéraire de la Fontaine* (Paris: P U P, 1970), pp. 163-226.

[8] Collinet, *op. cit.*, p. 155: "Cette éminente dignité de la fable est encore rehaussée par sa parenté avec les paraboles."

[9] The fable was not considered a genre in its own right either in classical antiquity or in the seventeenth century. Quintilian refers to the fable as a rhetorical device (*Institutio Oratoria*, V, XI, 19-21, London, 1921, Vol II, p. 282). Boileau omitted the fable from his *Art Poétique*. It is generally held that La Fontaine raised the fable to the level of a poetic genre. – The fable probably arose spontaneously in ancient Greece, and Hesiod's poem of the hawk and the nightingale in 8th century B.C. is the oldest known Greek fable. Aesop's fables are the first known repertory of Greek Fables which conveyed moral or satirical lessons in brief, dry verses. Phaedrus imitated Aesop but also invented many new fables and introduced political allusions. Babrius (2nd century A.D.) enlarged the formula of the genre in the direction of the satire and the bucolic. Marie de France was the best of the medieval fabulists who wrote in octosyllables. Gilles Corrozet in the sixteenth century was to use verses of different length, a form which La Fontaine perfected. The Indian apologues which were derived from the Panchatantra of 2nd century A.D. were translated into French in 1644 as *Le Livre de Lumières* and supplied some of La Fontaine's inspiration especially for the last six books.

[10] See Susan Tiefenbrun, "Mathurin Regnier's *Macette*: A Semiotic Study in Satire", in this volume, pp. 91-114.

[11] Jankélévitch, *l'Ironie*, p. 45: "L'ironie pourrait s'appeler, au sens propre, une allégorie. ..."

[12] Failure de recognize the sign value of animal archetypes results in myopic criticism. Jean Fabre, for example, criticized La Fontaine's inaccuracies in the description of the cicada for this insect never suffers from hunger in the winter, nor would a cicada even ask for "quelque grain de blé, quelque morceau de mouche ou de vermiceau." As Maurice Grammont so aptly put in in his *Essai*

de psychologie linguistique:" II (Fabre) auroit pu ajouter, pour être complet, que la cigale et la fourmi ne s'entretiennent pas en français."

[13] This archetypal motivation is substantiated historically in medieval literatures and in the Bible (Proverbs, VI, 6-8) and Epistles VI where the cicada is evoked as symbol of imprudence. The ant as a motif of prudence was used by Virgil in his *Georgics I*, 85 and by Horace in his *Satire I* (1, 33-35).

[14] Jankélévitch, *op. cit.*, p. 76.

[15] René Bray, *Les Fables de La Fontaine* (Paris: Malfère, 1929), pp. 66-67. Bray supplies an extended list of these errors.

[16] Gohin, p. 29: "Ce qui met tant de vie en effet, dans les Fables, c'est la présence même du poète."

[17] J. D. Biard has identified the mechanism of intersection, calling it appropriately an "incongruity," an "interference," and the "intersection of the human and animal planes." His discussion of the anthropomorphism on pp. 96-102 in *The Style of La Fontaine* is particularly illuminating.

[18] René Jasinski, *La Fontaine et le premier recueil des Fables* (Paris: Nizet, 1965). M. Jasinski places much emphasis on the topical level of interpretation, and he attributes sometimes excessive importance to the Foucquet incident throughout the collection of fables.

V

THEATRE: COMEDY

CHAPTER 7

MOLIÈRE'S *TARTUFFE:*
A PLAY WITHIN A PLAY*

Act IV Scene V of *Tartuffe* is a hilarious play within a play, and one
of the satiric highlights of Molière's theatre. Farcical, burlesque, and
gesticulative, the production of this mini-play evokes hearty belly
laughs as a vicious religious hypocrite is mercilously exposed. Subtly
ironic, topical and universal, shockingly realistic yet grossly exaggerated, this satire presents a passionate plea for human perception.
The players are Elmire, Orgon's reserved but recklessly committed
wife who portrays a coquette; Tartuffe, a villainous seducer posing
as a saint and here playing his unscrupulous self; Orgon, Tartuffe's
blind follower who assumes the function of the all-seeing but far
from omniscient audience. Elmire introduces and directs the production in Scene IV before the play begins. Firstly, she sets the stage by
placing the head of the household emphatically under the table.
Then, in a typical Tartuffe-like double-level language, Elmire informs
the audience of her ruse to catch the contemptuous hypocrite
in his licentious act. Finally, she appoints foolish Orgon as master of
production controls, capable of stopping the show instantaneously
at will. The outlandish incongruities and multiple oppositions within
the cast of characters and their roles, the scenic arrangements and
production management are merely a preliminary introduction to
the sophisticated linguistic trickery that emerges in Scene V, the
play within the play. While *explication de texte* is a method suited
to any text but less frequently applied to drama analysis, it is a fruitful and expedient means of breaking through this maze of verbal and
theatrical virtuosity. Because of the length and density of this selection whose underlying structural mechanisms are few and complex, I
think it advisable to perform a sequential and selective rather than
exhaustive explication in the hope of abstracting the models upon
which the comic and satiric effects are articulated.

    Scene IV functions as an informative and suspenseful prologue to
Elmire's play:

Elmire
Approchons cette table, et vous mettez dessous.

Orgon
Comment?

Elmire
Vous bien cacher est un point nécessaire.

Orgon
Pourquoi sous cette table?

Elmire
Ah, mon Dieu! laissez faire:
J'ai mon dessein en tête, et vous en jugerez.
Mettez-vous là, vous dis-je; et quand vous y serez,
Gardez qu'on ne vous voie et qu'on ne vous entende.
(v. 1360-1365)

As the proud and power-hungry head of a respectable household,
Orgon is hesitant to assume an ignoble posture on all fours. His exclamative language, tensely rapid pace, and redundant questioning bare
witness to his uneasiness. When Elmire persists explicitly ("Vous
bien cacher est un point nécessaire"), then implicitly through exclamative apostrophe ("Ah, mon Dieu!"), and, finally, gesturally
("Mettez-vous là, vous dis-je;"), the audience can not help but
perceive the symbolic function of Orgon's burlesque pose as *voyeur*.
Consistently blind to Tartuffe's despicable folly, deaf to his sensual
vulgarity encoded in spiritual jargon, and willfully enslaved by his
pretentious, mystical power, Orgon is the perfect character to play
the part, literally, of a table. Orgon's comic mask is a metaphoric
representation of Orgon the man, a concretization of the fool who is
about to be cuckolded under his very nose! But when the 'blind' man
is accorded the privileged role of 'seer,' the incompatibility of this
relationship produces ironic effects of antiphrasis. Orgon's role is
not a role, his mask is a true face, and appearances are transformed
into reality; in short, the archetypal opposition of Nature/Artifice
subsumed by these variants is shockingly invalidated. When an accepted antithetical relationship is rendered synonymic, this discrepancy
produces verbal ironies. But it is not until Elmire insists on Orgon's
role as master that a second level of simultaneous oppositions is
activated:

Comme c'est pour vous seul, et pour mieux le confondre,
Que mon ame à ses voeux va feindre de répondre,

> J'aurai lieu de cesser dès que vous vous rendrez,
> Et les choses n'iront que jusqu'où vous voudrez.
> C'est à vous d'arrêter son ardeur insensée,
> Quand vous croirez l'affaire assez avant poussée,
> D'épargner votre femme, et de ne m'exposer
> Qu'à ce qu'il vous faudra pour vous désabuser:
> Ce sont vos intérêts; *vous en serez le maître,*
> (v. 1377-1385)

Begging Orgon to assert his leadership, a role which Tartuffe has usurped and transformed into tyranny, Elmire is really asking Orgon to become Tartuffe and play God. Stylistically she places emphasis on Orgon's role as prime mover by the repetition of the pronoun "vous" and the relief-producing "c'est" constructions ("... c'est pour vous seul...", "c'est à vous d'arrêter son ardeur insensée;" "Ce sont vos intérêts;"). Elmire poses appropriately as a martyr, impatient ("dès que") to end the ordeal, willing but hesitant to sacrifice her honor for truth ("d'*épargner* votre femme et de ne m'*exposer* qu'à ce qu'il vous faudra "pour vous désabuser:").[1] Elmire's language is provocative, *précieuse,* and periphrastic:

> Je vais par des douceurs puisque j'y suis réduite,
> Faire poser le masque à cette âme hypocrite,
> Flatter de son amour des désirs effrontés,
> Et donner un champ libre à ses témérités. (v. 1373-1376)

Prudishly ladylike, Elmire refuses to name what it is she wants Orgon to see. She resorts to descriptive, metaphoric clichés ("un champ libre") and evasive euphemisms ("des douceurs," "les désirs effrontés," "les témérités") which are concretized appreciably by the plural form, a sign of Tartuffe's recurrent attempts at seduction. Why all this impressive valorization for a fool of a husband stooping under a table? Considered relationally as a pattern, Orgon's farcical posture and incongruously prestigious role as master are homologous reflections of the slave/master relationship which Orgon inflicts on his family, especially Mariane ("Qu'il faut qu'on m'obéisse, et que je suis le maître," v. 1130), and which Tartuffe has inflicted reciprocally on Orgon.

As the prologue ends and the culprit approaches the stage, Elmire displays her diplomatic evasiveness:

> Et ... l'on vient. Tenez-vous, et gardez de paraître. (v. 1386)

The generalized pronoun "l'on", a metonymic and *précieuse* representation for Tartuffe, is placed in emphatic position by the interruptive and suspenseful punctuation mark. The abuse of this pronoun both by Elmire and Tartuffe in Scene V will be one of the primary sources of textual ambiguity motivating Orgon's delayed silence. The scene ends as it began in a circular configuration with Elmire issuing scenic directions to one of the most laughable of theatrical concoctions: a blind seer, a husband who is his wife's own peeping tom, and a tyrannical master enslaved by a skirt-chasing savior.

A sense of continuity between Scenes IV and V is achieved when Tartuffe recalls the pronoun "On" in initial position:

> Tartuffe
> On m'dit qu'en ce lieu vous me vouliez parler.
>
> Elmire
> Qui. L'on a des secrets à vous y révéler.
> Mais tirez cette porte avant qu'on vous les dise,
> Et regardez partout de crainte de surprise.
> (v. 1387-1390)

Picking up the cue stylistically from Tartuffe, Elmire repeats his word and transforms its meaning in a baffling Marivaux-like banter. In "l'on vient" (v. 1386) the referent is Tartuffe; "On m'a dit" (v. 1387) is a passive construction in which "on" is unstressed and refers to a nebulous general public. In "L'on a des secrets à vous y révéler," "l'on" refers to Elmire, and the pronominal ambiguity establishes another identity between Orgon and Tartuffe since Elmire tells Tartuffe false secrets of her love while meaning to reveal true secrets to Orgon. In "avant qu'on vous les dise," "on" refers again to Elmire.

Elmire resorts to diverse strategies in order to win Tartuffe's confidence. First she feigns sympathy for him in the recent family upheaval, enhancing the value of the incident in which Damis is disinherited by superlatives and antepositioned hyperbolic comparisons:

> Une affaire *pareille* à celle de tantôt
> N'est pas assurément ici ce qu'il nous faut.
> *Jamais* il ne s'est vu de surprise *de même*; (v. 1391-1393)

Then she twists the truth, inconceivably focusing her attention on

Tartuffe's suffering and falsely attributing to Tartuffe's welfare ("pour vous") her motivation for intervention.

> Damis m'a fait *pour vous* une frayeur extrême
> Et vous avez bien vu que j'ai fait mes efforts
> Pour rompre son dessein et calmer ses transports.
> Mon trouble, il est bien vrai, m'a si fort possédée,
> Que de le *démentir* je n'ai point eu l'idée;
> Mais par là, grâce au Ciel, tout a bien mieux été,
> Et les choses en sont dans plus de sûreté.
> L'estime où *l'on* vous tient a dissipé l'orage,
> Et mon mari de vous ne peut prendre d'ombrage. (v. 1394-1401)

The ironic disjunction "il est bien vrai," placed in relief by the surrounding commas and repeated lexically by "démentir," is a stylistic marker of Elmire's pretense. The tactical error in her strategy is to exaggerate flattery in the word "l'on," whose ambiguous referent is potentially the entire family ("L'estime où l'on vous tient..."). Clearly the only persons who fit that description are Orgon and Madame Pernelle, a contradiction which arouses Tartuffe's suspicion. Even more incompatible with past history is Elmire's sudden intrusion of a courtly cliché "prendre d'ombrage," which in addition to its denotative significance imparts an appreciative connotation to Tartuffe as a potential rival. The subtle implications of love are rendered explicit in the following passage in which Elmire confesses to her passion metonymically ("coeur") and informs the audience of a causative past event. The recall of earlier scenes is a conventional device of narrative continuity which allows this small play within a play to function as a coherent unit:

> Pour mieux braver l'éclat des mauvais jugements,
> Il veut que nous soyons ensemble à tous moments;
> Et c'est par où je puis, sans peur d'être blâmée,
> Me trouver ici seule avec vous enfermée,
> Et ce qui m'autorise à vous ouvrir un coeur
> Un peu trop prompt peut-être à souffrir votre ardeur.
> (v. 1403-1408)

Elmire is endowed with the gift of imitating speech patterns. She parodies Orgon's obstinate and comically exaggerated decrees by repeating morphemically in "à tous moments" his hyperbolic "à toute heure":

> Non, en dépit de tous, vous la fréquenterez.
> Faire enrager le monde est ma plus grande joie,
> Et je veux qu 'à toute heure avec elle on vous voie. (v. 1172-1174)

Despite the radical change in Elmire's language, which Tartuffe comments upon skeptically in an emphatic couplet ("Ce langage à comprendre est assez difficile, Madame, et vous parliez tantôt d'un autre style." v. 1409-1410), her speech patterns still contain stylistic reminders of virtuous propriety ("sans peur d'être blâmée," un coeur un peu trop prompt peut-être..."). Unable to trick the supreme trickster, Elmire is forced to alter her strategy. Now she assumes the role of an experienced woman of the world, an expert on love matters. In fact, she accuses Tartuffe, in reverse psychology, of being ignorant about women:

> Ah! si d'un tel refus vous êtes en courroux,
> Que le coeur d'une femme est mal connu de vous!
> Et que vous savez peu ce qu'il veut faire entendre
> Lorsque si foiblement on le voit se défendre!" (v. 1411-1414)

Her speech, which parodies the confidence of expertise, is appropriately flourished with generalized abstractions like "pudeur," "honte," "amour," "honneur," hyperboles, proverbial expressions, the generalized first person plural, and "on":

> Toujours notre pudeur combat dans ces moments
> Ce qu'on peut nous donner de tendres sentiments.
> Quelque raison qu'on trouve à l'amour qui nous dompte,
> On trouve à l'avouer toujours un peu de honte;
> On s'en défend d'abord; mais de l'air qu'on s'y prend,
> On fait connoître assez que notre coeur se rend,
> Qu'à nos voeux par honneur notre bouche s'oppose,
> Et que de tels refus promettent toute chose. (v. 1415-1422)

Clever strategist, Elmire wins Tartuffe's confidence by identifying with him ("notre pudeur") and by telling him in his own terms what he already knows is true. To relay the message that surface appearances are not always accurate representations of reality. Elmire juxtaposes the concepts of word and deed in their respective paradigmatic forms: "refus," "s'en défense," "pudeur," "honte," "honneur," "s'oppose," represent variants of verbal pretense and "de tendres sentiments," "l'amour," "l'avouer," "on s'y prend," "nos voeux," "promettent toute chose" represent intended, hidden realities. In other words, Elmire is encoding into her speech yet another manifestation of the ironic mask which was formerly associated with religious hypocrisy and is now activated in a love context.

After insulting Tartuffe, she resorts to a more intellectual demonstration of her faith. She asks a series of unanswerable rhetorical questions:

> Aurois-je, je vous prie, avec tant de douceur
> Ecouté tout au long l'offre de votre coeur,
> Aurois-je pris la chose ainsi qu'on m'a vu faire,
> Si l'offre de ce coeur n'eût eu de quoi me plaire?
> Et lorsque j'ai voulu moi-même vous forcer
> A refuser l'hymen qu'on venoit d'annoncer.
> Qu'est-ce que cette instance a dû vous faire entendre,
> Que l'intérêt qu'en vous on s'avise de prendre.
> Et l'ennui qu'on auroit que ce noeud qu'on résout
> Vînt partager du moins un coeur que l'on veut tout?
> (v. 1427-1436)

Embedded in a series of dependent hypothetical clauses, Elmire falsely attributes her rejection of Mariane's marriage to a personal infatuation. What creates the intentional ambiguity in this passage is the intensely hypotactical structure, the metaphoric ("noeud") and metonymic ("coeur") associations, a recurrence of the polysemic "on" and interrogative, conditional mode.

Tartuffe, like Orgon, requires tangible proof of faith. His plan is, first, to profess love to Elmire in a polite manner and, then, to demand less formal action:

> C'est sans doute, Madame, une douceur extrême
> Que d'entendre ces mots d'une bouche qu'on aime:
> (v. 1437-1438)

Already in the first two lines of his speech Tartuffe displays his linguistic skill at superimposing two antithetical codes, the abstract and formal on the concrete and shocking. Polite, gallant language expressed in the substantivized, laudatory abstraction "une douceur extrême" and in the appellation "Madame," which is placed emphatically in apposition just before the cesura, coexists with the concrete metonymy ("bouche") which borders on comic vulgarity in its contrast to the preceding verbal formality.

> Leur miel dans tous mes sens fait couler à longs traits
> Une suavité qu'on ne goûta jamais. (v. 1439-1440)

The original abstraction "douceur extrême" is continued and concretized into the metaphor "leur miel dans tous mes sens," whose emotional content is heightened by the converging hyperboles "tous mes sens," "on ne goûta jamais," and "à long traits." The substantivized adjective "douceur" is also repeated morphemically in "suavité," whose seme of "fragrance" is semantically compatible with the contextual semes of "taste." In this one sequence, then, a paradigm of "sensuality" emerges with "leur miel," "sens," "traits," "goûté," and "suavité" as the components. What clashes in the series and constitutes an effective semantic superimposure is the "spirituality" implicit in "suavité," a lexeme recurrent in theological and mystical jargon.

> Le bonheur de vous plaire est ma suprême étude,
> Et mon coeur de vos voeux fait sa béatitude: (v. 1441-1442)

As the collocation of sensual and spiritual language continues, the following paradigms become identifiable:

SPIRITUAL	SENSUAL
le bonheur	plaire
suprême	de vos voeux
étude	mon coeur
béatitude	
mon coeur	

An intersection of the two codes and a resultant double-entendre occur in the term "mon coeur" which is a metonymic association for both spiritual and physical love. This double-level language is a stylistic marker of Tartuffe's idiolect and constitutes one of its major sources of verbal irony.

The contrastive conjunction "mais" signals an abrupt change in Tartuffe's line of reasoning:

> Mais ce coeur vous demande ici la liberté
> D'oser douter un peu de félicité.
> Je puis croire ces mots un artifice honnête
> Pour m'obliger à rompre un hymen qui s'apprête;
> Et s'il faut librement m'expliquer avec vous,
> Je ne me fierai point à des propos si doux,
> Qu'un peu de vos faveurs, après quoi je soupire,
> Ne vienne m'assurer tout ce qu'ils m'ont pu dire,
> Et planter dans mon âme une constante foi
> Des charmantes bontés que vous avez pour moi.
> Elmire. *Elle tousse pour avertir son mari.* (v. 1443-1452)

The ironies in this passage stem from the contrast of a high-toned language composed of courtly idioms ("Mais ce coeur vous demande...," "D'oser douter un peu...," "un artifice *honnête*," "je soupire"; "des charmantes bontés") and theological terms ("sa félicité," "une constante foi") which are inappropriate vehicles for the expression of base, primal drives. When Tartuffe prefaces his redundant plea for proof ("douter," "un artifice honnête," "fierai point," "m'assurer") by a profession of his sincerity ("demander ici *la liberté*," "Et s'il faut *librement* m'expliquer"), he is exposing himself as the archetypal satirist's adversary.[2] In formal verse satire a main speaker elaborates in persuasive, earthy, and proverbial language a vicious system of morality proferred as virtue. Tartuffe's rhetoric alternates concrete and abstract language, imparting to his speech patterns an unusually dynamic and ironic quality. Like Elmire, Tartuffe couches taboo desires in metaphoric ("planter dans mon âme . ."), euphemistic, ("un peu de *vous faveurs*"), and spiritual ("une constante foi") idioms. But this linguistic disguise does not cloak the vulgar innuendo in Tartuffe's reductivism. He minimizes Elmire's declaration of love by calling it "des charmantes bontés que vous avez pour moi" and "des propos si doux." Moreover, Tartuffe's sarcasm and "no-nonsense" attitude is transformed later into sheer blasphemy when he reduces God into "peu de chose" (v. 1482).

It is at this point in Tartuffe's persuasion that Elmire coughs. This interruptive and laughable act reminds the audience of Orgon's pervasive but silent presence, and activates an ironic discrepancy between what the audience sees and what Tartuffe knows. Suspense builds as the audience expects Orgon to call a halt to the farce. But Orgon, Tartuffe's alter ego, insists on more tangible evidence:

> Quoi? vous voulez aller avec cette vitesse,
> Et d'un coeur tout d'abord épuiser la tendresse?
> On se tue à vous faire un aveu des plus doux;
> Cependant ce n'est pas encore assez pour vous,
> Et l'on ne peut aller jusqu'à vous satisfaire,
> Qu'aux dernières faveurs on ne pousse l'affaire (v. 1453-1458)

The primary source of ambiguity in Elmire's intended message which motivates the continuation of the scene is her adamant refusal of mimesis and inability to pronounce the word 'love.' Had she been willing to call a spade a spade instead of euphemistically referring to Tartuffe's elusive term "vos faveurs" as "les dernières faveurs," the play might have ended right here. She does, however, intimate the shocking nature of Tartuffe's request by her exclamative "quoi," the repetition of the demonstrative pronoun ("cette vitesse," "cette tendresse") with its expressive immediacy effect, and the hyperbolic constructions "on se tue" and "des plus doux." Tartuffe will transform "aux dernières faveurs" to an equally abstract "des réalités," appreciably softening the obscenity of his uncompromising demands ("je ne croirai rien...") by the polite "Madame":

> Et je ne croirai rien, que vous n'ayez, Madame.
> Par des réalités su convaincre ma flamme. (v. 1465-1466)

Later "des réalités" become "d'assurés témoignages" (v. 1478), with comic insistence on a visual referent, an indirect reminder of Orgon's obtuse blindness. The final variant is intensified mildly by the comparative form "des témoins plus convaincants" (v. 1515). Even in a heated rage, when Orgon tries to convince Madame Pernelle of Tartuffe's fraudulence, he cuts himself short of pronouncing the word:

> Je devois donc, ma mère, attendre qu'à mes yeux
> Il eût ... Vous me feriez dire quelque sottise. (V, 3: 1688-1689)

Unable to evoke a response from her stubborn husband, Elmire changes her psychology and gnaws at his pride. Through an extended "empire" metaphor, symbolic of Orgon's masculinity, Elmire reminds him that he has not only been deposed of power but is about to be cuckolded:

> Mon Dieu, que votre amour en vrai *tyran* agit,
> Et qu'en un trouble étrange il me jette l'esprit!
> Que sur les coeurs il prend un *furieux* empire,
> Qu'avec *violence* il veut ce qu'il désire! (v. 1467-1470)

Then she tries sarcasm on Tartuffe:

> Mais comment consentir à ce que vous voulez,
> Sans offenser le Ciel, *dont toujours vous parlez*?
> Si ce n'est que le Ciel qu'à mes voeux on oppose,
> Lever un tel obstacle est à moi peu de chose,
> Et cela ne doit pas retenir votre coeur.
>   Elmire
> *Mais des arrêts du Ciel on nous fait tant de peur!* (v. 1479-1484)

The sarcastic irony in Elmire's language is activated by the hyperbole "toujours" and the heightening qualifier "tant." Merely implying that Tartuffe's exaggerated praise of heaven (a metonymy for God) is pretense, Tartuffe validates Elmire's implication by blasphemously minimizing God ("si *ce n'est que* le Ciel," "peu de chose," and "cela").

In Tartuffe's memorable and highly satiric speech, he identifies himself as a Christ-figure, a divine intermediary between man and God, the savior of man's soul, and endowed with special divination for saving sinful women!

> Je puis vous dissiper ces craintes ridicules,
> Madame, et *je sais l'art* de lever les scrupules.
> Le Ciel défend, de vrai, certains contentements,
> Mais on trouve avec lui des accommodements;
> Selon divers besoins, *il est une science*
> D'éntendre les liens de notre conscience
> Et de rectifier le mal de l'action
> Avec la pureté de notre intention.
> De ses *secrets,* Madame, on saura vous instruire;
> Vous n'avez seulement qu'à vous laisser conduire.
> Contentez mon désir, et|n'ayez point d'effroi:
> Je vous réponds de tout, et prends le mal sur moi. (v. 1485-1496)

Tartuffe tries to convince Elmire that he is the indispensable expert ("je sais l'art," "il est une science"), magnanimously willing to share divine secrets for the meager price of honor. Like Elmire, he poses as a sainted martyr ("et prends le mal sur moi") who shockingly proposes to substitute for religious absolutism a wickedly relativist system ("d'étendre les liens de notre conscience") in which an act is judged solely on its intention. At the dramatic moment, when Tartuffe's imperative pleas reach the height of their intensity ("Contentez mon desir, et n'ayez point d'effroi"), Elmire coughs and interrupts the energy flow with comic relief:

> Vous toussez fort, Madame.
>
> Elmire
> Oui, je suis au supplice.
>
> Tartuffe
> Vous plaît-il un morceau de ce jus de réglisse?
>
> Elmire
> C'est un rhume obstiné, sans doute; et je vois bien
> Que tous les jus du monde ici ne feront rien. (v. 1497-1500)

The audience invariably laughs here not only because of the mechanical repetition of Elmire's gestural pretense, but because of the ironic disparity between the literal and figurative significance of the act of coughing. Elmire's literal "supplice" (i.e., the cough, and in this sense a comic exaggeration) and figurative "supplice" (i.e., disgust at Tartuffe's hypocrisy; fear of the ultimate significance in Orgon's extended silence) are responded to inappropriately by "un jus de réglisse," a comic minimization of the inherent seriousness of Elmire's pathetic situation.

Tartuffe then continues his dissertation on ethical and moral compromise, imparting an undeserved sanctity to his wicked system by the use of proverbial constructions, abstractions, and the final, inductive "pointe." Three times he repeats the same immoral thought, turning it rhetorically on all its sides to expose its many blasphemous facets, and ending finally in what is intended to be a memorable, alliterative truism:

> Et le mal n'est jamais que dans l'éclat qu'on fait;
> Le scandale du monde est ce qui fait l'offense,
> Et ce n'est pas pécher que pécher en silence. (v. 1504-1506)

The bitter sweet truth in line 1506 applies as well to the silent and potentially sinful Orgon who has, without any apparent objection, been witnessing an attempted seduction of his wife. The implication of Orgon as referent is substantiated stylistically when Elmire coughs again.

Pretending to accept Tartuffe's proposition, but again reminding Orgon of her sacrifice, Elmire appeals to her husband in what can be considered a wife's pathetic realization of her loneliness:

> Enfin je vois qu'il faut se résoudre à céder,
> Qu'il faut que je consente à vous tout accorder,
> Et qu'à moins de cela je ne dois point prétendre
> Qu'on puisse être content, et qu'on veuille se rendre.
> Sans doute il est facheux d'en venir jusque-là,
> Et c'est bien malgré moi que je franchis cela;
> Mais *puisque* l'on s'obstine à m'y vouloir réduire,
> *Puisqu'on* ne veut point croire à tout ce qu'on peut dire,
> Et *qu'*on veut des témoins qui soient plus convaincants,
> Il faut bien s'y résoudre, et contenter les gens.
> Si ce consentement porte en soi quelque offense.
> Tant pis pour qui me force à cette violence; (v. 1507-1518)

In this passage the "l'on" and "les gens" are unquestionably Orgon who has fulfilled Elmire's metonymic description of him as a "rhume obstiné" (v. 1498) by the constancy of his imposing silence. The comic tensions rise as the audience waits impatiently to see just how far Elmire will be forced to go. Elmire is practically frantic ("facheux d'en venir jusque-là") and her bitter frenzy is evidenced by the hammering, anaphoric repetition of "puisque ... puisque ... et que," and the mordant sarcasm of "contenter les gens" which becomes direct invective in "Tant pis pour qui me force à cette violence:"

After a suspenseful and provocative omission by Tartuffe,

> Oui, Madame, on s'en charge; et la chose de soi ... (v. 1520)

which seems to signal the start of a truly theatrical spectacle if consumated, Elmire delays the ordeal by asking if Orgon is in sight. This dramatic ploy allows Tartuffe to pronounce the rare and fatal truth which will strip Orgon of his fantacized self-image:

> C'est un homme, entre nous, à mener par le nez; (v. 1524)

Like his spiritual "brother,"[3] Orgon has rechanneled his vanity and narcissistic pride into religious zeal. Each of these impostors has developed his imposture through the efforts of the other. When Orgon is finally betrayed by his brother, and is forced to see himself as a true reflection of this fraud, Orgon's own guilt compels him to end his complicity in deception and expose the hypocrisy of his idol.

Although Orgon is an obstinately egotistical man, he is not a complete fool, and it is the gravity of his flaw which saves the play from becoming a Farce. More serious a genre, this satire ends in Scene VI with a conventional, invective outburst and one of Molière's most stunning lines of poetry:

> Voilà je vous l'avoue, un abominable homme! (v. 1529)

This verse is memorable for its phonetic virtuosity. The first hemistiche is composed homogeneously of three short two-syllable segments, an explosive alliteration in fricatives and labials and an internally rich rhyme ("vous," "l'avoue"). This stridence is balanced contrapuntally in the second hemistiche by soft, homophonic, nasalized consonants which meld together to form what sounds like an interminably agonized moan. On the lexical and semantic levels this verse crystallizes many of the issues satirized in the course of the play. The initial term "voilà" is a demonstrative and potentially gestural preposition, Molière's subtle stylistic indication of Orgon's development from an inarticulate blind man to a poetic 'seer.' Never before was he able to distinguish much less point to the pollutant in his home. "Je vous l'avoue" marks, by the force of the verb "avouer," not only Orgon's change to sincerity but his bitter disappointment in losing his idolized confessor. "Un abominable home" substantiates this implication by underlining Tartuffe's mortality. He is just "un homme," and not the God-like myth Orgon had created.[4] The epithet "abominable" is perfectly suited to this defrocked saint in its etymological association with "abime," a metonymy for Hell, and a just ending for an unjust man. Orgon's sublime utterance closes the satire, reflecting the bitter sweet sincerity of a thwarted soul who has, finally, seen the truth about himself.

NOTES

* This chapter appeared as an article in *Teaching Language Through Literature* Vol XIII, No. 1 (December, 1973), 9-21.

[1] Despite Elmire's refusal to name the act of love and her frequent use of euphemisms like "les choses" or "de ne m'exposer qu'à ce qu il vous faudra" her choice of the conventional metaphor of love as a risk (épargner," "exposer") can leave little doubt in either Orgon's or the audience's mind as to the precise referent.

[2] See Alvin B. Kernan, *The Cankered Muse: Satire of the English Renaissance* (Yale University Press, 1959), pp. 1-36. "Every satirist is something of a Jekyll and Hyde: he has a public and a private personality. For the public personality ... the satirist always presents himself as a blunt, honest man with no nonsense about him ... preference for *plain terms* which express *plain truth*."

[3] Both Tartuffe and Orgon frequently refer to each other as brothers. Cf.

Tartuffe: "Oui, *mon frère*, je suis un méchant, un coupable,
Un malheureux pécheur, tout plein d'iniquité
Le plus grand scélérat qui jamais ait été; (III, 6: 1074-1076)
Orgon: (A Tartuffe) *Mon frère*, c'en est trop. Ton coeur ne se rend point,
Traitre? (A son fils)
Tais-toi, pendard. *Mon frère*, eh! Levez-vous de grace!
(III, 6: 1107-1109)

[4] Cf. Orgon's inarticulate but, here, appreciative description of Tartuffe: "C'est un homme ... qui ... ha! ... un homme ... un homme enfin." (I, 5: 272)

VI

THEATRE: TRAGEDY

CHAPTER 8

THE BIG SWITCH: A STUDY OF
CINNA'S REVERSALS*

In *Cinna* Corneille commits ideas to action and thoughts to form in an unusual combination of illusion and surprise. For illusion the deceptive mirror motif creates an eerie impression of déjà-vu which reproduces the familiar and satisfies anticipation. For surprise or *éclat*, the big switch is invoked.[1] Both processes are fundamentally necessary to the reversal model underlying the creation of *Cinna*. What is the big switch? By a varied and extensive use of poetic tools, Corneille manages to raise the expectation level of the reader to the heights of assurance only to have his self-confidence dashed soundly by the re-arrangement of a carefully established pattern.[2] The higher the expectation level, the greater the shock effect when anticipation is unfulfilled. And when what occurs on the stage is the exact opposite of expectation, a big switch is completed only to recur again and again in a ceaseless succession of Cornelian dazzlement.

The principles underlying the big switch technique are not new. The theory of tragic reversals dates back to Aristotle. Novelists of the first half of the seventeenth century abused the literary potentials of the unexpected and were subsequently accused of breaching the rule of verisimilitude.[3] Changing all things into their contrary, as Plato put it, is not only the essence of divine power but the very stuff of tragedy itself. Just as Plato implied a relationship between tragic reversals and the irony of fate, I am suggesting a necessary relationship of the structure of reversal to dramatic and verbal ironies.

Irony is a complex term involving a basically incongruous equation of disparate elements, a disquieting identity of incompatibles, and when most thought-provoking, a simultaneity of mutually exclusive oppositions as in Emilie's celebrated epithet, *l'aimable inhumaine*, a well-turned oxymoron with resonant, internal assonance. The perceptual process which stuns the reader into the realization of an illogical or impossible identity of opposites is fundamentally the same as a reversal. Thus irony is structurally inherent to tragedy.

In *Cinna* through hidden linguistic tricks, the suggestion of character[4] identities and exchanges, and the creative application of a reversal model in the structural designs of the play, Corneille formally dramatizes the irony of his message: the power of pardon and the hatred of love.

REVERSAL MODEL IN THE STRUCTURAL DESIGN OF ACT I

Cinna begins on a note of alarm Emilie's soliloquy is a curtain raising plea for immediate action designed to capture the attention of a complacent audience. The unleashing of Emilie's impatient energies and the vitality of her revenge are expressed by the erotic metaphor of birth (*désirs, naissance, enfants, séduite, embrasse*) which affectively conveys the visceral torment of her cross-purpose emotions. What more appropriate vehicle for the expression of impatience than an extended, post-positioned enjambement which delays the substance of thought long enough for its opposite meaning to rush forth in the very next verse:

> Impatients désirs d'une illustre vengeance
> Dont la mort de mon père a formé la naissance
> Enfants impétueux de mon ressentiment,
> Que ma douleur séduite embrasse aveuglément (1-4)[5]

Emilie delivers her impassioned apostrophe to will at the beginning of the first scene in a moving double personification of vengeance and sadness whose binary pattern is echoed at the end of the scene by a dismissal of fears and weakness called "tendresses." The simultaneity of opposing wills is already hinted in the first few verses by the use of strong antithesis (*mort/naissance*), chiasmus[6] (*impatients désirs/enfants impétueux*), and parallel synonymity (*vengeance, ressentiment*). Each of these tropes reinforces the structures of similarity and difference basic to the reversal model. Emilie's eagerness to determine the direction and strength of her will reflects the universal search for self affecting each of the characters in *Cinna*.[7] Tormented by her conflict of duty, Emilie is suddenly awakened to Love's paradoxical accompaniment by hatred and enslavement. She describes the conflict through the metaphor of combat in a memorable apostrophe to Love:

> Amours, sers mon devoir, et ne le combats plus. (48)

The cyclical pattern of Hatred-Fear-Love recurs in Scene II. Emilie crystallizes her emotional torment in a series of antitheses whose differential is emphasized by the similarity of surrounding repetitions:

> Mon esprit en désordre à soi-meme *s'oppose*:
> Je veux et ne veux pas, je m'emporte et je n'ose; (121-122)

The literalization of the seme of reversal is observed in the semic component of the kernel verb "s'opposer" and similarly throughout *Cinna* by the recurrence of such like terms as *renverser* (30), *revers* (440, 496), *contraire* (162, 1554), *dédire* (138) and *retour* (1368, 335). These morphemes are linguistic signs of a hidden structure, lexical variants of an invisible master plan of reversal continuously functioning within the play's poetic discourse.[8] When any member of the paradigm of reversal appears, a signal of the structure of reversal is instantaneously activated with the accompanying effect of repetition producing similarity. The effect of similarity, which is achieved by the duplication of dialectical and ternary patterns in Scenes I and II, is most dramatically evidenced by verbal repetition at the transition point in Emilie's thinking. In both scenes a switch from revenge to forgiveness is initiated by association with precisely the same verb "exposer."[9] Like an alarm the word calls forth strong fears ("frayeurs") which momentarily arrest the flow of Emilie's vengeful thoughts, switching her temporarily from obsessive hatred to the equally passionate force of love.[10] Emilie's surging impatience for death which effectively opens the play also ends Scene II by the striking repetitions in initial and final position of constancy's ever-encroaching enemy, time, "aujourd'hui." Caught in the frenzy of urgent action, Emilie's craze for retribution sets a rapid, stalking pace for the rest of the play whose characters, too, are caught up in the dramatic, history-making moment of political upheaval. Emilie's own death wish which appropriately closes the scene reveals the depths of her despair at this point in time when life is valued for the sole purpose of Auguste's death. The pathos of Emilie's renunciation is matched only by Auguste whose heart-rending loneliness will evoke the pity of tragic moments:

> *Il est tard*, après tout, de m'en vouloir dédire.
> *Aujourd'hui* on s'assemble, *aujourd'hui* l'on conspire;
> L'Heure, le lieu, le bras se choisit *aujourd'hui*;
> Et c'est à faire enfin à mourir après lui. (137-140)

Although Scenes I and II are structural replicas of each other
following the characteristic mirror motif, Scene II fulfills essential,
dramatic functions and introduces an atmosphere of irony which
will continue throughout the play on many different levels. Emilie's
ultimatum reaffirms the dominant force of this *adorable Furie*, as
Corneille's contemporaries called her, and defines Cinna's role as
agent in the execution of revenge:

> S'il me veut posséder, Auguste doit périr. (55)

The very structure of the ultimatum is programmed to elicit surprise
at Emilie's unnatural rigor and unusual resolution.[11] The force and
symmetry of the alliterative verbs "posséder" and "périr" are
enhanced by the categorical and increasingly intense copulatives
"vouloir" and "devoir." The shock value is derived grammatically
by the sudden and unexpected switch in subjects from "il" (meaning
Cinna) in the subordinate clause to "Auguste" in the independent
clause whose syntax indicates the order of Emilie's priorities. Fulvie's
portrayal of the presently repentent and paternal Auguste is a
preparation for his ultimate clemency. However, the irony of this
reversal is seized only by retroaction. Auguste's special relationship
to Emilie alternates between "fille" and "femme" – one critic
called her "la fille adoptive d'Auguste," and another suggested she
might be Auguste's next wife.[12] The nature of their relationship is
purposely left unclear in order to enhance the irony of Emilie's
heroic sacrifice in instigating the murder of Auguste and to establish an identity and exchange between Livie and Emilie, on the one
hand, and August and Emilie's father on the other hand like
Cinna, Emilie's perception of the act of revenge ranges at any
moment from voluntary betrayal to its opposite, a necessary but
distasteful fulfillment of filial duty. Moreover, in view of Emilie's
recurrent indecisiveness, her now unshakeable confidence in the
constancy of her own mind takes on ironic implications:

> *Je suis* ce que *j'étois* et je puis davantage, (78)

> Je demeure *toujours* la fille d'un proscrit. (72)

The irony of potential contradiction is matched by her commitment
to personal involvement – "C'est une lâcheté que de remettre à
d'autres" (105) – all the while allocating responsibility for the act
of murder to her alter-ego, Cinna.

In Scene III the spotlight focuses on Cinna. He displays an uncanny likeness to his irresolute mistress as he pledges her an "execrable" oath of love and allegiance, categorically affirming an inborn hatred for Auguste.[13] Unlike Emilie, however, his thinking is steadfast, his purpose unshakeable. But like the whimsy of public opinion which can shift "et dans un même instant, par un effect *contraire*" (162), Cinna comprehends the changeability of his identity and the inevitability of its rapid dissolution. Through the force of antithesis and paradox, Cinna expresses the agonizing insecurity of a man who, like Auguste, is undergoing a self-defeating and re-creating identity crisis:[14]

> Demain j'attends la haine ou la faveur des hommes,
> Le nom de parricide ou de libérateur,
> César celui de prince ou d'un usurpateur. (249-251)

Never before is the irony of self-destruction so poignantly expressed as in Cinna's scathing denunciation of Auguste whose brutality was met with the people's incomprehensible devotion. In a perverted ethos where kindness breeds defeat and evil assures victory, Auguste's legions were absurdly committed to fight for their enslavement.[15] The vigor of Cinna's argument against political tyranny and the sincerity of his personal detestation indirectly transfer motivating strength to his so-called second half. For Emilie and Cinna are undeniably one, united in purpose by Auguste's death and in spirit by mutual love, a courtly union which is carefully established to justify Emilie's abdication of responsibility.[16] But for Emilie public glory gained through Cinna's deed is secondary to her lust for personal retribution which she encodes in appropriately oxymoric terms:

> Joignons à *la douceur de venger* nos parents,
> La gloire qu'on remporte à punir les tyrans, (107)

The force of Cinna's conviction in Scene III is an ironic preparation for his sudden about face in the following act. All three scenes of Act I which end similarly on a vigorous appeal for vengeance, tend to minimize the weakening effect of Emilie's fleeting hesitations. Thus against a backdrop of imposing forcefulness, Emilie's decision in Scene IV to shrink away from duty functions as an unexpected reversal of a pattern. This rupture is ingeniously set up by the traditional *coup de théâtre* in which Auguste majestically summons Cinna and Maxime to his chambers. This symbolic gesture signifying

Cinna's peril assumes the same function as the earlier verb "exposer" which automatically elicited Emilie's re-assessment of values.

> Cinna; ne porte point mes maux jusqu'à l'extrême; (297)
>
> Ne me réduis point à pleurer mon amant. (304)

The second half of Scene IV reverses the first, restituting Emilie's initial plea for immediate revenge which she aptly calls "cette mâle assurance." Masculinity, then, is indirectly defined by what Emilie lacks, the inner strength of constancy. Feminine insufficiency will be alluded to later in Act IV by Auguste who reacts with abhorrence to his wife Livie's pleas for clemency. At that point, masculinity as defined by Auguste is an outward strength characterized by the assertion of authority and the public display of power. These points of view do not constitute a real difference but rather an extension of definition. The totality of man and his unique potential for heroism is the invariant which is counterbalanced only temporarily by the frailty of woman. But like everything Cornelian, 'constants' are subject to change and victimized by time. Thus the definitions of masculinity, femininity, and above all heroism remain in a dynamic state of becoming until the end of the play when Livie's unprecedented wisdom looms forth as more than manly and Auguste's sudden choice for the quiet peace of humanitarianism approaches the divine grace of the gods.

The final verse of Act I is a sibillant whisper of the tenderness that Emilie feels is weakness:

> Et souviens-toi seulement que je t'aime. (354)

Beginning on hatred and ending on love, Act I closes off a cycle which will regain momentum and regenerate with each curtain fall creating the impression that the same thing is happening over and over again. The structural design of the first act of *Cinna*, which represents in miniature the architecture of the entire play, is an actual model of reversal whose effectiveness is dependent upon the principles of similarity and difference, intensifying repetition and the sporadic break in an established pattern. The perception of an anomaly or difference engenders a momentary stop in the reading flow, an interruption which formally imitates and illustrates a familiar Cornelian thematic constellation: the impossibility of constancy (i.e. similarity), the power of *éclat* (i.e. difference), and the nobility of distinction, which is a culturally accepted deviation or difference. Thus a perfect superimposition of form and content is established in *Cinna*, an identity which is the foremost sign of an artistic discourse, and which might explain the many moments of reading and thinking pleasure which *Cinna* has continued to provide for more than three hundred years.

IRONY OF DUPLICITY IN ACT II

Expectation depends on archetypes, myths, and conventions. Auguste's first appearance in Act II fulfills our expectations of the Emperor. He exudes majesty by commanding complete privacy and pontificating power. But all this inflation in an extended enjambement is an ironic preparation for Auguste's brutal debunking of the joys of limitless grandeur:

> Cet empire absolu sur la terre et sur l'onde
> Ce pouvoir souverain que j'ai sur tout le monde,
> Cette grandeur sans borne et cet illustre rang
> Qui m'a jadis coûté tant de peine et de sang,
> Enfin tout ce qu'adore en ma haute fortune
> D'un courtisan flatteur la présence importune,
> N'est que de ces beautés dont l'éclat éblouit,
> Et qu'on cesse d'aimer sitôt qu'on en jouit. (355-364)

Like Emilie, Auguste perceives constancy as idealization and fears the reality of transcience. Since the linguistic trace of permanence is repetition, Auguste cleverly reproduces this figure in his speech as if to will its hopeless arrival:

> L'ambition déplaît quand elle est assouvie,
> D'une contraire ardeur son ardeur est suivie; (365-366)

Auguste's soliloquy contains the essence of *Cinna*'s tragic and iconoclastic message. Realistic, sated with empty power, and disenchanted with a meaningless life, Auguste dissolves traditionally accepted Judeo-Christian beliefs into mere illusions. He demonstrates that history does not necessarily repeat itself and that the efficacy of its teaching is subject to the caprice of fate.[17] He expresses his pessimistic outlook through the metaphor of the deceptive mirror:

> Mais l'exemple n'est qu'un miroir trompeur. (384)

The up-rooting effects of Auguste's delayed re-orientation of values accounts for the depression which has clearly altered his personality to the point of passivity. Disappointed with the fantasy of so-called success where enemies and death lurk everywhere, Auguste yearns for the quiet serenity of inner peace (*repos*). Grief-stricken, he expresses his princely solitude in an extraordinary verse built on the dynamics of internal antithesis:

> Et monté sur le faîte, il aspire à descendre. (370)

Auguste's conception of himself as a soft, suffering soul with regrets is a portrait which contradicts that of the corrupt and ruthless tyrant – "Ce tigre altéré de tout le sang romain." (167) A monarch is the living image of God on earth.[18] Nevertheless, the willful abandonment of his empire and the relegation of precious power to the people is more than symbolic suicide; it is contrary to logical expectation and a reversal of nature.[19] Auguste's unsettled mind and indecisive will – "Je veux être empereur ou simple citoyen" (404) – do not correspond to the head-strong usurper who, according to Cinna, stopped at nothing to achieve a political goal. But in the contemplation of Auguste's evolution from this unbecoming weakling to the quintessential hero in total possession of himself – "Je suis maître de moi comme de l'univers,/Je le suis, je veux l'être ..." (1696-1697) – the reader is experiencing preparations for the dynamic irony of long-term character reversal.[20]

Auguste's proposal of friendship to his chiefs of treason – "mes chers amis," "traitez-moi comme ami" – adds irony to betrayal and reaffirms the truth of Auguste's pessimistic philosophy of life. Traitor and friend are mutually exclusive categories. Auguste speaks truer than he knows when he willingly accords power to these traitors:

> Rome, Auguste, L'Etat, tout est en votre main (400).

The irony of this affirmation is in its double and contradictory meaning. On the literal level, and through the constantly recurring metonymy of the hand which symbolizes responsibility and the much respected ethic of personal involvement, Cinna and Maxime are designated to decide *intellectually* the fate of Rome. On the hidden and figurative level, Cinna and Maxime will virtually nullify Auguste's voluntary abdication by the *force* of their assassination. That Auguste finally decides to retain the empire, to selflessly disregard his need for inner peace and opt altruistically for Rome's salvation, is in keeping with the princely virtue of a great Caeser and his *Raison d'Etat*. But his unduly generous transferral of decision-making power to the leaders of conspiracy magnifies what was formerly Auguste's mere ignorance to his victimization, albeit dupery. How true and yet untrue are Auguste's pregnant remarks; like Orgon, who is comically unable to see through Tartuffe's hypocrisy, Auguste's innocent but tragic blindness is encoded appropriately in the paradigm of *voir* and its complementary mask motif:

> Je *vois* trop que vos coeurs n'ont point pour moi de *fard*,
> Et que chacun de vous, dans l'avis qu'il me donne,
> Regarde seulement l'Etat et ma personne. (628-630)

With every effect of verbal irony, there is usually one word in the verse whose multiple or contradictory meaning surges to the foreground as if to command explanation. For example, Auguste naively attributes 'love' of the emperor to Maxime's and Cinna's intellectual disagreement:

> Votre amour en tous deux fait ce combat d'esprit, (631)

Love it is, but not for Auguste. Cinna's love first and foremost of himself, then of Emilie, and Maxime's dedication to the principle of political freedom constitute the underlying causes of their opposing counsel.

Cinna's political position in favor of monarchy continues the established ironic atmosphere and raises the discourse to new heights of verbal duplicity.[21] How else can the reader account for the obvious contradiction in Cinna's speeches in Acts I and II? In the first, he is steadfastly republican, vehemently opposed to the tyranny of monarchy and the humiliations of servitude:

> Lui mort, nous n'avons point de vengeur ni de maître:
> Avec la liberté, Rome s'en va renaître. (1225-1226)

In the second he rallies for monarchical protection. I can not agree with Serge Doubrovsky who claims that Cinna is and always has been a sincere monarchist.[22] Cinna's speech in Act II is a jewel of deception, a masterful display of Cornelian duplicity, which is set up in parallel opposition to Maxime's speech of unprecedented truth – Maxime, the supreme hypocrite, second in baseness only to

Euphorbe whose name symbolizes his treacherous character. Cinna's pretense in Scene I is subsequently exposed and his political affirmations categorically reversed in Scene II when Cinna, himself, explains the selfish motivation for his sudden attachment to monarchical principles.[23]

That Cinna's speech is ironic is rather simple to support stylistically. A careful comparison of his soliloquy in Act I and his dialogue in Act II will reveal the use of blatent contradiction. A study of such ironic techniques as antiphrasis, hyperbolic inflation, and sarcasm are proof enough without comparison to dispel any beliefs that this speech is truth. Cinna speaks the language of a sly politician, cleverly supporting an argument that he does not necessarily believe but which is practical for his purpose. He begins on a note of professed sincerity achieved through the refusal of politeness which Cinna knows too well to be the sign of hypocrisy. His beginning is that of the traditional satirist whose commentary is not always reliable:

> Je vous obéira Seigneur ...
> Et mets bas le respect qui pourroit m'empêcher
> De combattre un avis où vous semblez pencher, (406-408)

Then Cinna uses a series of accepted generalizations which, because they do not apply to Auguste's specific case, lend an air of speciousness to all his remarks. His statements are never false but ironic by antiphrasis, and delivered with characteristic tongue-in-cheek. When the ironic, ambivalent, and double-edged term is in final rhyming position, the power of poetic form is particularly persuasive:

> On ne renonce point aux grandeurs *légitimes*;
> On garde sans remords ce qu'on acquiert sans crimes; (413-414)

In view of Cinna's speech in Act I outlining the details of Auguste's despicable criminal history, this hyperbolic couplet takes on the weight of sarcasm.

Cinna's unwarranted flattery of the monarch is another signal of his duplicity:

> N'imprimez pas, Seigneur, cette honteuse marque
> A ces *rares* vertus qui vous ont fait monarque; (417-418)

Here the irony is encoded in the connotative and denotative ambivalence of the word "rare." On the connotational level, "rare," in the sense of strange and unique, contains the potential for simultaneous praise and blame and is thus the perfect vehicle for satire whose rhetorical category is *laus et vituperatio.* Moreover, the multiple meanings of "rare" imply mutually exclusive connotations. The appreciative and highly positive connotation of "rare" meaning 'unique' and that kind of distinction which the seventeenth-century valued as noble, worthy of admiration, runs counter to the negative connotation of "rare" meaning infrequent or that which is encountered less often than expected. Thus Cinna praises and blames the king simultaneously but without self-incrimination through the use of what I call double-level language.

Contradiction is another sign of suspicious narrator reliability. Cinna's insistent repetition of Auguste's 'justice' is excessive and antiphrastic when compared to his former vehement denunciation in Act I of Auguste's 'injustice.'

> Vous l'êtes *justement*, et c'est sans attentat
> Que vous avez changé la forme de l'Etat. (419-420)

> Gouvernant *justement*, ils s'en font *justes* princes: (426)

> César fut un tyran, et son trépas fut *juste*, (430)

Cinna's hypocrisy in Act II is corroborated by comparison with his former vehement denunciation in Act I of Auguste's injustice. Moreover, the proximity of the two speeches enhances the obvious contradictions and reduces the possibility of sincere intellectual reversal:

> J'ajoute en peu de mots: "Toutes ces cruautés,
> La perte de nos biens et de nos libertés,
> Le ravage des champs, le pillage des villes,
> Et les proscriptions, et les guerres civiles,
> Sont les degrés sanglants dont Auguste a fait choix (215-220)

In Act II the reader can not help but suspect Cinna's ulterior motives for opportunism. Couched in a double level language of ironic disinvolvement, Cinna insinuates others and signifies himself:

> Un plus puissant démon veille sur vos années: (434)

> Il est des assassins, mais il n'est plus de Brute: (438)

Hoping to conserve Auguste only to kill him for glory and for love, Cinna cleverly uses the verb "se conserver" in a context of false good will:

> Conservez-vous Seigneur, en lui laissant un maître.
> Sous qui son vrai bonheur commence de renaître; (617-618)[24]

The beginning of Maxime's opposing speech will resume as in cyclical recurrence the same hypocritical flattery and play on Auguste's virtue that we observed in Cinna's argument for monarchy. He reproduces the same hyperbolizing adjectives which are signs of ironic intention:

> Oui, j'accorde qu'Auguste a droit de conserver
> L'Empire où sa vertu l'a fait *seule* arriver, (443-444)
>
> Il a fait de l'Etat une *juste* conquête (446)

By agreeing with Cinna, Maxime's difference of opinion will be all the more emphatic based on the principles of the big switch. In accordance with the mirror motif, Maxime's subsequent speech in favor of republican liberty is constructed as a parallel but opposite recall of Cinna's argument for monarchy. The correspondences achieved by verbal repetitions are truly remarkable. A whole system of repetitions develops whereby verse 400 recalls 435, 495 echoes 439, 497 recalls 410, and 496 repeats 449 word for word.[25] In ironic preparation for Auguste's not so tragic reversal and most memorable pronouncement – "Je suis maître de moi comme de l'univers" – the two conspirators in alternate succession and for different arguments pronounce the same pithy aphorisms:

> Il est beau de mourir maître de l'univers. (440) (496)

The importance of this type of proximal verbal repetition is its high perception potential. It is a rhetorical device which signals the function of only one half the structure of reversal, that is, similarity. To complete the structure, difference must be perceived. A profusion of repetitions in a system of correspondences such as that obtained between Maxime and Cinna simulates a curious sense of déjà-vu which I feel is one of the outstanding properties of *Cinna*.

In Scene II Cinna will confess his duplicity more explicitly but not with complete honesty. Refusing to tell Maxime about Emilie, he imputes his intellectual deception to a disguise for the personal revenge of political tyranny:

Un chef de conjurés la (la tyrannie) veut voir impunie. (650)

Again in Act III he will unfold the motivations for the ruse to Emilie:

Moi seul j'ai raffermi son esprit son esprit étonne,
Et pour vous l'immoler ma main l'a couronné. (955-956)

Sans moi, vous n'auriez plus de pouvoir sur sa vie; (962)

Thus we see that Cinna's political speech to Auguste is and was meant to be a hoax. To say that Cinna was always a monarchist is a contradiction of terms, for Cinna is incapable of constancy. If one were to study the zig-zag pattern in all of Cinna's speeches and his seemingly conflicting allegiance sometimes to Auguste and sometimes to Emilie, it would be clear that Cinna is a truly severed character whose intellectual and emotional loyalties are flighty and indecent. His most despicable betrayal occurs in the fifth act when he steals away Emilie's hope for glory by claiming complete responsibility for the act of revenge. That Cinna's name should bear the honors of the title I believe to be the greatest of all Cornelian ironies for no one in the play is so lacking in the heroic stance as Cinna, whose repugnant "lâcheté" oppresses him.[26]

Another actantial reversal set up in Act II and continued in Act III is the switch from Maxime "ami" to Maxime "ennemi." References to friendship are made throughout the play[27] in ironic preparation for the most stunning of reversals which is political parricide, treason on a grand scale by a close friend or relative, much like Auguste's inhuman betrayal of Emilie's father, Toranius, who was Auguste's own tutor. Constant analogous references to the Caesar-Brutus event reinforce the topos of parricide.[28] In fact, Auguste rightly questions the very existence of friendship under a system of subjugation:

Si donnant des sujets il ôte les amis, (1124)

Maxime's treason is prepared as early as Act I through the vehicle of reversal:

Un ami déloyal peut trahir ton dessein;
L'ordre mal concerté, l'occasion mal prise,
Peuvent sur son auteur renverser l'entreprise, (28-30)

Cinna's categoric affirmation of safety in an atmosphere of peril underlines the irony of Maxime's betrayal:

> Rien n'est pour vous à craindre: *aucun* de nos amis
> Ne sait ni vos desseins, ni ce qui m'est promis: (339-340)

In Act III Emilie reiterates this naive blindness:

> *Aucun* de tes amis ne t'a manqué de foi, (907)

Cinna's blindness reflects the tragedy of man's insensitivity, his undeveloped awareness, and low-level self-consciousness. *Cinna* is a play about not knowing – not knowing oneself, and not knowing others for what they really are. Auguste's friends are really his chief conspirators; Maxime betrays Cinna, the treason of a traitor; Maxime betrays himself by continuously refusing to assume full responsibility for his crime. And finally, the double infidelity when Cinna betrays his beloved Emilie and in so doing his own second self by depriving her of public glory and himself of the more substantial personal glory.

In Act III Scene I Maxime, who is sincerely horrified by the thought of betrayal (734), is polarized against Euphorbe, the Machiavellian *fourbe* who literally espouses the legitimacy of evil:

> L'amour rend tout permis; (735)
> Un véritable amant ne connaît point d'amis, (736)
> Contre un si noir dessein tout devient légitime: (741)

Maxime is rendered purposely sympathetic in order to enhance the shock of his subsequent treachery. But whether innocent or guilty, all the main characters in *Cinna* are somehow involved in their own self-destruction. Realizing that Cinna's successful murder of Auguste will mean his own defeat with his secretly beloved Emilie, Maxime exclaims his distress in a pun which evokes the ironic synonymity of *amitié* and *amour*:

> J'avance des succès dont j'attends le trépas,
> Et pour m'assassiner je lui prête mon bras.
> Que l'amitié me plonge en un malheur extrême!
> (727-730)

The life and death instincts (Eros and Thanatos), which are in a notorious state of constant imbalance, can be switched on and off instantaneously by changes in environmental pressures. Emilie's recurring death wish echoes Auguste's whose self-destructive instinct is most symbolically expressed by his abdication of sovereign power. His latent death wish is rendered manifest by the shouting force of anaphora in Act IV after Cinna's cataclysmic betrayal is revealed to him:

> Meurs, et dérobe-lui la gloire de ta chute;
> Meurs; tu ferois pour vivre un lâche et vain effort,
> ...
> Meurs, puisque c'est un mal que tu ne peux guérir;
> Meurs enfin, puisqu'il faut ou tout perdre, ou mourir.
> ...
> Meurs; mais quitte du moins la vie avec *éclat*; (1170-1179)

In this extraordinary passage built on the literary power of similarity and repetition, the word that looms to the foreground is the final *éclat*, that symbol of *difference* which constitutes the very essence of Cornelian heroism.

Cinna, too, in his moments of unsettling anguish contemplates the liberties of suicide. In the oxymoric language of courtly galantry, Cinna allies love and death in one of Corneille's most poetic chiasmus:

> *Mourant* pour te servir, tout me semblera *doux* (260)

Later he hints at death:

> Ah! plutôt ... mais hélas! j'idolâtre Emilie, (813)

Here the diacritic stop signs (exclamation points, suspension points, comma and semi-colon) are mimetic of death's suspension. More explicitly but never literally Cinna commands death's end to come:

> Périsse mon amour, périsse mon espoir. (887)

Maxime does not seek death itself, but fears that unwittingly he is the cause of his own undoing.

STRUCTURAL AND ACTANTIAL IDENTITIES IN ACT III

Acts I and III are structured like a mirror, an equal but opposite reflection of the original. In Act I Emilie is irresolute, wavering between strength and weakness first in secret solitude in Scene I and then in the presence of Fulvie in Scene II. In Act III, Scenes IV and V repeat this dialectic with the same characters present like an echo from afar. Moreover, Emilie's conflict in her Act I Scene I soliloquy corresponds perfectly in Act III to Cinna's indecision displayed before Maxime in Scene II and privately in Scene III. Thus the patterns are identical but the order is reversed – the dialectic strength/weakness is maintained, the double scenes are reproduced, but the soliloquy now succeeds the dialogue and the attributes of strength and weakness formerly ascribed respectively to Cinna and Emilie are now reverted to the opposite character. In Act I Emilie momentarily tries to discourage Cinna from killing the evil Auguste for fear of "mille et mille tempêtes." In Act III recalling this metaphor of peril "mille et mille fois" (1060), Cinna tries to discourage his "aimable inhumaine" from harming the now good Auguste (970-972). Cinna's conflict is in the difficult choice between *bonté* and *beauté*, both of which in their own way are forms of slavery. Formerly against the bonds of political enslavement, Cinna now reverses his stance and welcomes the evils of dictatorship as illogically as Auguste's blind legions, who fought only to regain their detestable shackles:

> Emilie: Il fuit plus que la mort la honte d'être esclave.
> Cinna: C'est l'être avec honneur que d'être d'Octave; (981-982)

Cinna's change of opinion in Auguste parallels his continued switch in the use of the proper names Caesar, Octavius, and Auguste. The specific figurative use of these proper names creates their own mythology. Caesar is evoked as the Emperor, the archetypal father and largest of categories including the positive attributes of princely virtue and *Raison d'Etat*, and the symbol of sovereign power, both just and unjust:

> Au seul non de César d'Auguste et d'empereur,
> Vous eussiez vu leurs yeux s'enflammer de fureur, (159-160)

Octave is the criminal usurper, the incarnation of Evil itself:

> Sa mort dont la mémoire allume ta fureur,
> Fut un crime d'Octave, et non de l'Empereur (1607-1608)

The name Auguste represents a double antithetical attribute, the evolution of the hateful to the beloved – the equivalent in form to Emilie's Cinna:

> J'*aime* encore plus Cinna que je ne *hais* Auguste, (18)
>
> *Auguste* chaque jour, à force de *bienfaits*, (63)
>
> Cette *bonté* d'Auguste ... (930)

Like a reflection of Cinna's other self, Emilie, the pillar of strength in Act III Scene IV, now assumes Cinna's former role as the blood-thirsty whip who spurs on conspirators with political platitudes and nerve-crackling pleas for vengeance. To express the extremity of her emotion and the strength of her convictions she employs a rhetorical figure describing the reversal of nature, the adynaton:

> Il peut faire trembler la terre sous ses pas,
> Et changer à son gré l'ordre de tout le monde;
> Mais le coeur d'Emilie est hors de son pouvoir. (940-945)

Full of the passions of hate, she reverses morality, turns black into white in parallel antitheses that shake up the order of world politics and religion by legitimizing evil:

> Je fais gloire, pour moi, de cette ignominie:
> La perfidie est noble envers la tyrannie;
> Et quand on rompt le cours d'un sort si malheureux,
> Les cours les plus ingrats sont les plus généreux. (973-976)

More than manly, she emasculates her lover with the crack of her tongue:

> Pour être plus qu'un roi, tu te crois quelque chose. (990)

Her lash is no more impressive than Auguste's in Act V who bursts Cinna's bubble of self-esteem, reducing him to nothing more than a puppet on Auguste's string:

> Ma faveur fait ta gloire, et ton pouvoir en vient:
> Elle seule t'élève, et seule te soutient;
> C'est elle qu'on adore, et non pas ta personne:
> Tu n'as crédit ni rang qu'autant qu'elle t'en donne,
> Et pour te faire choir je n'aurois aujourd'hui
> Qu'à retirer la main qui seule est ton appui. (1527-1531)

And like Auguste who in a moment of inner strength pardons all, Emilie, in a moment of weakness reverses the tidal flow of vindictive spirit. The rapidity of the switch, increasing its unexpectedness, is mimetic of the incalculable speed of thought:

> Helas! cours après lui, Fulvie,
> Et si ton amitié daigne me secourir,
> Arrache-lui du coeur ce dessein de mourir: (1070-1073)

The effect of the structural homologue of Acts I and III is to reinforce an identity and exchange between Cinna and Emilie, which has been established thematically by definition of their love. The exchange motif has been examined in detail by Jacques Ehrmann on the stylistic level, and the present study extends the categories of analysis to the structural and actantial levels. Identities are signalled most obviously by proximal repetition:

> Emilie: Je suis toujours moi-même, et mon coeur n'est point autre (914)
>
> Cinna: Je suis toujours moi-même, et ma foi toujours pure (945)

The ironic persuasion of constancy by the two most inconstant people in the play is a direct recall of Emilie's self-confident assertions in none other than Act I, the homologous text:

> Je suis ce que j'étais, et je puis davantage. (78)

That Emilie and Cinna are one is noted pathetically by Maxime who understands regretfully that a betrayal of Cinna is a betrayal of his beloved. Wanting Emilie willingly and not as a conquest, he says deceitfully to her in Act IV:

> En faveur de Cinna je fais ce que je puis,
> Et tache à garantir de ce malheur extrême
> La plus belle moitié qui reste de lui-même. (1332-1335)

Later Maxime reiterates his hypocrisy in a similar allusion to their unification:

> Cet amour en naissant est toute fois extrême:
> C'est votre amant en vous, c'est mon ami que j'aime, (1369-1370)

Identities of this sort which are noticeable throughout the play reinforce the structures of similarity and account for what I referred to earlier as the eerie feeling of *déjà-vu*. Even Auguste and Cinna share certain attributes. Auguste killed Emilie's father and warranted the title "parricide." Emilie, who replaces Julie and may also be replacing Livie,[29] now bears the dishonorable title of "parricide" (1594). Cinna, now eternally ingratiated to Auguste for his magnanimity, refers to himself as "le parricide" in a verse that recreates identity ("je deviens, je suis") and recalls the bondage inherent in "le serment exécrable" that Cinna willingly chose to accept:

> Je deviens sacrilège ou je suis parricide. (817)

And in view of Auguste's paternal attachment to Emilie, Cinna, like Auguste who murdered Emilie's father, will now reproduce the same crime by assassinating Auguste.

And yet, despite the quantity of identities and their lasting impression of similarity, difference is what predominates in *Cinna, éclat*, and all that is worthy of admiration. Emilie and Cinna are no longer at equal purposes in Act III. What was once lovable to Cinna now becomes hateful, inhuman, execrable, and odious. What was once cruelty, now becomes goodness, virtue, and princely magnanimity. Cinna's fluctuation stems ironically from the constancy of egotism. He is and always has been an opportunist, whose self-interest prevents him from resisting external pleasures be they Emilie's beauty or the goodness of Auguste's gifts. Time, the present moment, now is what determines Cinna's choices in his perpetual quest for immediate gratification.

SYSTEM OF IDENTITIES AND EXCHANGES IN ACT IV

In Act IV the system of identities is continued and developed. Auguste's soliloquy reproduces the same fluctuational indecision observed in the speech patterns of both Emilie and Cinna. Act IV begins abruptly *in medias res* with Euphorbe's precipitous unmasking of conspirators and his sly and unexpected cover-up for Maxime. Following the intertext of Caesar's legendary "et tu Brute," Auguste's wide-eyed and pathetic disappointment in Cinna is expressed succinctly in a poetic apostrophe:

> O trop sensible coup d'une main si chérie!
> Cinna, tu me trahis ... (1098-1099)

Through the everpresent image of the hand, symbol of man's direct
responsibility, Corneille supports the irony of fate with a verbal
irony or the association of incompatible oppositions: *coup* and
chérie. For Emilie the reconstruction of the intertext is more obvious:

> Et toi, ma fille, aussi! (1564)

The irony of parodic imitation in this verse is highly effective but in
no way comic. Irony and comedy need not be an automatic association. The noble passion of vengeance, a highly-charged and intensifying emotion, creates and consumes the tragic atmosphere of *Cinna* in
this weighty moment of human, and political seriousness.

Auguste's flaw, like Oedipus,' is insufficient vision, symbolic blindness, and like Sophocles, Corneille makes full use of the literary
potentials of ironic language to convey the tragic limitations of Man.
Auguste suspects no one except the most faithful, his wife. He accuses
Livie of self-interest:

> Ayez moins de foiblesse ou moins d'ambition (1256)
>
> C'est l'amour des grandeurs qui vous rend importune. (1261)

Auguste's supercilious insolence towards his wife[30] makes us wonder
again about the nature and intensity of his attachment to Emilie.
Auguste's marriage gift to Cinna could potentially be a heroic and
sacrificial gesture bestowed in preparation for his final noble act of
grace. But not even Auguste, who disdains Livie's "conseils d'une
femme" (1245), can deny her perspicacious observation of life's
inevitable reversals:

> Mais gardez que sur vous *le contraire* n'éclate. (1230)

Auguste's soliloquy is an unmasking, a sincere and vital plea for
self-knowledge which runs counter to the hypocrisy in Maxime's
soliloquy at the end of the act. Remorseful to a degree and per-
ceiving his own treason as evil, Maxime ascribes the onus of guilt,
nevertheless, to Euphorbe. The two speeches are arranged in the
characteristic mirror format. Auguste's sincerity begins with a call
for introspection and self-reassessment through increased awareness:

> Rentre en toi Octave, et cesse de te plaindre. (1130)

Auguste's detailed confession of past sins then follows, an autoflagellation which posits the justice of treason for past tyranny and confirms Cinna's unmitigating denunciation of Octavius in Act I. In contrast, Auguste then displays a childlike bewilderment at Cinna's betrayal, and a pitiful innocence in the face of all the addictive and encroaching deception about him. The evil which is hypocrisy is beautifully expressed through the metaphor of the hydra, that inescapable, ever-increasing enemy:

> Rome a pour ma ruine une hydre trop fertile:
> Une tête coupée en fait renaître mille, (1165-1166)

The numerical configurations in this metaphor involve a subtle and long-range recall of Emilie's initial plea for revenge in Act I:

> Je m'abandonne toute à vos ardents transports,
> Et crois, pour *une* mort, lui devoir *mille* morts (15-16)

The ironic identity between Auguste and Emilie, victim and murderer, continues during Auguste's suicidal self-abandonment. Like Emilie whose ultimate weapon against Cinna's hestitation is the threat of her glorious death,[31] Auguste's plea for an end to his misery similarly engenders thoughts of glory attained through punitive retribution. Emilie's initial joy and quiet serenity in Scene IV Act IV, like the opposite side of Auguste's tormented spirit, will instantaneously be switched by Fulvie who brings alarming news of Cinna's danger. Now Emilie, on a similar path of despair and self-destruction – "Et je veux bien périr" (1303) – pronounces the key to *Cinna*'s thematic puzzle – the equation of fate's contrariness with man's emotional reversals:

> A chaque occasion le ciel y fait descendre
> Un sentiment *contraire* à celui qu'il doit prendre: (1293-1294)

Although Auguste's soliloquy ends suspensefully, just as his talk with Livie casts a doubt on his decision to pardon or punish, both Scenes II and III suggest punishment as Auguste's choice. This preparation accounts for the intensity of the shock at Auguste's unexpected display of self-domination and heroic sacrifice.[32]

The last of the identities is established less successfully with fewer points of correspondence between Maxime and Cinna; both conspirators, both lovers of the same woman, both unfaithful by nature. Maxime forces Emilie to perceive the identity for his own self-interest and to encourage an exchange (*rendre, perdre*) between himself and Cinna:

> Ouvrez enfin les yeux, et connoissez Maxime:
> C'est un autre Cinna qu'en lui vous regardez;
> Le ciel vous rend en lui l'amant que vous perdez (1345-1347)

Emilie sees through Maxime's deceit and accuses him of the same "lâcheté" (1380) which is to be Cinna's eternal punishment. And finally she invites Maxime to die with her, just as she expected Cinna to die a sweet death in service to his mistress:

> Cinna: Mourant pour vous servir, tout me semblera doux (260)
>
> Emilie: Mais si mon amitié par là ne te délivre,
> N'espère pas que je veuille te survivre.
> Je fais de ton destin des règles à mon sort,
> Et j'obtiendrai ta vie, ou je suivrai ta mort. (349-352)

The triple identity of principle characters reinforces the drama of resemblance. For Auguste, Cinna, and Emilie the choices are the same in substance – pardon or punish. Cinna takes advice from his hatefilled mistress, Emilie, and Auguste listens reluctantly to his beneficent wife, Livie, the Christian conscience of the play. Auguste appears to despise Livie's feminine weakness derived from an adherence to the Christian virtue of tolerance (which surfaces as practicality), just as much as Cinna loathes Emilie's inhuman strength for vindication. Auguste and Emilie, victim and murderer, are on similar paths of despair and self-destruction. *Cinna*'s Rome is basically a topsy-turvy world in continuous transition:

> Un ami déloyal peut trahir ton dessein
> L'ordre mal concerté, l'occasion mal prise
> Peuvent sur son auteur *renverser* l'entreprise. (28-30)

The pathetic pagan inhabitants of this whirlwind cosmos are shook ceaselessly by the wrath of fate until their distorted values turn up right at the end of the play in a miraculous apotheosis.

THE BIG SWITCH: ACT V

The fifth act of *Cinna* confirms a remark made in passing by Greimas that all textual analyses should start not at the beginning but at the end of the text. When I read the fifth act of *Cinna*, which is the high point of the play and the total unmasking of the hypocrits by a master trickster, I can not hlep but think of Molière's *Tartuffe*. Like Madame Pernelle, who displays her domineering bent in the first act by matter of factly denouncing in comic succession the evils of each member of the family (with the striking exception of Tartuffe, of course, the worst perpetrator), Auguste, too, assumes a dominant posture and promptly berates, questions, and degrades first Cinna then Emilie and passes over Maxime. Auguste blindly calls this last and worst of traitors his only friend. With each character except Maxime Auguste suggests retribution by the term "supplice" which occurs at the end of Scene I and Scene II in preparation of the big switch towards clemency. And like father Orgon who tries in vain to present an argument in the midst of Dorine's incessant interruptions, Auguste not so conically and for dramatic irony insists on Cinna's absolute silence. In *Tartuffe* the silence motif accompanied by Orgon's threats is comical, slapstick. In *Cinna* the same motif engenders a twist, a wry kind of humor rarely involving the comic per se.

> Auguste: Parle, parle il est temps,
> Cinna: Je demeure stupide; (1540-1541)

Cinna proposes two opposing explanations for his behavior. The first is a hypocritical denial of involvement and the second a forthright confession with justifications. Emilie, on the other hand, remains consistently faithful to her duty, and even breaks with Cinna on the question of her honor:

> Cinna, qu'oses-tu dire? Est-ce là me chérir
> Que de m'ôter l'honneur quand il me faut mourir. (1639-1640)

Maxime confesses his betrayal, acknowledges his role in the master plan of reversals as the worst of all criminals, but again places blame on Euphorbe.

In the face of base deception and trivial bickering, Auguste's forgiveness takes on the virtue of divinity. By the act of forgetting, a superhuman and voluntary control of the involuntary mind, Auguste attempts the impossible which is friendship under rule by one:

> Soyons amis, Cinna, c'est moi qui t'en confie: (1701)

Auguste has achieved the colossal feat Emilie could not – the exercise of will to eradicate a desire for vengeance. The force of Auguste's extraordinary contradiction of nature[33] is to provoke more of the unexpected like the erasure of Emilie's eternal hatred, her miraculous conversion to monarchy, the cessation of fate's contrariness, and the praise of political subjugation:

> Après cette action vous n'avez rien à craindre:
> On portera le jour désormais sans se plaindre;
> Et les plus indomptés, renversant leurs projets,
> Mettront toute leur gloire à mourir vos sujets;
> ...
> Jamais plus d'assassin ni de conspirateurs:
> Vous avez trouvé l'art d'être maître des coeurs. (1757-1764)

In a contagious moment of insight, Auguste wins a victory over evil, restores faith in providential history and free will, and reverses his own fleeting attraction to fatalism. And the thunderous effect of the pardon brings vision to those blinded by hatred and love:

> Emilie:
> Je me rends, Seigneur, à ces hautes bontés;
> Je recouvre *la vue* auprès de leurs *clartés*: (1715-1716)

> Livie:
> Ce n'est pas tout, Seigneur: une céleste flamme
> D'un rayon prophétique illumine mon âme. (1753-1754)

But when a convergence of the unexpected reaches an ill-defined point of excess, believability is threatened and an about face occurs. The reader-spectator begins to question whether or not all this miraculous magnanimity and conversion are not just more of the same duplicity, a political ploy, and a logical extension of the ironic context whose reversal model presupposes unreliable narration. The not so innocent but nonetheless ignorant victims of this cruel kindness are duped by Auguste into the adulation of a false god. But more preposterous is the joke played on the spectators who play an active role in the transmission of the ironic message. The fifth act can be read as a big hoax on the spectator whose initial gullibility and belief in Auguste's converted selflessness identifies him with the tragic ignorance of the characters. That man is ultimately unable to fight destiny is the deep-seated tragedy which reverses the superficial optimism normally associated with Cornelian theatre.

Auguste's pardon is a unique display less of magnanimity than of "générositéé" in the classical sense, a sacrifice predicated on *orgueil* and ultimate self-interest.[34] That this egotism is a universal trait is a Freudian hypothesis which does not contradict Christian doctrine but which is nevertheless open to continued question. Auguste achieves public and personal honor by self-domination, and complete self-consciousness through learning about others. His fatherly and final words of advice to Cinna contain a heart-filled appeal to increased awareness by learning:

> Apprends à te connaître et descends en toi-même: (1517)

When the tragedy ends happily,[35] reversing the very definition of tragedy itself by a blissful return to an innocent state of ignorance, the last of the big switches turns off and the audience is left with the enlightened pleasure of continued contemplation.

> Qu'Auguste a tout *appris*, et veut tout oublier. (1780)

NOTES

* This chapter is an extended version of a paper delivered at the Northeast Modern Language Association on April 8, 1976, at Burlington, Vermont.

[1] Roland Barthes in *Sur Racine* (Paris: Seuil, 1963) commented on the fundamental role of reversals in tragedy and the importance of antithesis, "la frappe" (which we call "éclat"), and symmetry: "Or ce qui fait toute la spécificité du revirement tragique, c'est qu'il est exact et comme mesuré. Son dessin fondamental est la symétrie." (p. 52) "Ce jeu réversif a d'ailleurs sa rhétorique: l'antithèse, et sa figure versifiée: la frappe." (p 53).

[2] See M. Riffaterre, *Essais de stylistique structurale* (Paris: Flammarion, 1971), pp. 64-95, for a discussion of stylistic context and contrast. This study shows the function of contextual contrast and what I called 'neutralization' by redundance. (See Chapter 3, "Hidden Patterns in the French Classical Novel," especially pp. 68, for a discussion of this on the structural and actantial levels.)

[3] René Godenne, *Histoire de la nouvelle française au XVIIe et XVIIIe siècles* (*Geneva: Droz, 1970*).

[4] 'Actantial' is a term coined and developed by Greimas in his *Sémantique structurale* (Paris: Larousse, 1966), pp. 172-189. It refers to the concept of 'character' as an acting model, structure, or form rather than the conventional static conception of character as actor. I will use this term rather than 'character'.

[5] All citations in my text are from the Marty-Laveaux edition of *Oeuvres de P. Corneille*, III (Paris: Hachette, 1862), 362-462.

[6] Cf. P. J. Yarrow, *Corneille* (London: Macmillan and Co., 1963), on the

poetry of Corneille (pp. 286-319). Yarrow is one of the rare critics who understands and discusses the role of irony and its stylistic and rhetorical vehicles such as chiasmus, antithesis, repetition, parallelism, paradox and symmetry.

[7] Cf. *Cinna*:

Auguste: Rentre en toi, Octave, et cesse de te plaindre. (IV, 2, 1130)
Emilie: Me connois-tu, Maxime, et sais-tu qui je suis? (IV, 5, 1331)
Auguste: Apprends à te connoitre et descends en toi-même: (V, I, 1517)

[8] Umberto Eco, *La Structure Absente* (Paris: Mercure de France, 1971).

[9] *Cinna*: Et je sens refroidir ce bouillant mouvement
Quand il faut pour le suivre, *exposer* mon amant. (I, 1, 19-20)
Pensez mieux, Emilie, à quoi vous l'*exposez*, (I, 2, 115)

[10] Cf. Claude Abraham, *Pierre Corneille* (New York: Twayne, 1972), p. 69: "... in all dramatic literature there are few rôles more difficult, more demanding than that of Emilie, a young lady who fluctuates repeatedly from anger to tenderness, from love to hatred, from youthful ejaculations to considered power (as in III, 4 where tenderness alternates with sarcasm and even violent hatred)."

[11] Perhaps this is the scene motivating Antoine Adam's somewhat onesided view of Emilie's personality — "Le personnage d'Emilie semble d'une raideur mécanique... On la prend pour une Kantienne." *Histoire de la littérature française au XVIIe siècle*, I (Paris: Del Duca, 1962), 532.

[12] Cf. Marie Tastevin, *Les Héroines de Corneille* (Paris: Librairie Champion, 1924), p. 73, and Serge Doubrovsky, *Corneille et la dialectique du héros* (Paris: Gallimard, 1965 p. 190: "Emilie va jusqu' à envisager d'épouser Auguste et de satisfaire ainsi sa vengeance par une double trahison envers lui et envers Cinna: 'Je recevrais de lui la place de Livie," (I, ii. 81).

[13] The history of this natural hatred between Auguste and Cinna is explained in Act V, 1, 1440.

[14] Cf. Jacques Ehrmann, "Les Structures de l'échange dans *Cinna*," *Les Temps Modernes*, 246 (Novembre, 1966), 929-960. Ehrmann discusses the nature of the identity crisis as a confusion between the "donateur" and "objet donné" (p. 940).

[15] The absurdity of civil war, of man's allegiance to enslaving monarchy, and of the perverted conversion of treason to heroism, is forcefully conveyed by Cinna's enumeration of paradoxes (I, 3, 178-188).

[16] Emilie Faguet refuses to see the function of love in *Cinna*. In his *En lisant Corneille* (Paris: Hachette, 1914) he says: "l'amour est inutile dans cette pièce," and "Emilie ôtée la pièce subsisterait tout entière." (p. 123). Without going this far, I would agree that the love theme is subordinated to the more serious re-evaluation of the nature of political and personal power. Corneille, himself, expressed a need for the enlargement of the scope of tragedy: "La tragédie demande quelque grand intérêt d'Etat, ou quelque passion plus noble et plus mâle que l'amour, telles que sont l'ambition ou la vengeance, et veut donner à craindre des malheurs plus grands que la perte d'une maîtresse. Il est à propos d'y mêler l'amour, parce qu'il a toujours beaucoup d'agrément, et peut servir de fondement à ces intérêts, et à ces autres passions dont je parle; mais il faut qu'il se contente du second rang dans le poème, et leur laisser le premier."

Discours du poëme dramatique, Coll. Les Grands Ecrivains de la France, 12 vols. (Paris: Machette, 1862), I, 24.

[17] André Stegmann, *L'Héroisme Cornélien: Genèse et signification*, II (Paris: Armand Colin, 1968), p. 289: "la conception de l'histoire providentielle restera la seule constante vraiment immuable du théâtre cornélien. Pour cette raison toutes les tragédies sont toujours, d'une certaine manière, des tragédies 'à fin heureuse."

[18] Cf. Corneille, *Horace*, v. 844.

[19] Shakespeare played with the unnaturalness of abdicating power in *King Lear*. Lear's division of his kingdom before the play even begins is the first sign of his approaching tragic defeat.

[20] See George Poulet, *Etudes sur le temps humain* (Paris: Plon, 1949), pp. 89-103. "Il veut (le héros cornélien), et en voulant ce qu'il veut, il veut être ce qu'il est. La volonté pose l'existence." (p. 92).

[21] La Harpe, *Cours de littérature ancienne et moderne*, 3 vols. (Paris: Firmin Didot, 1851), I, 488, cited in Herbert Fogel's *The Criticism of Cornelian Tragedy* (New York, 1967), p. 42. La Harpe, agreeing with Voltaire on Cinna's hypocritical nature, saw the deception in Cinna's speech: "... le rôle de Cinna est essentiellement vicieux, en ce qu'il manque à la fois, et d'unité de caractère et de vraisemblance morale ... n'a-t-il pas fait le rôle d'un malhonnête homme quand il s'est jeté aux genoux d'Auguste pour le déterminer à garder l'empire? Et qui l'obligeait à tant d'hypocrisie ... il paraissait bien plus simple de laisser cette bassesse hypocrite à Maxime, qui n'est dans la pièce qu'un personnage entièrement sacrifié." (I, 488).

[22] Serge Doubrovsky, *Corneille et la dialectique*, p. 197.

[23] This bipartite design is rather conventional for the formal verse satire and other forms of verbal duplicity. The first part of the text argues in favor of either an irrational, ridiculous, or unexpected form of behavior which is then reversed in the second part. See Mary Claire Randolphe's brilliant essay entitled "Structural Design in the Formal Verse Satire," *Philological Quaterly* 2 (1942), 368-384.

[24] The duplicity of Cinna's platform is signalled primarily by contradiction. But the effectiveness of contradiction as a rhetorical figure is dependent upon the subtle mechanism of perception. I wonder how many readers will associate verse 617 and 1226 which reproduce the same rhyme "maître-renaître" but change the subjects from "*Rome* va renaître" to "*son vrai bonheur* commence de renaître." In this instance the period between repetitions is probably longer than that required for a first reading perception to take place.

[25] *Cinna*:

Que vous allez souiller d'une tache trop noire,	(410)
Mais la plus belle mort souille notre mémoire.	(497)
On a dix fois sur vous attenté sans effet,	(435)
On a fait contre vous dix entreprises vaines,	(490)
Enfin, s'il faut attendre un semblable revers	(439)
Ne vous exposer plus à ses fameux revers.	(495)
Il est beau de mourir maître de l'univers.	(440)
Il est beau de mourir maître de l'univers;	(496)

[26] The subtitle of the play noted in the original edition of *Cinna* was *La Clémence d'Auguste*.

[27] Cf. *Cinna*, verses 28, 171, 399, 701, 704, 735, 851, 1350, 1370, 1402, 1665, 1689, 143, 163, 290, 309, 339, 393, 716, 736, 907, 1081, 1124, 1307, 1579, 1701, 1736.

[28] See references to Brutus in verses 265, 438, 667, 829, 842, and 1169. For the immediate retrieval of this type of distribution I am grateful to M. Quemada whose Concordance, Index and Statistical data on *Cinna* were invaluable to me (Paris: Librarie Larousee, 1971) in Vol. VII of *Documents pour l'étude de la langue littéraire.*

[29] *Cinna,*

Je recevrais de lui la place de Livie
Comme un moyen plus sûr d'attenter à sa vie. (I, 2, 81-82)

[30] *Cinna,*

J'ai trop par vos avis consulté là-dessus;
Ne m'en parlez jamais, je ne consulte plus. (IV, 3, 1220-1221)

Vous m'aviez bien promis des conseils d'une femme:
Vous me tenez parole, et c'en sont là, Madame. (IV, 3, 1245-1246)

[31] See Emilie's speech (Act III, 4, 1013-1048) for her constant threats of death, especially 1045-1048:

Je descends dans la tombe où tu m'as condamnée
Où la gloire me suit qui t'étoit destinée:
Je meurs en détruisant un pouvoir absolu;
Mais je vivrois à toi, si tu l'avois voulu."

[32] Cf. Doubrovsky, *Corneille et la dialectique* p. 212: "... l'effort de l'homme pour se récupérer sur et contre sa nature. Le héros n'est jamais ce qu'il veut; il ne le devient que dans la mesure où *il se fait* au terme d'un dur, long et déchirant combat contre autrui et contre soi-même."

[33] In *Le Sentiment de l'amour dans l'oeuvre de Pierre Corneille* (Paris: Gallimard, 1948), Octave Nadal sensed the importance of the hidden structure of reversal, but he revealed his awareness only indirectly through his choice of words: "Il (le pardon) traduira chez Auguste, *un changement radical,* en profondeur, dans sa manière de voir et de comprendre les choses, ... *un renversement* total chez Auguste de la façon de comprendre la puissance" (p. 19).

[34] Cf. Serge Doubrovsky, *Corneille et la dialectique,* p. 214, and Robert J. Nelson, *Corneille: His Heroes and Their Worlds* (Philadelphia: University of Pennsylvania Press, 1963), p. 98, who both agree with this observation.

[35] Marie-Odile Sweetser, *Les Conceptions dramatique de Corneille d'après ses écrits théoriques* (Paris, Genève: Droz, 1962), p. 77: "Lancaster souligne que l'auteur fait preuve d'originalité en donnant un dénouement heureux à une tragédie et en faisant de ses héros des êtres dignes d'admiration plutôt que de crainte et de pitié. Par là il est évident que Corneille ne s'est soumis que très superficiellement aux canons aristotéliciens."

CHAPTER 9

SIGNS OF THE HIDDEN: SEMIOTIC STUDY OF RACINE'S *BAJAZET*

> Ils ont beau se cacher. L'amour le plus discret
> Laisse par quelque marque échapper son secret.
> (III, viii, 1119-1120)

Bajazet is the poetic illustration of a Cartesian quest for certainty. In this philosophical theatre the players pose the same questions raised in the *Discours*: Can one know for sure? What is proof of knowledge? By what method is truth distinguished from illusion? Truth is a function of vision, an essence hidden deeply 'within' but discernible from 'without' by seers endowed with phenomenological power. Like Descartes who systematically doubted all knowledge −

Ainsi à cause que nos sens nous *trompent* quelquefois, je voulus supposer qu'il n'y avait aucune chose qui fût telle qu'ils nous la font imaginer ... je me résolus de *feindre* que toutes les choses qui m'étaient entrées en l'esprit m'étaient non plus vraies que *les illusions* dans mes *songes*.[1]

− the characters caught up in *Bajazet*'s network of conspiracies, undercover surveillance, and unreliable communication systems crave the truth, demanding evidence of fact before the senses. But unlike Descartes who put faith in the power of reason, they rely on an intuitive reading of verbal and non-verbal signs to arrive at the essence of truth. The atmosphere of distrust and resultant uncertainty in *Bajazet* stems mainly from the indirect nature in which information is necessarily transmitted in the seraglio. Owing to the formal exigencies of the unity of place, the respect for the awesome *bienséances*, and staging limitations, actions are rarely visible either to the spectators or to the characters. Thus Racine has recourse to intermediaries and "récits" in order to report accounts of actions that take place off stage. In *Bajazet* the *récit* is more than just the conventional indirect discourse. Unreliable commentary is the structural essence motivating a tragic and poetic quest for truth.

Doubt develops naturally and immediately in *Bajazet*. As the
play opens, the spectator realizes that a new and different order has
been established.[2] The very first dialogue between Acomat and
Osmin represents a vital and urgent appeal for reliable information
from the outside world, knowledge which Acomat threatens could
change the destiny of the entire Ottoman Empire.[3] Suspicion is
aroused by the strangeness of the play's exotic setting in Byzance
or Constantinople, a referent endowed with seductive and poetic
associations. Mysterious echoes are heard from the far-off Babylonian
battlefield, dark silence lurks about the walls of an enclosed palace
surrounded by waters; ghostly mutes within its walls carry secret
messages to shadow dwellers; deeply hidden treasures of delight are
imagined within the inner chambers of the Sultan's private and once
prohibited harem.[4] He who ventures forth into this series of inner
circles, like the players and spectators who reach for the core of
forbidden pleasure, experiences an infernal voyage[5] guided from
without by the devil Amurat and from within by his henchman, the
mutes, the slaves, and the odious Orcan. Acomat, whose name
significantly resembles that of Amurat, is the real, hidden power
inside the Inferno, in contrast both to Amurat, who strikes from
afar, and to Roxane, whose power is illusory, temporary, and
dependent ultimately upon the will of her master, Amurat. Acomat's
obsession for total power[6] provokes the revolutionary opening of
the closed palace, an accessibility of the forbidden, and a dramatic
change in the established order of things.[7]

   Characters caught up in this extraordinary place having the dual
properties of both prison and paradise are all engaged in a quest –
Acomat for power, Bajazet for freedom, Atalide for love, and
Roxane for all of these. The obscure path of this quest is marked by
silent, secret communications between the outside and inside sources
of threatening power – Babylon and Byzantium, Amurat and
Acomat. Coded[8] communications are transmitted with the speed of
lightning through the channels of false tales, rumors, gossip, and
espionage by disguised conspirators acting in a desperate fear of distant oppression. The messages of this communication system have
various sign systems – some gestural, some verbal, some physical –
and two major operative principles: truth and illusion, *gages certains*
and *gages trompeurs*. The receiver must first distinguish truth from
illusion by sheer perception, and then decode the message according
to the accepted cultural significance of that particular sign. Thus a
peculiar ethos develops in *Bajazet* in which virtue lies not in the
good but in the power of vision, in the ability to interpret signs of

the hidden. Since Acomat is clearly the visionary[9] and Amurat the all-powerful and all-knowing, the two most vilainous creatures of illusion, Acomat, through sheer trickery, and Amurat, by virtue of his oppressive presence in absence, acquire extraordinary and ironic potentials as symbols of goodness. This perversion of the Judeo-Christian ethos sets the tragic tone of the play.

The only reliable channel of communication between the two powers of the inner and outer worlds is represented by Osmin whose critical eye witness accounts significantly begin and end the play.[10] By nature of the generally appreciative historical, cultural, and literary associations attached to the concepts of 'harem' and 'palace,' the inner world of the Seraglio has the significance of an idyllic enclosure, the crux of an unobtainable happiness which is virtually destroyed by Acomat at its unprecedented opening before the play begins. 'Harem' has the positive connotations of privacy, mystery, seduction, beauty, and sensual pleasures for the privileged. But the *sérail* in Racine's play has its own mythology fraught with the negative social connotations of imprisonment, slavery, interdiction, and the pains of death. At its opening an illusory sense of freedom is granted which marks the destruction of all save Acomat:

> Elle-même a choisi cet endroit écarté
> Où nos coeurs à nos yeux parlent en liberté.
> (207-208)

The 'palace' is traditionally the place of ultimate beauty, vastness, and luxury reserved for the nobles. But for a man as proud as Acomat[11] who knows the ins and outs of this curious palace full of lowly slaves — "esclaves obscurs, nourris loin de la guerre, à l'ombre de ses murs" (1415-1416) — the seraglio is the womb of the palace's immoral leisure, "une molle oisiveté" (106) he calls it, an enclave of shadiness in which conspiracy and deception now reign supreme in a new order of illusion.

Shadows, darkness, blackness, and obscurity belong to the palace's sign system of evil transmitted through the metaphoric code of light absence. Shadow, the metonym of the hidden, is the cause of an evil effect of darkness throughout the palace:

> Par un chemin obscur une esclave me guide (209)

The seraglio, or the most hidden, is thus the symbol of Evil. Orcan, the feared executioner and harbinger of death, is born in darkest

Africa, and his description suggests the fires and blackness associated with Hell:

> Orcan ...
> Né sous le ciel *brûlant* des plus *noirs* Africains (1105)

The very sight of Orcan inspires shivering thoughts of death:

> Ah! sais-tu mes frayeurs? Sais-tu que *dans ses lieux*
> J'ai vu du *fier Orcan le visage odieux*?
> En ce moment *fatal*, que je crains sa venue! (1123-1126)

Orcan is the microcosm of this infernal palace seething with the passions (*feux, flammes*) of illicit love couched in the shadows of dark secrets. Acomat is hidden by Amurat's power from the much sought after political limelight:

> Un Visir aux sultans *fait toujours quelque ombrage* (185)

Roxane, the Sultan's favorite and supreme untouchable, is hidden from the truth by virtue of seclusion and by Atalide's veiled interception. This epistemological conflict is encoded in the shadow metaphor:

> Je veux que devant moi sa bouche et son visage
> Me *découvrent* son coeur, sans me *laisser d'ombrage* (329-330)

The palace, container of the inner Seraglio, is the metonymic symbol of all that is evil in illusion. Roxane, a slave herself, describes the motley inhabitants of the palace with supercilious disrespect and ironic arrogance:

> Cette foule de chefs, d'esclaves, de muets,
> Peuple que dans ses murs renferme ce palais (435-436)

The palace is a microcosm of Man's imprisonment (*renferme*) in the tragic universe (*cette foule, peuple*), where leaders and followers (*chefs, esclaves*) coexist with those fortunate enough to give orders (*chefs*) and those destined to silence in the receipt and obedience of orders (*esclaves*), very much like the lot of the palace mutes who are the hyperbolic and symbolic manifestations of slavery's imposed passivity and virtual insignificance.[12] The mutes, like Orcan, are messengers of Death. Irony lurks in the illusion of freedom for the privileged, in the curious and oxymoric juxtaposition of the depreciative "foule" with the appreciative "chef," an incompatible association which poetically destroys any illusion of grandeur. The real world for the old soldier, Acomat, is not the palace of shadows but the battlefield, the place of reckoning where power is won by hand-to-hand combat and where fear of false testimony is inoperative.

The difference in *Bajazet* between the terms *palais* and *sérail* is not what critics conjecture to be insignificant. There is a significant seme of interiorization and closedness attached to the term "sérail" and not necessarily to "palais." When Roxane says:

Que le Serrail soit désormais fermé (571)

she is commanding a return to the previous order of seclusion, of prohibition of vision, an aspect of the a cultural mores whose value is rendered explicit in the following verse:

Et que tout rentre ici dans l'ordre accoutumé. (572)

When Atalide relates what Roxane has commanded, she employs the term "palais" synonymically, yes, but more importantly metonymically to mean the inner chambers of the harem:

Mais laissez-nous. Roxane, à sa perte animée,
Veut que de ce palais la porte soit fermée. (661-662)

The figurative closing of the palace doors, a literal absurdity, is clearly a metaphoric expression for the re-establishment of an atmosphere of constraint attached most naturally to the concept of harem and seraglio but not to palace.

Roxane's pronouncement is also in a larger sense a call for the return to a former master-slave relationship in which 'entrance' or freedom is bestowed only upon the receipt of and obedience to orders. Zaire, commenting upon Roxane's famous decree, interprets it as a figurative expression signifying the restriction of sight and the reinstatement of a feudal system:[13]

Il ne peut plus la voir sans qu'elle le commande. (1129)

Thus Acomat's devious scheme to spark in Roxane an illicit desire not only for the planned love but for marriage – the outrageous

union of a slave and a sultan – and his clever arrangement of the
favorite's accessibility through the interception of Acomat's intended,
Atalide, constitute not only a dangerous breach of social mores but
the compromising transgression of a sacred taboo of open communication. But because of an even greater system of secrecy in the
strength of Bajazet's silent and sacred love for Atalide, the defeat
of Acomat's plan is ironically prepared from the very beginning. The
violation of the rigorous laws of seclusion and closedness[14] in the
Sultan's private palace signify at once a courageous but futile
attempt at a tragic slave rebellion begun, ironically, by a man of
rank and former power. Roxane's main objective is to transcend
her slavery by marriage with a Sultan, be it Amurat who has already
promised this unusual but not unprecedented union, or Bajazet, her
preferred but secretly committed loved one. For clearly everyone
but the cruel Amurat is a slave in *Bajazet* – even Bajazet, the Sultan's
brother calls himself "un esclave":

> Je chéris, j'acceptai, sans tarder davantage,
> L'heureuse occasion de sortir d'esclavage (1505-1506)

The master, Amurat, is feared by all[15] and particularly detested by
Acomat, who has a secret faith in free will and in the power of
individual determination by physical prowess. He cleverly protects
his blasphemous optimism by contradiction:

> Ce combat doit, dit-on, fixer nos destinées,
> Et même, si d'Osmin je compte les journées,
> Le ciel en a déjà réglé l'événement. (221-223)

To continue the undercurrent of irony, at the end of this most
tragic of tragedies[16] the only survivor and benefactor of the grandiose
plot is the inner world's prime mover, Acomat, who flees the threat
of onrushing death only to take up his life again in another country.
There he is to perform, at last, his necessary and vital function.[17]
Acomat's aim, even when he suspects defeat, is to create a sign of
his existence by his deeds, a reputed name, a trace, a lasting identity
in this world of illusion:

> Par une belle chute il faut me *signaler*,
> Et *laisser un débris* du moins après ma fuite (1401-1402)

One of the subtle sources of irony in *Bajazet*, which also confirms

the play's hidden political and social message, is the historical intertext regarding the unusual marriage of a sultan named Suliman with a
slave, curiously named Roxelane, in defiance of a tradition established by a sultan named none other than Bajazet. By an over-
whelming number of similarities both of incidents and names,
Bajazet becomes the parody or rewriting of history.[18] Both Roxane,
in order to shake off subjugation, and Acomat, in accordance with
his belief in self-determination, invoke the historical argument of
Suliman's cultural bravery in order to persuade Bajazet to marry
Roxane.[19] Without ever saying whom he actually loves, Bajazet
temporarily wheedles his way out of a commitment to Roxane. In a
long-winded comparative argument distinguishing Suliman's great
power from Bajazet's meager dependence on the people's wishes
(v. 471-497), Bajazet demonstrates the primary need for a good
public image. Later he can perform feats of a revolutionary order.
The essence of his argument is to delay and thereby gain the force
of curative time:

> Maître de leur suffrage,
> Peut-être avec le temps j'oserai davantage. (493-494)

Bajazet's diverse ploys to hide the truth run the linguistic gamut
from intellectual trickery to actual silence:

> Madame, ignorez-vous que l'orgueil de l'Empire. ...
> Que ne m'épargnez-vous la douleur de le dire? (453-454)

He may openly evade direct questions:

> Acomat
> Mais vous aimez Roxane.
>
> Bajazet
> Acomat, c'est assez. (606-607)

Bajazet is a man of integrity who prefers legitimacy to deception
but who, by love's weakening powers, has been put in the uncomfortable position of forced pretence. Acomat, the master deceiver,
admires Bajazet's unique faith in the power of truth:

> O courage inflexible! O trop constante foi,
> Que même en périssant j'admire malgré moi! (655-656)

More forceful than faith is Bajazet's intrinsic inability to play the subtle games of deception. Atalide, who knows him longest, can most accurately and truthfully describe his hidden personality trait:

> Car enfin Bajazet ne sait point se cacher (391)

In *Bajazet* there is a constant alternation between speech and silence, between Roxane's frenetic pleas for verbal confirmation of unreliable messages and Bajazet's hesitation to disclose the reality of his feelings. Bajazet's faltering speech provides the opportunity for Roxane to display her whiplike discourse:

> Bajazet
> Je vous dois tout mon sang: ma vie est votre bien;
> Mais enfin voulez-vous. ...
>
> Roxane
> Non, je ne veux plus rien. (519-522)

She holds the threat of immediate death over him. His only escape is speech:

> J'ai l'ordre d'Amurat, et je puis t'y soustraire.
> Mais tu n'as qu'*un moment: parle*. (1541-1542)

In a perfect correspondence between signifier and signified, the rapidity and force of Roxane's speech imitates the content of her recurring urgent ultimata: Her running pace is breakneck; her time is now or never:

> Commencez *maintenant*. C'est à vous de *courir*
> *Dans le* champ glorieux que j'ai su vous ouvrir. (439-440)
>
> N'en doute point, j'y *cours*, et dès ce moment même. (537)
>
> Pour la dernière fois, je le vais consulter (259)
>
> Pour *la dernière fois*, veux-tu vivre et règner? (1540)

Roxane lives passionately in the most immediate present. At the very first sight of Bajazet she displays the classic signs of love: involuntary speech and confession of the sacred:

> Roxane vit le prince. Elle ne put lui taire
> L'ordre dont elle seule étoit dépositaire. (153-154)

Her love is instantaneous like that described as "Eros-événement" by Barthes,[20] or the conventional *coup de foudre*, whose immediacy is translated linguistically by the subtle use of verbal repetition and the unexpected appearance of the simple past tense:

> Il vit que son salut
> Dépendoit de lui plaire, et bientôt il lui plut. (155-156)

But a higher order of love is signalled in *Bajazet* by a sacred silence, like "Eros-sororal" or the longterm childhood romance between Bajazet and Atalide, a love of strength which needs no tests of faith:

> Quoi? cet amour si tendre, et né dans notre enfance
> Dont les feux avec nous ont crû dans *le silence* (713-714)

A system of signs different from the *coup de foudre* is observable linguistically in a verse describing the permanent love between Bajazet and Atalide:

> Nous avons su toujours nous aimer et nous taire. (366)

In this case temporal duration, slowness, maturation, and resultant depth loom to the foreground. The repetitive use of the longer form "nous" rather than "on," the more delayed *passé composé* in contrast to the immediate simple past, and the adverb "toujours" with double, long nasalized vowels that slow down the rhythm of the verse are some of the phonetic and morphological components supporting the message of a longstanding, deep love. The fatal blow is struck, however, when Love's enemy, jealousy, destroys the sacred silence and inspires in Atalide a need to test the faith of her lover's speech.[21]

Unlike signs which, according to Saussure, are arbitrary, unmotivated, and subject to interpretation within the system of cultural values in which the sign appears, literary symbols are not wholly arbitrary. A symbol is a relatively stable association of contiguity or resemblance between two elements on the same level, between two signifiers or between two signifieds.[22] The important determinant in symbolization is a certain sense of regularity in the association between the signifiers or signified, for although all words are signs, not every sign is a symbol. One symbol may refer to two different concepts in the very same text. Silence, represented by the mutes who accompany Orcan in his mission of death, is the symbol of

evil by association with death and the symbol of the good by metonymic association with Bajazet's sacred love for Atalide. Bajazet
explicitly but falsely ascribes his unwillingness to confess this love as
verbal insufficiency. Not directly but by the power of question's
suggestion, he intimates the frustration of his reticence:

> Roxane
> Achève, parle.
>
> Bajazet
> O ciel! que ne puis-je parler? (559-560)

Despite her frequent appeals for more speech, Roxane actually
disdains verbal discourse:

> Les moments sont trop chers pour les perdre en paroles. (1470)

She is herself a woman of few words. In fact it is her short, pointed,
and highly dramatic discourse which makes her a figure of such
exceptional strength and appeal in French classical theatre. Barthes
calls her "un mâle prostitué," virile, emasculating.[23] Her famous
lines are the short ones: "Sortez," "Retirez-vous," "Qu'on la
retienne," etc.[24] Her entering words as she confronts Bajazet face to
face for the first time resound with the drama of a death knell:

> Prince, l'heure fatale est enfin arrivée (421)

She possesses a rare kind of sadistic humor and sarcasm that makes
skin crawl. When Atalide promises Roxane the freedom of her own
death, Roxane retorts inhumanly by suggesting the joyous sight of a
lover's murdered body:

> Je ne mérite pas un si grand sacrifice:
> Je me connois, Madame, et je me fais justice.
> Loin de vous séparer, je prétends aujourd'hui
> Par *des noeuds éternels* vous unir avec lui.
> Vous *jouirez* bientôt de son aimable *vue*. (1621-1625)

Roxane knows the sign value of words and uses them with effective
discretion to reveal and reinforce the intensity of her inner emotions,
sealed messages of the heart. Act II, Scene i, Roxane's first direct
contact with Bajazet, is an outstanding example of the expressive
potentials of the pronouns *tu* and *vous* which Roxane alternates to

correspond with the fluctuation of her highly changeable emotional states. The diverse cultural sign values of these pronouns in French are well known and depend upon their immediate context for interpretation.[25] For example, at the very beginning of the scene, Roxane uses the form "vous" as a sign of politeness which she supports by such appreciative forms as the twice repeated "Seigneur," and the subtle, somewhat obsequious reference to her subserviance in the verb "servir." But at the first signs of Bajazet's hesitation, she switches her tone from polite determination to sarcastic outrage. The pronoun "vous," now in a context of sarcasm, carries the additional value of distanciation, conveying coldness, and potential anger:

> Je vous entends, Seigneur: je vois mon imprudence;
> Je vois que rien n'échappe à votre prévoyance. (497-498)

Anger hidden under the irony of sarcasm is rendered manifest in the second half of her speech by the sudden switch to direct threat in the form of a series of rhetorical questions:

> Mais avez-vous prévu, si vous ne m'épousez,
> Les périls plus certains où vous vous exposez?
> Songez-vous ...
> Songez-vous ...
> Songez-vous, en un mot, que vous ne seriez plus? (503-512)

When Bajazet counters her threats with displays of gratitude which are hidden signs of indifference (the same kind of indifference achieved by his formality in the later "discours glacé"), Roxane's outrage is uncontrollable, and she employs the form "tu," a manifest sign of her contempt. Attached to the contemptuousness implicit in the form "tu" is a subtle nuance of social class value. (Well-known is the social commentary hidden in the famous "Va-t'en" addressed to Jean Valjean.) That Roxane, the slave, can suggest social class superiority to none other than the Sultan's brother is one of the more latent verbal ironies achieved by the use of the form "tu." But coming once more to her senses, and eager to persuade her lover, Roxane sweetens the bitterness of her outraged discourse, this time, interestingly enough, by switching to "vous" and its accompanying value of respect. Its sign value of distanciation is now inoperative:

Bajazet, écoutez: je sens que je vous aime.
Vous vous perdez. Gardez de me laisser sortir. (538-539)

Continuing to plead for Bajazet's love, linguistically she moves closer and closer to her lover by switching to the familiar and endearing "tu":

Dans son coeur? Ah! crois-tu, quand il le voudroit bien,
Que si je perds l'espoir de régner dans le tien,
D'une si douce erreur si longtemps possédée,
Je puisse désormais souffrir une autre idée,
Ni que je vive enfin, si je ne vis pour toi? (547-551)

The exclamation "Ah!," a polyvalent verbal sign, actually prepares the slight change in tone from persuasion to entreaty. The divergent sign values of the frequently occurring exclamation "Ah!," which opens up choices for multiple interpretation, is another example of the ironic potential of *Bajazet*, and by irony, here, I refer to multiplicity of meaning or senses.[26]

Roxane's sweet endearment is shortlived. As soon as Bajazet shows signs of verbal insufficiency and the concomitant fears of truth – "O ciel! que ne puis-je parler?" – Roxane displays her outrage by the sudden use of the formal "vous":

Quoi donc? Que dites-vous? et que viens-je d'entendre?
Vous avez des secrets que je ne puisse apprendre!
(561-562)

When Bajazet finalizes his preference for death over the illegitimate usurpation of the throne, Roxane's fury and impatient rage are transmitted through a multitude of linguistic signs: a proliferation of exclamative expressions ("Ah! Hola! c'en est trop enfin"), a final switch to the form "tu" with its affective and here ironic connotations of inexorable detestation ("tu ne seras satisfait"), and a terse command signifying death – "Qu'on vienne."

In this theater of deception, Bajazet is a poor player suffering from the virtue of sincerity. Finally agreeing with reluctance to please Atalide and partake in the plot to deceive Roxane, Bajazet naively seeks linguistic advice for the interpretation of his own role:

Hé bien! Mais quels discours faut-il que je lui tienne?
(786)

Acomat needs no advice about duplicity. Roxane's initial, continued, and fatal error is to have placed unusual confidence in Acomat's multipurpose and deceitful language:

> La Sultane d'ailleurs se fie à mes discours. (1423)

Acomat resorts to non-verbal signs like looks and tones in order to discern truth from illusion. Nevertheless he artificially insists on the importance of verbal declaration:

> Acomat
> Déclarez-vous, Madame; et sans plus différer. ...
>
> Roxane
> Oui, vous serez content: je vais me déclarer.
>
> Acomat
> Madame, quel regard, et quelle voix sévère,
> Malgré votre discours, m'assure du contraire? (1339-1342)

Bajazet's speech is too transparent and Roxane's mind too cunning for her not to discern from the very beginning of the play the secret truth within the cloaks of an unconvincing language disguise. When Bajazet offers his best but still inadequate intellectual argument against marriage, Roxane feigns belief, attacks his innocence as blindness by falsely flattering his "prévoyance," and prepares his ultimate annihilation – "Rentre dans le néant dont je t'ai fait sortir" (524). Roxane's duplicity is actualized by the force of sarcasm and by a pretense of faith in discourse:

> Je vous entends, Seigneur: je vois mon imprudence;
> Je vois que rien n'échappe à votre *prévoyance*.
> Vous avez pressenti jusqu'au-moindre danger
> Où mon amour trop prompt vous alloit engager.
> Pour vous, pour votre honneur, vous en craignez les suites,
> Et *je le crois, Seigneur, puisque vous me le dites.* (497-502)

The real proof of her sarcasm and suspicion appears in the involuntary, almost unconscious emission of embittered thought encoded in the sudden and unexpected appearance of the *style indirect libre*. The former obsequious *Seigneur* is now transformed by opposition into the more sincere "ingrat":

> L'ingrat est-il touché de mes empressements?
> L'amour même entre-t-il dans ses raisonnements? (527-528)

The polyvalent adjective "même" reveals Roxane's questions to be rhetorical. Despite many desperate attempts to arrive at the truth through diverse languages of the mouth, eyes, and hand, signs of the face called "discours du visage" and the beautiful oxymoron "des regards éloquents" (887), Roxane really knows, but does not want to know, the truth about Bajazet.[27] Her insight, the clarity of her vision, and the acuteness of her sensitivity are the sources of her agony. Roxane actually yearns for a return to the hidden. At the sight of Atalide's fainted body, a blatant sign of the lovers' involvement, Roxane encodes this wish for figurative blindness in the metaphoric language of the eyes:

Sur tout ce que j'ai *vu fermons plutôt les yeux* (1236)

She literalizes her wish at the very end of the soliloquy, reinforcing its significance by placing it in the emphatic final position:

Je veux tout ignorer. (1250)

Roxane has been blinded voluntarily by her own love, "*mon amour aveugle*" (1071), to the truth which she knows but cannot accept about Bajazet. He does not and will not love her. Even before the convincing presentation of evidence, before Atalide's tears, before her fainting spell, before the receipt of Bajazet's letter, Roxane knew everything, and she revealed her knowledge to Atalide in a pregnant retort which achieves the force of an ironic preparation:

Je conçois vos raisons mieux que vous ne pensez. (1060)

Despite this intuitive knowledge, Roxane systematically doubts its veracity, a voluntary Cartesian skepticism which is understandable given the suspicious atmosphere of conspiracy, secrecy, and silence within the palace. Her skepticism is manifested linguistically by a proliferation of questions (v. 1065-1096). Roxane's willful ignorance is the greatest of all ironies in a play written as a quest for certainty.

Racine is an excellent 'rhetorician,' and by that I mean he knows how to persuade by the most artful and extravagant schemes of dramatic irony. To convey the philosophical message about the unreliability of phenomenological knowledge, Racine involves his readers and spectators directly, forcing them to experience the characters' frustrations in their quest for truth. This spectator involvement results structurally from a behind-the-scenes action, a reconciliation between Roxane and Bajazet that has taken place somewhere between the end of Act II and the beginning of Act III. The truth of what was actually said between Roxane and Bajazet is not known either to the spectators or to the characters. It takes two witnesses to report the incident's significance, both of whom are either misleading or unreliable: first Zaire[28] and then the loathsome trickster Acomat, who never really lies blatantly but subtly by the false and incriminating interpretation of signs in what might be called a language of the eyes:

> J'ai longtemps immobile observé leur maintien.
> Enfin *avec des yeux qui découvroient son âme,*
> *L'une a tendu la main* pour gage de sa flamme;
> L'autre, avec des *regards éloquents*, pleins d'amour,
> L'a de ses feux, Madame, assurée à son tour. (884-887)

Ironically, words were never actually exchanged during the reconciliation; only gestural and facial signs that we will see later in Bajazet's reliable testimony are subject to diverse interpretations. Even the thought of uttering a deceptive discourse is repugnant to Bajazet:

> Moi, j'aimerois Roxane, ou je vivrois pour elle,
> Madame! Ah! croyez-vous que loin de le penser,
> *Ma bouche seulement eût pu* le prononcer? (978-980)

When he explains the error of sign interpretation to Roxane, he employs the significant subjunctival conjunction "soit ... soit" which translates the element of cultural diversity inherent to language interpretation:

> Et soit qu'elle ait d'abord expliqué mon retour
> Comme un gage certain qui marquoit mon amour,
> Soit que le temps trop cher la pressât de se rendre,
> A peine ai-je parlé, que sans presque m'entendre
> Ses pleurs précipités ont coupé mes discours.
> ...
> Moi-même, rougissant de sa crédulité
> Et d'un amour si tendre et si peu mérité,
> Dans ma confusion, que Roxane, Madame,
> Attribuoit encore à l'excès de ma flamme (983-994)

The value and significance of signs like physical presence,[29] blushing, and crying, vary within different systems. Blushing, for example, is normally associated with embarrassment, but by metonymic transference of two semantic fields in which the color red is ascribed to the heat of passion, the two emotions, embarrassment and love, are superimposed by a common denominator and potentially inter-related. Thus the cause of blushing, i.e. embarrassment, may be due to inhibitions about love. In his explanation of the reconciliation, Bajazet does not mention the handshake, falsely interpreted by Acomat as a sure sign of love, probably because the handshake signified at the time of occurrence nothing more than the conven-tional greeting of two people. Bajazet's omission of the detail is proof of its cultural value as automatic and traditional and of little substantive significance in the love system.

Unable to put faith in verbal discourse, the characters in *Bajazet* develop various other sign languages to communicate knowledge. Unfortunately these sign systems are not universally coded and, as we saw earlier, signs which are subject to diverse interpretations are dependent upon the immediate context for reliable decoding. Never before was the distinction between spoken and written word so effectively illustrated as in *Bajazet* where direct eye witness is deman-ded, where form and expression, *la bouche et les yeux*, are invoked to verify the content of messages sent through unreliable com-munication systems:

> Ces mots ne me suffisent pas.
> Que sa bouche, ses yeux, tout l'assure qu'il l'aime. (1157-1158)

When direct spoken communication is rendered impossible by distance, in the case of Amurat, or by prohibition, in the case of Atalide and Bajazet, then the written word or letter is adopted as a relatively reliable source of truth. Bajazet's letter to Atalide is an avowed refusal to feign love for Roxane and an explicit declaration of eternal love. By this categoric tone and clearly defined language, there is no possibility of misinterpretation:

> Puisque jamais je n'aimerai que vous. (1144)

When Amurat's letter is sent from afar, the legitimacy of its contents is checked by confirmation of scriptural signs. The seal and the handwriting, or "la main," are metonyms of orthography referred to also as "la lettre":

> Roxane
> Voyez: lisez vous-même.

Vous connoissez, Madame, et la lettre et le sein.
Atalide
Du cruel Amurat je reconnois *la main*. (1182-1184)

There is a similar confirmation by Zatime of the scriptural signs in Bajazet's letter. The second reading of the written communication is by an unintended receiver:

Du prince votre amant j'ai reconnu *la lettre* (1261)

Convinced by the qualities of permanance and sincerity attributed to the sacred written word, Roxane's faith in the spoken word dwindles progressively:

Je ne vous dis plus rien. Cette lettre sincère
D'un malheureux amour contient tout le mystère (1489-1490)

But the spoken word nevertheless and necessarily predominates a theatrical production. What differentiates *Bajazet* from other plays is the disdain of indirect discourse, the specific insistence on the actual presence of the speakers, the obsession, in short, with perception. The verb *voir* recurs so frequently in *Bajazet* that a new lexicon must be developed to determine its multiple meanings. *To see* is not only 'to perceive', in the ordinary sense, but 'to see beyond the obvious,' 'to read signs of the unspoken':

Vois-tu dans ses discours qu'ils s'entendent tous deux? (1252)

To see is 'to conceive,' as of an idea:

Roxane ... ne put voir sans amour ce héros trop aimable (369)

To see is 'to understand,' as in "je vois tes desseins" (52.9). Sight implies the immediate presence of the object observed ("Non, vous ne verrez point cette fête cruelle," 709). *To see* is to remove the darkness of the absent or hidden:

Souffrez que Bajazet voie enfin la lumière. (237)

Thus *to see* is 'to know' in the philosophical sense.[30] Frequent references to the verbs *sembler, croire,* and *paraître* form a paradigm of the elusive, linguistic signs of external appearances which mask the internal essence of truth.

To see is also 'to love.' The semantic correlation of *voir* and *aimer* is confirmed by a long literary and philosophical history dating back to Plato. Subsequently, the relationship of sight to love is concretized in the medieval literature as the 'dard' which passes through the lover's eye. Cupid's victim, enslaved forever by the beauty of his loved one, revels in the peace of idyllic contemplation.[31] Thus the logical association of Love, the sight of Beauty and Truth, had been perceived and poeticized long before Keats immortalized them:

> Beauty is truth, truth beauty. (*Ode on a Grecian Urn*)

Racine, who has written a tragic play about the beauty of truth and the pervading ugliness of duplicity, evokes the motif of the eyes in order to 'read,' as it were, "le discours du coeur." Communication in *Bajazet* is depicted metaphorically as the reading of signs where the eyes of the reader assume the vital function of the lens, and the face of the observed is the book on which signs are written:

> Dans le secret des coeurs, Osmin, n'as-tu rien lu?
> Amurat jouit-il d'un pouvoir absolu? (31-32)
>
> Mon malheur n'est-il pas écrit sur son visage? (1222)

The eyes are the mirror of the heart,[32] the source of Love's seduction,[33] the prime receiver of communicated knowledge, and the tester of its certainty. Thus characters in *Bajazet* make a point of speaking 'to one's eyes,' a thought which Racine renders poetic by an extraordinary use of double personification:

> Et comme enfin Roxane *à mes yeux s'est montrée*
> ...
> Elle-même a choisi cet endroit écarté,
> Où *nos coeurs à nos yeux parlent* en liberté. (202-208)

Moreover, punishment in *Bajazet* comes in the form of an interdiction of sight. When jealousy clouds Atalide's vision, she retaliates in kind:

> Il ne me verra plus. (939)

Eyes are unquestionably the Good, the light source for truth, the enemy of dark shadows. Racine plays antithetically with the enlightenment of truth and the darkness of ignorance through the eye motif and its associated properties:

Je plaignis Bajazet; je lui vantai ses charmes,
Qui par un soin jaloux dans l'ombre retenus,
Si voisins de *ses yeux*, leur étoient inconnus. (138-140)

But like Descartes who feared the illusion of dreams, Roxane too suspects hallucinations and perceptual distortion:

De quel étonnement, ô ciel! suis-je frappée!
Est-ce un songe? et mes yeux ne m'ont-ils point trompée?
(1033-1034)

Eyes must be trained by experience to distinguish true from false signs. Signs in *Bajazet* are called *gages, marques*, and *témoins*. Some signs of love are quite unusual for they are governed by the ethos of a foreign culture, not only exotic Byzantium but seventeenth-century France. Other signs of love are quite conventional. Willingness to marry before proof of fertility and capacity to fulfill primogenitural demands are sacrificial signs of such magnitude that Roxane is easily convinced of Sultan Amurat's real devotion. He is willing to marry a slave "avant qu'elle eût un fils" (102). Show of political favor is for Roxane another sure sign of true love. Guided by the narrow confines of her ambitions for social class, Roxane cannot understand why Bajazet could possibly prefer Atalide who offers him no throne (1083-1084). Certain words which Roxane uses are signs of the metaphoric love code which is a literary convention represented most emphatically by Scudéry's *Carte de Tendre*. Abstractions like "trouble" and "ardeur," which are conventionally associated with love in seventeenth-century French literature, occur in *Bajazet*. Reciprocity and the transferral of power are indications of a deeply committed romance. Roxane, for example, is Bajazet's master of life and death, his *arbitre souveraine*, a power bestowed upon his slave by Amurat. Racine suggests reciprocity more subtly by attributing the same epithets to two different people:

Amurat est *content* (33)

l'heureux Amurat (59)

l'heureuse Roxane (101)

Some signs of love in Bajazet are more difficult to read because of their inherent polyvalence. Returned presence, like Bajazet's presence before Roxane during the reconciliation, the handshake, and the adjective "chagrin" require interpretation. The ironic potential of these polyvalent signs is due not only to their different meanings in different systems, but to their variable denotations and concomitant connotative changes. For example, the term "chagrin," normally associated with love by the metaphor "chagrins d'amour," is denotatively a rather vague emotional discontentment (*tristesse, mélancolie*) which Atalide describes as "des soins." Racine uses the associative powers of words for ironic purpose. Thus when Roxane asks Atalide to explain Bajazet's "chagrin" at the time of his "discours glacés," she indicates by her choice of words that she clearly knows more about the love between Atalide and Bajazet than her surface language tells. In the significant presence of Atalide Bajazet uses conventional signs of emotional distanciation like formality, politeness, and a profusion of abstractions (*devoir, complaisance, reconnaissance, bienfaits,* and *bontés*) to signify a real lack of love to Roxane, the immediate receiver of the communication.

> Répondez-moi, comment pouvez-vous expliquer
> *Ce chagrin* qu'en sortant il m'a fait remarquer? (1047-1048)

Atalide responds to Roxane's question by referring only to the denotation of "chagrin":

> Bajazet s'inquiète, et qu'il laisse échapper
> Quelque *marque des soins* qui doivent l'occuper?

Moreover, Atalide chooses to refer only to the literal significance of Bajazet's discourse, not to its sign value. Whereas "bontés" for Roxane is an insult because of its formality, Atalide tries to show that "bontés" means just what the signifieds denote – a positive, general statement of appreciation:

> Madame, *ce chagrin* n'a point frappé ma vue.
> Il m'a de *vos bontés* longtemps entretenue. (1049-1050)

But by employing the term "chagrin" and its association with love, Roxane was already encoding the answer in the form of her question. This type of subtle play with words involving code intersection has the same ironic force of preparative discourse which can only be perceived retroactively. For example, when in Act IV Zatime hints at the *coup de théâtre* and unexpected tragic reversal that will occur at the end of the play, Zatime's ironic preparation can only be appreciated after Roxane's murder by the all-powerful Amurat:

Et qui sait si déjà quelque bouche infidèle
Ne l'a point averti de votre amour nouvelle? (1289-1290)

Similarly Roxane by her choice of words suggests but does not state an awareness of Bajazet's love for another. She will deduce that the other is Atalide, who by the transparency of her signs and lack of control actually cries, blushes,[35] and even faints before her rival. As luck would have it, even the letter, Atalide's written proof of Bajazet's love, reaches the eyes of Roxane.

But before these more convincing facial, gestural, and scriptural signs persuade Roxane of the complicity, in the privacy of her own thoughts she actually suspects her own reasoning. She is aware of the inherent weakness of these non-verbal sign systems whose semantic fields are superimposed, whose codes are not standardized, and whose cultural values are not explicitly defined. To avoid the traps of 'over-reading' or 'misinterpretation,' Roxane suggests the need for some distance, an objectivity which could guide her in the quest for certainty:

> Mais peut-être qu'aussi, trop prompte à m'affliger,
> J'observe *de trop près* un *chagrin* passager. (1075-1076)

Despite frequent warnings, Atalide allows her involuntary system to function like blatant signs of hidden feelings. Zaire warns:

> Suspendez ou cachez l'ennui qui vous dévore
> N'allez point par vos pleurs déclarer vos amours. (410-411)

Even Bajazet suspects the weakness of Atalide's powers of control:

> Belle Atalide, au nom de cette complaisance,
> Daignez de la Sultane éviter la présence.
> Vos pleurs vous trahiroient: cachez-les à ses yeux. (673-675)

Roxane identifies Atalide's tears as a test of certainty, confirmed shortly after by her fainting:

> Cache tes pleurs, malheureuse Atalide. (1193)

Like an obsession before her own eyes, and in the absence of Atalide, Roxane speaks directly to her, repeatedly evoking the incident of tears and implying by its very recall the force of its sign value:

> Mais dans quel souvenir me laissé-je égarer?
> Tu pleures, malheureuse? Ah! tu devois pleurer. (1307-1308)
>
> Tu pleures? et l'ingrat, tout prêt à te trahir. (1311)

When Atalide faints, Zatime takes recourse in signs to describe her state of lifelessness:

> Madame, elle ne marque aucun reste de vie
> Que par de longs soupirs et des gémissements. (1254-1255)

Crying, fainting, blushing, signs, moans, these are some of the many "discours du visage" and body languages which *Bajazet*'s characters must learn to decode in order to penetrate the hidden messages of the heart. For as Roxane knows:

> L'amour le plus discret
> Laisse par quelque marque échapper son secret. (1119-1120)

Just as the eyes are the mirror of the heart, and the heart the source of life, so the face in *Bajazet* is the signpost of man's emotions, the heart and soul of his living body. When Osmin learns that the slave secretly sent by Amurat to execute Bajazet was himself drowned by orders from the inside, Osmin refers metonymically to the shocking reality of Bajazet's live body as "son visage":

> Quoi, Seigneur? le Sultan reverra son visage,
> Sans que de vos respects il lui porte ce gage? (77-78)

Suspicious of false testimonies, Amurat will later insist on more concrete evidence of truth — Bajazet's head in his hand:

> Ne vous montrez à moi que sa *tête* à la *main*. (1192)

The face is like an open book relating tales of hidden emotion better even than words can tell:

> Ils ne m'ont point parlé; mais mieux qu'aucun langage
> Le transport du Visir marquoit sur son visage (797-798)

The face reveals, even in a man as cunning as Acomat whose own experience and sensitivity provide him with the extra-ordinary sensory ability to read manifest and latent signs. On the battlefield he knows the persuasive effects of Mahomat's banner, the signal of danger and contingent death.[36] Not an expert in matters of romance, he nevertheless sees through Roxane's hesitations as a sure sign of love and hope:

> Tu vois combien son coeur, prêt à le protéger,
> A retenu mon bras trop prompt à la venger.
> Je connois peu l'amour. (1407-1409)

Unlike the master trickster, Bajazet is incapable of engaging in deception. Atalide knows that it would constitute a sacrifice for him to don a mask:

> Bajazet va se perdre. Ah! si, comme autrefois,
> Ma rivale eût voulu lui parler par ma voix!
> Au moins si j'avois pu *préparer son visage!* (395-397)

Even the absence of signs is, in itself, a sign. Bajazet's silence, which he calls a "témoin de trouble caché," is undeniable evidence, for him at least, of his innocence in this grandiose play within a play.

> Ai-je pu vous tromper par des promesses feintes?
> Songez combien de fois vous m'avez reproché
> Un silence témoin de mon trouble caché. (1514-1516)

The polyvalence of signs creates ambiguity and justifies multiple interpretations. For example, "mon trouble caché" is a vague description of an effect whose more significant causation is a secret kept hidden from Roxane. The lack of referential precision, frequent use of abstraction, and general refusal to identify deep-seated causes result in an attenuation which Leo Spitzer called the *Klassische Dämpfung*. The refusal of precision and holding-back techniques are some of the characteristics of classical discourse that render its reading auto-reflexive and highly poetic.[37]

Unmitigating scrutiny, the impossibility to hide from the inescapable and hostile "regards d'autrui," this is the claustrophobic atmosphere of the Racinian tragedy so effectively expressed in *Bajazet* where words, gestures, facial expressions, and even silence reveal the sacred hidden.[38] Attempting hopelessly to mask private emotions by strategies of public deception, the Racinian tragic hero in search of that which is hidden in others is a victim of his failing vision, ceaselessly groping for the insightful interpretation of signs from the far-reaching regions of the soul. Exposure and disguise, lucidity and deception, vision in darkness, certitude and doubt – these are the Racinian dialectics which transform the world of the palace into a hellish nightmare.

NOTES

[1] Descartes, *Discours de la methode pour bien conduire sa raison et chercher la vérité dans les sciences* (Paris: Garnier-Flammarion, 1966), 4ème Partie, p. 59.

[2] Doubt is signalled stylistically by the form of Osmin's first discourse which is significantly an interrogative construction:

> Et depuis quand, Seigneur, entre-t-on dans ces lieux,
> Dont l'accès étoit même interdit à nos yeux?
> Jadis une mort prompte eût suivi cette audace. (3-5)

Roxane's famous speech in Act II, Scene ii renders this cultural revolution explicit:

> Sortez. Que le Serrail soit désormais fermé,
> Et que tout rentre ici dans *l'ordre accoutumé*. (571-572)

[3] Cf. (v. 14-15)

> Songe que du récit, Osmin, que tu vas faire
> Dépendent *les destins de l'empire ottoman*.

The irony in this remark is perceived retroactively, for in fact Acomat's involvement in matters of state, his underhanded manipulations performed in secret, will, he believes, change the destiny of the empire and reinstate his power under a new leader, Bajazet. He has faith, therefore, in the free will of man, faith that will prove futile by the end of the play when Amurat's supreme will annihilates all the members of the palace in a "grande tuerie." Irony lies in the play on words and recall of Acomat's lines 14-15 by Osmin:

> Mais enfin le succès dépend des destinées. (58)

Critics have falsely united these two thoughts as being equivalent. They are in fact a reversal of significance, one being a sign of free will and the other a sign of fatalism.

[4] The word "sérail" means not only harem but palace in general. Cf. Dr. E. van der Starre, *Racine et le théâtre de l'ambiguïté: Etude sur Bajazet* (Leiden, (1966), p. 92. The choice of the term "sérail," a foreign sounding word to the French language, has the stylistic effect of exoticism, a sign of *'dépaysement'* which functions in conjunction with the earlier but less accurate name "Byzance" (in contrast to Constantinople) and "Babylone" (in contrast to

Bagdad) to produce a poetic effect despite the anachronisms. The effectiveness of this *dépaysement* or distanciation for the seventeenth-century public is doubtful, for, as Corneille said, "Tous ses personnages, sous les habits turcs, sont Français" (cited by A. Adam, *Histoire de la littérature française du XVIIème siècle*, IV (Paris: Del Duca, 1968), p. 350.

[5] The inferno-hell motif, while never corroborated explicitly, is actualized diversely by a process of association and similarity with the literary symbol immortalized by Dante. Other critics make reference to the motif (e.g. Judd Hubert, *Essai d'exégèse racinienne* (Paris: Nizet, 1956), p. 148: "Dans le monde infernal que Racine nous dépeint dans *Bajazet*"; cf. Odette de Mourgues, *Racine or the Triumph of Relevance* (Cambridge University Press, 1967), p. 133: "In *Bajazet*, too, order becomes a destructive force, ... Hence the alarming negativeness of the framework in this tragedy: *Bajazet* takes place in Hell."

[6] Acomat's plot is encoded as a vengeful act to reinstate his due power. Amurat has virtually reduced Acomat to the illusory rank of a city dignitary with no actual power:

> Il commande l'armée; et moi, dans une ville,
> Il me laisse exercer un pouvoir inutile.
> Quel emploi, quel séjour, Osmin, pour un Visir! (89-91)

For a soldier with a sense of his true worth, this titular position is sheer humiliation, the sense of which is signalled stylistically by the exclamations.

[7] See Judd Hubert, *Essai d'exégèse racinienne* (Paris: Nizet, 1956), pp. 141-159. The entire chapter entitled "L'Ordre Accoutumé" is particularly useful in our study of the signs of hidden truth.

[8] The word 'code' in linguistics and semiotics is misleading because of the current diverse uses. Code is used imprecisely by analogy to mean 'language' in general, or more specifically to mean any set of signs used conventionally within a given signifying system in order to communicate. We use the term in the more precise sense to mean a set of transformations (correspondences, equivalents, variants) which provide the key to change from one sign system to another. An interesting and informative discussion of the term 'code' by Eliseo Veron is found in "Pertinence idéologique du code," *Degrés*, II (Juillet-Octobre 1974), 3-13.

[9] Acomat is not only the prime mover in the complex plot to depose the sultan, Amurat, and name Bajazet the new Sultan, but he is capable of the most perspicacious interpretations of signs. In Act IV, Scene vii, Acomat defines himself as a seer through the comparative metaphor of blindness:

> Prince aveugle! ou plutôt trop aveugle ministre! (1378)

He later literalizes his power of vision:

> Mais *moi, qui vois plus loin*, qui par un long usage (1389)

Acomat reads Roxane's inner thoughts by identifying her hesitation to have Bajazet killed as a sign of continued love:

Tu vois combien son coeur, prêt à le protéger,
A retenu mon bras trop prompt à la venger. (1407-1408)

[10] In Act I, Scene i, Acomat urges Osmin to deliver an honest testimony:

De ce qu'ont vu tes yeux parle en témoin sincère (13)

Zaire says in Act V, Scene x:

Par la bouche d'Osmin vous serez mieux instruite.
Il a tout vu. (1673-1674)

[11] Acomat's pride and self-esteem are the motivations behind his revenge. To Osmin he says:

Mourons: moi, cher Osmin, comme un Visir; et toi,
·Comme le favori d'un homme tel que moi. (1427-1428)

[12] Imprisonment is a leitmotif in *Bajazet* which is intricately related to the theme of free-will and determinism. The Seraglio's intrinsic imprisonment is a metaphoric representation of man's bondage which is literalized by Bajazet's *real* imprisonment. Variants of this thematic structure are social slavery, the question of free will and self-determination, and the slavery of love:

Ainsi donc pour un temps Amurat désarmé
Laissa dans le Serrail Bajazet *enfermé*. (127-128)
Venez en d'autres lieux *enfermer* vos regrets. (415)
Sortez. Que le Serrail soit désormais *fermé. (571)*

The metaphoric representation of imprisonment becomes literalized again in Act V when Atalide is captured in reciprocal response to Bajazet's initial imprisonment:

Cependant on m'arrête, on me tient *enfermée (1449)*
Gardes, qu'on la retienne. (1453)

[13] Odette de Mourgues, *Racine or the Triumph of Relevance*, p. 133: "The interesting point in *Bajazet* is that the order is a wicked order, that it is based on slavery and goes against the conception of order of a seventeenth-century audience. ..." "Sortez que la porte du Sérail soit désormais fermée" is a figurative expression signifying closedness, a restriction on the liberty of sight, and the re-establishment of a system of commands and obedience. Corroboration of this interpretation is seen in Zaire's explanation of Roxane's pronouncement:

Il ne peut plus la voir sans qu'elle le commande. (1129)

[14] "Et craignoit du Serrail les rigoureuses lois" (204)
[15] 　　　　　　　　Amurat en furie
S'approche pour trancher une si belle vie. (265-266)

Moi-même j'ai souvent entendu leurs discours;
Comme il les craint sans cesse, ils le craignent toujours. (43-44)

[16] Both Barthes and Odette de Mourgues consider *Bajazet* the most tragic of tragedies, but for different reasons. Odette de Mourgues in *Racine or the Triumph of Relevance* states: "Bajazet remains a superb play, perhaps the most harrowingly tragic in the theatre of Racine (the lack of a moral background increasing the terrifying feeling of claustrophobia) and is certainly his boldest experiment" (p. 134). Barthes in *Sur Racine* states: "Roxane cependant se débat dans le mileu le plus étouffant qu'ait connu la tragédie racinienne" (p. 103). Interestingly enough Lucien Goldmann in *Le Dieu caché* (Paris: Gallimard, 1955) refuses to label *Bajazet* a tragedy at all: *"Bajazet* est la première pièce de l'essai de vivre et du compromis. *Bajazet, Mithridate* et *Iphigénie* ... qui ne sont pas des tragédies" (p. 383). The compromise Goldman refers to is in Bajazet's hesitating but ultimate capitulation in duplicity and in a depiction of a world that is not altogether evil. Jacques Scherer in *Racine: Bajazet*, "Cours de la Sorbonne" (Paris: Centre de documentation universitaire, n.d.), referring to the last act and the famous "grande tuerie," reminds us of young Racine's tendency to equate the number of deaths with the tragicness of a tragedy (p. 4).

[17] "Je cours où ma présence est encore nécessaire" (1718).

[18] Cf. René Jasinski, *Vers le vrai Racine* (Paris: Librarie Armand Colin, 1958), pp. 1-90, for a detailed study of the actual historical events leading to Bajazet's death, and life in Amurat's seraglio around 1635. Cf. Jacques Scherer, *Racine: Bajazet*, pp. 17-46, for the genesis (historical, romanesque, and theatrical) of *Bajazet*. Scherer also studies how and to what extent Racine changed history for poetic effects.

[19] Cf. v. 455-496, 598-599, 603-604.

[20] Cf. Roland Barthes, *Sur Racine* (Paris: Seuil, 1963), p. 22. Despite Roxane's constant verbal appeals for Bajazet's immediate action, her own non-verbal behavior manifests the opposite. She delays, knows the truth but prefers to forget, refuses, despite the persuasive evidence, to take a real stand. Cf. Jules Brody's excellent article *"Bajazet* or the Tragedy of Roxane," *Romanic Review* 4 (12.1969), 273-291, esp. pp. 273-275.

[21] Ferdinand de Saussure, *Cours de linguistique générale* Edition R. Engler, (Wiesbaden: Otto Harrassowitz, 1967-1974), 4 vols., p. 100.

[22] Cf. Oswald Ducrot, Tzvetan Todorov, *Dictionnaire encyclopédique des sciences du langage* (Paris: Seuil, 1972).

[23] Barthes, p. 102: "Cette ambiguité sexuelle atteint son comble dans *Bajazet.* Bajazet n'est qu'un sexe indécis, inversé, transformé d'homme en femme ... on le sent lentement désexué par la virile Roxane."

[24] Eugène Vinaver, *Racine et la poésie tragique* (Paris: Nizet, 1963), p. 59: "La couleur tragique qu'on a coutume de prêter au 'Sortez!' de l'Acte V se trouve démentie par le sang froid de Roxane elle-même qui ne songe désormais qu'à multiplier les meurtres." According to Vinaver *Bajazet* represents a poetic silence in Racine's theatre: "... même les quelques trouvailles qu'on y relève – telle la *tranquille fureur* de Roxane – restent dans l'atonie générale, trop dispersées pour rétablir le courant poétique" (p. 60). He ranks *Bajazet* in the

category of "une pièce à complot qui s'achève sur un affreux massacre ... une grande tuerie ..." (p. 58).

26 Cf. Louis-Jean Calvet, *Pour et contre Saussure: Vers une linguistique sociale* (Paris: Payot, 1975), pp. 130-133, for the socially and culturally based signification of *vous* and *tu*. His discussion is not by any means complete.

26 See La Harpe's comment on the significance of this exclamation, cited in *Bajazet*, Les Grands Ecrivains de la France, II (Paris: Hachette, 1865), p. 504: "Quand la célèbre Clairon prononçait ce vers, son accent ... son geste, ses yeux, toute son action dans cette seule exclamation Ah! exprimaient le conflit tout entier, au point qu'avec un peu d'intelligence on aurait deviné tout ce qu'elle allait dire."

27 John Lapp, *Aspects of Racinian Tragedy* (Toronto University Press, 1955), p. 24: "It is this terrible lucidity, by which Roxane sees both her own true motives and the futility of her hope, that distinguishes her from earlier heroines like Hermione, who, in her wavering, her fits of hope alternating with rage or despair, never really rises to the consciousness of her position."

28 Zaire's testimony is not false but misleading:

> Zaire
> Je n'en ai rien appris.
> Mais enfin, s'il n'a pu se sauver qu'à ce prix,
> S'il fait ce que vous-même avez su lui prescrire,
> S'il l'épouse, en un mot. ...
>
> Atalide
> S'il l'épouse, Zaire! (811-814)

29 Atalide fears what her physical proximity to Bajazet will signify to Roxane. This fear is encoded in a recurrence of accumulating imperatives showing the desire for displacement ("Allez ... allez ... allez," v. 785-792). Roxane also renders manifest and more explicit the cultural significance of their dangerous proximity:

> Allez: entre elle et vous je ne dois point paroître (789)
> Allez, encore un coup, *je n'ose m'y trouver*. (791)

30 The verbs *voir* and *savoir* are frequently collocated.

> Je *verrai* Bajazet. Je ne puis dire rien,
> Sans *savoir* si son coeur s'accorde avec le mien. (255-256)

31 See Jules Brody, *Boileau and Longinus* (Geneva: Droz, 1958), p. 135, note 1 for a discussion of this topos. See also Starobinski's excellent book *L'Oeil vivant* (Paris: Gallimard, 1961) devoted to this subject. "La vue" is sacred in love, for it is the slate on which the sense impressions of beauty will fall:

> C'est par d'autres *attraits* qu'elle plaît à ma vue (181)

and

> La Sultane éperdue
> N'eut plus d'autres désirs que celui de sa vue.

32

> Peut-étre en la voyant, plus sensible pour elle,
> Il a vu dans ses yeux quelque grâce nouvelle. (917-918)

[33] Cf. "Ses yeux ne l'ont-ils point *séduite*?" (1674).

34

> Je ne retrouvois point ce trouble, cette ardeur
> Que m'avoit tant promis un discours trop flatteur (283-284)

[35] Atalide:

> Pensez-vous que cent fois en vous faisant parler
> Ma rougeur ne fût pas préte à me déceler? (771-772)

36

> Déployez en son nom cet étendard fatal,
> Des extrêmes périls l'ordinaire signal. (239-240)

[37] See Roman Jakobson, *Essais de linguistique générale* (Paris: Minuit, 1963), and his *Questions de poétique* (Paris: Seuil, 1973).

[38] See John Lapp's final chapter of *Aspects of Racinian Tragedy*, especially pp. 134-151, for an excellent comparison of the motif of inescapable scrutiny in Madame de Lafayette and in Racine (p. 134).